D1595964

OXFORD ENGLISH MONOGRAPHS

HENRY JAMES

HISTORY,
NARRATIVE,
FICTION

ROSLYN JOLLY

CLARENDON PRESS · OXFORD

Oxford University Press, Walton Street, Oxford OX2 6DP
Oxford New York
Athens Auckland Bangkok Bombay
Calcutta Cape Town Dar es Salaam Delhi
Florence Hong Kong Istanbul Karachi
Kuala Lumpur Madras Madrid Melbourne
Mexico City Nairobi Paris Singapore
Taipei Tokyo Toronto
and associated companies in
Berlin Ibadan

Oxford is a trade mark of Oxford University Press

Published in the United States
by Oxford University Press Inc., New York

© Roslyn Jolly 1993

First published 1993

British Library Cataloguing in Publication Data
Data available

Library of Congress Cataloging in Publication Data
Jolly, Roslyn.
Henry James : history, narrative, fiction / Roslyn Jolly.
(Oxford English monographs)
Includes bibliographical references.
1. James, Henry, 1843–1916—Knowledge—History. 2. Historical fiction,
American—History and criticism. 3. Literature and history. 4. Narration
(Rhetoric) 5. Fiction—Technique.
I. Title. II. Series.
PS2127.H5J64 1993 813'.4—dc20 93-10066
ISBN 0-19-811985-2

3 5 7 9 10 8 6 4 2

Printed in Great Britain
on acid-free paper by
The Ipswich Book Company Ltd.,
Suffolk

Preface

COMMENTING on James's argument that the novelist should claim the status of the historian, Joseph Conrad described Henry James as 'the historian of fine consciences'. This gloss on one of James's most important theoretical statements about the novel is misleading, as it effaces the difficulties produced for both James and his characters by the idea of history. Conrad manages to suggest that James's novels embody at the same time an unproblematic alignment with the discourse of history and a graceful retreat from the material of history; for he goes on to explain that the fineness of the consciences James represents resides in their capacity for idealistic acts of renunciation which place them beyond the appeal of the 'shadows' that constitute worldly, human history. James is presented as the historian of those who give up the attempt to struggle with history.

But James's relation to history was less serene than this formulation suggests, as is evident from the anxious ways in which he spoke about history as it affected the novelist. In 1884 he argued that if the novel 'will not give itself away . . . it must speak with assurance, with the tone of the historian'; but in 1915 he found that, under pressure of historical events, 'The subject-matter of one's effort has become *itself* utterly treacherous and false—its relation to reality utterly given away and smashed.' The first remark is a major theoretical statement from 'The Art of Fiction', the second a private confession of despair about the value of his whole career as a novelist. Yet the two statements are continuous in their anxiety, and the panic expressed in the second is, while controlled, discernible in the first. The panic is that fiction will 'give itself away', or be 'given away', as *not history*, and the novelist's whole enterprise will be thereby invalidated.

What is at stake here for James is the novelist's authority to speak about human experience—an authority rendered precarious by long-standing philosophical and moral charges against fiction's false epistemology. When, as in Victorian culture, these epistemological concerns were made the channel for other kinds of social and political anxiety, and used to justify various forms of censorship, the need to establish the novel's freedom and authority intensified. The younger James's response was to attempt to turn history from a problem into a solution for the novelist. Fiction was to be authorized—and, he hoped, liberated—by history: reality effects produced by an alliance of fictional with historiographical narrative would help to secure the novelist's cultural position and validate his or her pretensions to represent life.

Such a response worked with, rather than against, the whole philosophical, social, and political complex of hostility to fiction in English culture. James's early novels were grounded in an anti-romance tradition in which 'the tone of the historian' was produced through the exposure and correction of fiction's false view of the world. The novel's effort not to 'give itself away' as fiction committed it to disciplining and blocking expressions of the fictive imagination dramatized *within* the novel. The 'historical' status of the novel was guaranteed by the antipathy to fiction that was also a defining feature of the new scientific historiography of the nineteenth century.

In dramatizing and disciplining his characters' novelistic imaginations James drew on various social and literary practices which expressed his culture's anxieties about fiction: the imagination and manipulation of different reading communities, a questioning of the morality of readership and authorship, and even such acts of censorship as he himself, as a novelist, wished to escape. The second and third chapters of this book explore the ways in which the fabric of historical narrative was both woven and unravelled by James's engagement, in the works of his early and middle periods, with the censorious practices of a culture at odds with its own fictions. The disciplinary, anti-romance enterprise of the novel-as-history depended on distinctions between characters and author which became increasingly unstable and, indeed, untenable, and James's position as a historian was constantly assailed by his own characters, whose unruly acts of authorship contest the power of history to define their world. The characters precede their author in articulating new theories of fiction based on an opposition to history, rather than an alliance with it. This new, radically anti-historical approach to experience is the subject of the fourth and fifth chapters, which trace the efforts of Lambert Strether and Maggie Verver to use fiction as a means of solving problems in moral and social life. *The Ambas-*

sadors and *The Golden Bowl* suggest a major strand in James's late theory of the novel: the belief that fiction is most valuable not as a record of experience, but as a mode of encountering and shaping it.

'Oh, I'm not afraid of history!', declares Maggie Verver, overturning the epistemological hierarchy that had caused such anxiety for her creator and the whole literary culture within which he wrote. But in 1914 it became impossible not to be afraid of history. The authority of the fictive imagination endorsed in James's late novels and criticism was thrown deeply into question by the seemingly incontestable historical power represented by the Great War. The final chapter of this book examines how James's late theories of fiction were tested by the experience of war, which left fiction's relation to reality 'utterly given away and smashed' but which also seemed to James to demand the production of 'counter-realities'—what he had come to regard as the novelist's proper work—as the only possible response.

The diachronic argument of this study of James's changing relations to history could not have been based on the synchronizing version of James's career embodied in the *New York Edition*. I have therefore chosen to use the first authorized English book editions of his works, or reprinted versions of these. The *New York Edition* has been used for purposes of comparison.

The writing of this book was supported by equipment and travel grants from the Research Management Committee of the University of Newcastle (Australia). I would also like to acknowledge travel grants received from the Graduate Research Funds of the University of Oxford and Lincoln College.

Many people helped with the production of this book, and it is a pleasure to thank them. Bernard Richards was an unflaggingly generous and supportive supervisor when I was working on an earlier version of this study as a D.Phil. thesis at Oxford. Simon Petch and Kate Flint made invaluable contributions to my thinking about fiction and history, and I wish to thank them for sharing insights arising from their own areas of expertise which allowed me to start thinking in new ways about James. I am also grateful for comments offered by Vivien Jones, Barbara Everett, Philip Horne, and Jennifer Gribble, who read various versions or sections of this study. The completion of this work also owes much to the help and friendship of Neil Berman, Victoria Rowbotham, Lisa Handley, Dana Cohen, Suzanne Lewis, and Judith Hawley. Finally, I would like to thank my parents for their unfailing support.

This book is dedicated to Simon Petch.

Contents

List of Abbreviations

References to works by James are included in the text, using the following abbreviations:

Amb.	*The Ambassadors* (London: Methuen, 1903).
TA	*The American*, first pub. 1877 (London: Macmillan, 1879).
AS	*The American Scene* (London: Chapman & Hall, 1907).
CT	*The Complete Tales of Henry James*, ed. with introd. by Leon Edel, 12 vols. (London: Hart-Davis, 1962–4).
TE	*The Europeans: A Sketch*, 2 vols. (London: Macmillan, 1878).
GB	*The Golden Bowl*, first pub. 1904 (London: Methuen, 1905).
HJ & EW	*Henry James and Edith Wharton: Letters: 1900–1915*, ed. Lyall H. Powers (New York: Scribner's, 1990).
Letters	*Henry James: Letters*, ed. Leon Edel, 4 vols. (i–iii: London: Macmillan, 1974–81; iv: Cambridge, Mass.: Belknap Press, 1984).
LC	*Henry James: Literary Criticism*, ed. Leon Edel and Mark Wilson, 2 vols. (New York: Library of America, 1984); i: *Essays on Literature, American Writers, English Writers*; ii: *French Writers, Other European Writers, the Prefaces to the New York Edition*.
ITC	*In the Cage* (London: Duckworth, 1898).
LD	'Is There a Life After Death?', in W. D. Howells *et al.*, *In After Days: Thoughts on the Future Life* (New York: Harper, 1910), 199–233.
Lubbock	*The Letters of Henry James*, ed. Percy Lubbock, 2 vols. (London: Macmillan, 1920).
NYE	*The Novels and Tales of Henry James: New York Edition*, first pub. 1907–9; 24 vols. (London: Macmillan, 1908–9).
PS	*Parisian Sketches: Letters to the* New York Tribune *1875–1876*, ed. with introd. by Leon Edel and Ilse Dusoir Lind (London: Hart-Davis, 1958).
PL	*The Portrait of a Lady*, 3 vols. (London: Macmillan, 1881).
PC	*The Princess Casamassima: A Novel*, 3 vols. (London: Macmillan, 1886).
QS	*The Question of Our Speech, The Lesson of Balzac: Two Lectures* (Boston: Houghton, Mifflin, 1905).
RH	*Roderick Hudson*, first pub. 1876, rev. edn., 3 vols. (London: Macmillan, 1879).

SF	*The Sacred Fount* (London: Methuen, 1901).
SL	*Selected Letters of Henry James*, ed. with introd. by Leon Edel (London: Hart-Davis, 1956).
SP	*The Sense of the Past* (London: Collins, 1917).
SBO	*A Small Boy and Others* (London: Macmillan, 1913).
TM	*The Tragic Muse*, 3 vols. (London: Macmillan, 1890).
TS	*The Two Magics: The Turn of the Screw, Covering End* (London: Heinemann, 1898).
WS	*Washington Square, The Pension Beaurepas, A Bundle of Letters*, 2 vols. (London: Macmillan, 1881).
WR	*Within the Rim and Other Essays 1914–15* (London: Collins, 1918).

Fiction and History:
James's Early Theory of the Novel

IT IS impossible to imagine what a novelist takes himself to be unless he regard himself as an historian and his narrative as a history. It is only as an historian that he has the smallest *locus standi*. As a narrator of fictitious events he is nowhere; to insert into his attempt a backbone of logic, he must relate events that are assumed to be real.

(*LC* i. 1343)

THE ANALOGY between the novel and history, put forward so uncompromisingly in these lines from the essay 'Anthony Trollope' (1883), dominated James's early theory of fiction. Implicit in his constant calls for fiction to represent life, James's tendency to define the novel in terms of history was strengthened by the increasing commitment to realism in his theory and criticism of the 1870s and 1880s. A historiographical model for the novel had been outlined explicitly as early as his 1867 review of the historical novelist Anne Manning, and was most famously stated in 'The Art of Fiction' (1884), in which James claimed that 'the novel is history. That is the only general description (which does it justice) that we may give of the novel' (*LC* i. 46).

What is so striking about the passages in 'Anthony Trollope' and 'The Art of Fiction' that discuss the novel as history is the extreme and defensive language used. Alternatives to the historiographical model are 'impossible to imagine' (*LC* i. 1343), infringements of it 'a terrible crime' (i. 46); it is offered as the 'only' way to do 'justice' to the novel (i. 46) or to gain for it even 'the smallest *locus standi*' (i. 1343). Yet this theory of fiction proposed by a working novelist involves an extraordinary act of self-erasure, for it states that 'As a narrator of fictitious events he is nowhere' (i. 1343).

The defensive tone and sense of limited options are explained in 'The Art of Fiction', in which James contextualizes his theoretical model as a response to a deep, if 'dissimulated' (*LC* i. 46), cultural contempt for and distrust of fiction. Claiming historical status for the novel is seen as the 'only effectual way to lay . . . to rest' (i. 46) the lingering suspicion of fiction in English culture. James wrote: 'The old superstition about fiction being "wicked" has doubtless died out in England; but the spirit of it lingers in a certain oblique regard directed toward any story which does not more or less admit that it is only a joke' (i. 45). According to James, the reception of fiction in nineteenth-century England was either hostile or dismissive. Distrust or outright antagonism were legacies of the 'old evangelical hostility to the novel' (i. 45) which, on the grounds that a record of imaginary events was not literally true, had condemned fictional narrative for providing false pictures of life which were deceptive and dangerous to the reader. James believed that residual distrust of this kind still operated in Victorian culture, and might be allayed only if the novel were to 'renounce the pretension of attempting really to represent life', admitting that it was 'only a "make-believe" ' (i. 45). If it made no claim to represent life, the novel could not be accused of misleading its readers, but this meant that it could escape hostility only by giving up the right to serious consideration. James felt that in England the novel was expected to be 'in some degree apologetic' (i. 45), to 'make itself humble in order to be forgiven' (i. 46). Above all, it must never seek serious consideration on artistic grounds, for:

'Art,' in our Protestant communities, where so many things have got so strangely twisted about, is supposed in certain circles to have some vaguely injurious effect upon those who make it an important consideration, who let it weigh in the balance. It is assumed to be opposed in some mysterious manner to morality, to amusement, to instruction. (i. 47)

In nineteenth-century England, the evangelical distrust of fiction merged with the philistine distrust of art in general, and hostile and non-serious responses towards the novel were inextricably linked in a complex of negative attitudes which the writer of fiction would, James argued, find almost impossible to negotiate. Moral distrust might be deflected with a pose of jocularity, but even this would 'not always succeed in passing for orthodoxy', and in renouncing any serious cultural pretensions, the novel might fall victim to 'the weight of the proscription that was formerly directed against literary levity' (i. 45). Given these attitudes, the identification of the novel with history seemed the only way of asserting its capacity to represent life truly and of justifying a serious attitude towards it. The novel, James argued, 'must take itself seriously for the public to take it so' (i. 45), and therefore 'it must speak with assurance, with the tone of the historian' (i. 46).

Why did James put forward the analogy between history and the novel with such urgency and intensity, offering it as a theoretical contribution to what he hoped was a new 'era of discussion' (*LC* i. 44) about fiction, when what he was proposing was essentially the same technical manœuvre used by Defoe and countless other early novelists in their attempts to circumvent a widespread cultural distrust of fiction? His insistence on aligning the novel with history seems at first both culturally anachronistic and technically redundant. Victorian culture recognized the novel as its major literary form. As a reviewer of Trollope's novels wrote in 1858:

The present age is the age of novels. There is no department of literature which has by the existing generation of writers been more successfully cultivated, none which has been more in favour with the existing generation of readers, than that of prose fiction.[1]

It is difficult to reconcile such testimony with James's description, nearly thirty years later, of the novel as a form barely tolerated in English culture. Moreover, the idea of non-fictionality advocated by James was already implied in the narrative conventions of the realist novel, as narrators were commonly presented as historians, biographers, or witnesses, and the verbs of narration often borrowed from the evidential procedures of historiography and law. Meanwhile, an analogy with history was a staple element in Victorian theories of fiction, giving rise to some of the most characteristic questions of Victorian novel criticism: is the narrative true to life? is it a reliable report on the world? The idea of history was entrenched in Victorian

---

[1] [Percy Greg], 'Mr. Trollope's Novels', *National Review*, 7 (1858), 416.

thinking about the novel, and the novel was entrenched in Victorian culture.

James's writings on realism and censorship show that he considered both these commonly held views to be hollow propositions. His strong sense of living in a culture hostile to fiction is dramatized in 'The Author of Beltraffio', a short story about the domestic relations of a modern novelist, which was serialized a few months before 'The Art of Fiction' and published in book form the following year. The titular 'author', Mark Ambient, is a spokesman for 'the gospel of art' (*CT* v. 303); his wife combines the puritan's traditional hostility to the novel with the philistine's distrust of art in general. Mrs Ambient's fears focus on a perennial topic in anti-fiction polemics—the effect of novels on the young—but her conflict with her husband over his possible influence on their child provides the occasion for a broader articulation of two opposed sets of views on fiction generally. Ambient's artistic credo is truth to life (v. 331), an interest in all aspects of human energy, and a 'passion for form' (v. 323); he is so seriously committed to art that he regards bad writing as a social as well as an aesthetic offence (v. 333). Mrs Ambient, 'the angel of propriety' whose only passion is for philistinism (v. 336–7), finds 'his writings immoral and his influence pernicious' (v. 329), for to her, the only acceptable novel is one in which life is 'blinked and blinded', 'dodged and disfigured' (v. 336). Their irreconcilable views lead to tragedy, and when their child is sacrificed, not to fiction but to the fear of fiction, James makes an extreme point about the destructive energies of hostility to the novel. Ambient warns the narrator that, as a novice writer, he should know about the 'hatred' of art and literature still to be found in modern culture (v. 336), and the tale as a whole is an allegory on this theme. Although her actions are melodramatic, Mrs Ambient's opinions are no more extreme than many of those expressed in the debates on realism and censorship which raged in England in the 1880s and 1890s, and the domestic drama embodies the violent feeling with which the right of the novelist to 'represent life' was contested in England at this time.

The melodrama of 'The Author of Beltraffio' is the counterpart, in plot, to the linguistic excess that erupts into James's usually urbane critical idiom when the historical analogy is discussed in 'The Art of Fiction' and 'Anthony Trollope'. In each case, the resort to an extreme and emotional form of expression reflects how inflammatory an issue in Victorian culture was the question of whether novels should be free to represent all aspects of life. The emotion generated by this debate brought to the surface the distrust of fiction latent in Victorian culture and exposed the hollowness of the loose analogy with history which was inscribed, with bland conventionality, in most novel theory and criticism of the period, but which failed to guarantee for the novelist the historian's freedom from censorship. The historical analogy was a dead—or dormant—metaphor in English criticism, which had to be revitalized if any serious attempt were to be made at gaining for the novelist the right to represent life.

James sought to give the conventional analogy between history and the novel a new force by bringing it up to date with changes in historiographical practice over the century. He was attracted to the new 'scientific' historiography of the later nineteenth century as offering a narrative model of great cultural prestige, based on an epistemological authority associated with a set of technical manœuvres which were available for imitation by the novelist. Reference to the nineteenth-century project of scientific historiography allowed him to invest the old historiographical analogy with a new significance as the basis of his attempt to prove that the novel 'is at once as free and as serious a branch of literature as any other' (*LC* i. 49). The cultural politics and technical implications of James's idea of the novel as history were produced by the intersection of a new discourse on history with an old discourse on fiction, and the term 'history', as it appears in his early theory and criticism, must be glossed by contemporary developments in historiography, as well as by the English tradition of hostility to the novel.

HOSTILITY TO FICTION

A correspondent to the *Christian Observer* in 1815 declared: 'Were I called upon to name at once the most fruitful source both of individual and national vice, and the most convincing evidence of both, I should name novels, as at once cause and effect.'[2] The 'old evangelical hostility to the novel' (*LC* i. 45) was at its height in the second half of the eighteenth and the first quarter of the nineteenth centuries, and was part of a broader complex of antagonistic attitudes towards the novel at a time when the huge popularity of this relatively new genre appeared to many as a threat to moral, social, and literary values.[3] Religious attacks on the novel drew on charges and rhetoric inherited from earlier traditions of hostility to other fictional genres such as stage plays and romances,[4] and were reinforced by utilitarian objections to fiction, which expressed a pattern in Western thought traceable to Plato's attacks on poetry for falsehood and inutility.[5] When the distrust of imaginative literature became focused on the novel in the eighteenth century, anti-fiction diatribes confirmed the categories established in the rhetoric against poetry and stage plays: contrasted with history, which was considered serious and useful, fiction was characterized as frivolous or pernicious, the province of jokes and lies.

While fiction was largely denied serious critical attention during this period—novels were labelled light literature and consigned by critics to a kind of literary junk culture[6]—it attracted a significant body of moral commentary. Opponents of the novel

---

[2] 'A.A.', 'On the Practice of Novel-Reading', (letter), *Christian Observer*, 14 (1815), 513.

[3] Overviews of hostility to the novel during this period are found in John Tinnon Taylor, *Early Opposition to the English Novel: The Popular Reaction from 1760 to 1830* (New York: King's Crown Press, 1943); and W. F. Gallaway, Jr., 'The Conservative Attitude toward Fiction, 1770–1830', *PMLA*, 55 (1940), 1041–59. American attitudes resembled those of the English: see G. Harrison Orians, 'Censure of Fiction in American Romances and Magazines, 1789–1810', *PMLA*, 52 (1937), 195–214.

[4] See e.g. Stephen Gosson, *The School of Abuse, Containing a Pleasant Invective against Poets, Pipers, Players, Jesters, &c.*, first pub. 1579 (London: Shakespeare Society, 1841). A similar attack on stage plays is combined with opposition to novel-reading in John Kendall, *Remarks on the Prevailing Custom of Attending Stage Entertainments; Also on the Present Taste for Reading Romances and Novels; and on Some Other Customs*, 3rd edn. (London, 1801).

[5] Plato, Book 2, *Republic*, *The Dialogues of Plato*, trans. B. Jowett, 4th edn., vol. ii (Oxford: Clarendon Press, 1953), 222. Jeremy Bentham's utilitarian objections to imaginative literature are quoted in C. K. Ogden, *Bentham's Theory of Fictions* (London: Kegan Paul, Trench, Trubner, 1932), p. xciii.

[6] Taylor, *Early Opposition*, 11–20. Typical disparagements of fiction in comparison with poetry are found in S. T. Coleridge, *Seven Lectures on Shakespeare and Milton*, ed. with introd. by J. Payne Collier (London: Chapman & Hall, 1856), 3; 'Mr. Colburn's List', *Athenaeum*, 47 (1828), 735–6; and 'Antiquus' [J. S. Mill], 'What is Poetry?', *Monthly Repository*, NS 7 (1833), 61–2.

claimed that its focus on romantic love (attended by adventure and intrigue) encouraged readers to become dissatisfied with their own lives and to crave fictional excitements. The correspondent to the *Christian Observer*, 'A.A.', analysed the process by which this effect on the reader was achieved:

The imagination, once deceived, becomes itself the deceiver; and instead of embellishing life, as it is falsely represented to do, it heightens only imaginary and unattainable enjoyments, and transforms life itself into a dream, the realities of which are all made painful and disgusting, from our false expectations and erroneous notions of happiness.[7]

The novel was condemned as a false mode of knowledge about the world, declared educationally invalid on the grounds that it is impossible to teach by feigned example or to argue from fictitious premises. Hugh Murray argued in 1805 that 'no good purpose can be answered by an attempt to draw inferences from imaginary events',[8] while 'A.A.' claimed that because their subject matter was invented, novels could never give 'a true knowledge of ourselves and of the world', only 'a fictitious acquaintance with both'.[9] Bentham's utilitarian objections to the poet's 'false morals, fictitious nature' coincide with the evangelicals' claim that the aesthetic qualities of a novel could do nothing to redeem a genre which was simply epistemologically 'wrong': 'The foundation of the building is radically wrong, and the superstructure and ornaments are of little consequence.'[10] However, the false nature attributed to the novel was as much a question of ideology as epistemology; the views of life offered in fiction were often labelled 'false' not because they represented unrealities or impossibilities, but because they were sexually, domestically, socially, or politically subversive. Such sliding between epistemological and socially constructed categories of the 'false' was an important part of anti-fiction rhetoric, both in its early, explicit, narrow expressions, and in later, more subtle, Victorian manifestations.

---

[7] 'A.A.', 'On the Practice of Novel-Reading', 513.
[8] H. Murray, *Morality of Fiction; Or, an Inquiry into the Tendency of Fictitious Narratives, with Observations on Some of the Most Eminent* (Edinburgh, 1805), 10.
[9] 'A.A.', 'On the Practice of Novel-Reading', 514.
[10] Ogden, *Bentham's Theory of Fictions*, p. xciii; 'A.A.', 'On the Practice of Novel-Reading', 516.

Outright hostility to the novel became less common after the first quarter of the nineteenth century. The author most often credited with changing critical and public perceptions was Scott; according to Trollope he precipitated a 'revolution' in attitudes to the novel, making it both aesthetically and morally respectable and causing the 'embargo' placed on it in many circles to be lifted.[11] The ever-increasing importance of fiction in English life and literature was summed up by Edmund Gosse in 1892: 'Since the memorable year 1837 the novel has reigned in English literature; and its tyranny was never more irresistible than it is to-day. The Victorian has been peculiarly the age of the triumph of fiction.'[12] Central to this sense of the novel's importance was a general acceptance that it exercised a profound influence over the lives of its readers. The character Baldwin in Vernon Lee's 'A Dialogue on Novels' (1885) speaks for the educated middle class:

I believe that were the majority of us, educated and sensitive men and women, able to analyze what we consider our almost inborn, nay, automatic, views of life, character, and feeling; that could we scientifically assign its origin to each and trace its modifications; I believe that, were this possible, we should find that a good third of what we take to be instinctive knowledge, or knowledge vaguely acquired from personal experience, is really obtained from the novels which we or our friends have read.[13]

Trollope went further, claiming that 'Novels are in the hands of us all; from the Prime Minister down to the last-appointed scullery-maid',[14] and arguing that fiction had become 'the former of our morals, the code by which we rule ourselves, the mirror in which we dress ourselves, the *index expurgatorius* of things held to be allowable in the ordinary affairs of life'.[15] This description of the novel as an '*index expurgatorius*' cleverly expresses Trollope's sense of the increased power of fiction: he reverses the

[11] Anthony Trollope, 'On English Prose Fiction as a Rational Amusement' (1870), in *Four Lectures*, ed. Morris L. Parrish (London: Constable, 1938), 114. See also Taylor, *Early Opposition*, 97, and Richard Stang, *The Theory of the Novel in England 1850–1870* (London: Routledge & Kegan Paul, 1959), 7.

[12] Edmund Gosse, 'The Tyranny of the Novel', *National Review* (Apr. 1892); reprinted in *Questions at Issue* (London: Heinemann, 1893), 7.

[13] Vernon Lee [Violet Paget], 'A Dialogue on Novels', *Contemporary Review*, 48 (1885), 390.

[14] Trollope, 'Prose Fiction', 108.

[15] Id., 'Novel-Reading', *Nineteenth Century*, 5 (1879), 26.

former proscribed position of the novel to represent it as a new censoring authority which dictates what may be considered 'allowable in the ordinary affairs of life'. Yet it was precisely this sense of the novel's powerful influence over its readers that made the critic W. R. Greg call it 'that branch of the intellectual activity of a nation which a far-seeing moralist would watch with the most vigilant concern, and supervise with the most anxious and unceasing care'.[16] For as Trollope himself frequently testified, 'still there remains something of the bad character which for years has been attached to the art'.[17] Similarly, Walter Besant, whose paper on 'The Art of Fiction' prompted James's essay of the same title, launched his defence of the art of novel-writing in the face of a general tendency to 'regard the story-teller with a sort of contempt':

The general—the Philistine—view of the Profession, is, first of all, that it is not one which a scholar and a man of serious views should take up: the telling of stories is inconsistent with a well-balanced mind; to be a teller of stories disqualifies one from a hearing on important subjects.[18]

Despite its popularity, the cultural status of the novel was by no means secure, and its influence over readers was more often than not conceived of in negative rather than positive terms. The power of novels was undeniable, but surprisingly few attempts were made to harness that power for educational or social ends. When in 1888, writing on 'The Profitable Reading of Fiction', Thomas Hardy drew attention to 'the humanizing education found in fictitious narrative' and 'the aesthetic training' imparted by a well-constructed novel, he conceded that his argument was unusual: 'To profit of this kind, from this especial source, very little attention has hitherto been paid.'[19] Fiction had no place in

---

[16] [W. R. Greg], 'False Morality of Lady Novelists', *National Review*, 8 (1859), 145.
[17] Trollope, 'Novel-Reading', 27. See also id., 'Prose Fiction', 94; and id., *An Autobiography*, 2 vols. (Edinburgh: Blackwood, 1883), i. 195.
[18] Walter Besant, *The Art of Fiction* (London: Chatto & Windus, 1884), 6.
[19] Thomas Hardy, 'The Profitable Reading of Fiction', *Forum* (Mar. 1888); reprinted in *Life and Art: Essays, Notes and Letters*, ed. with introd. by Ernest Brennecke, Jr. (New York: Greenberg, 1925), 68. For a rare defence of the educative value of fiction, see [Anne Mozley], 'On Fiction as an Educator', *Blackwood's Magazine*, 108 (1870), 449–59. In 'The Rhetorical Use and Abuse of Fiction: Eating Books in Late Nineteenth-Century America', *Boundary* 2, 17 (1990), 133–57, Steven Mailloux discusses nineteenth-century American attempts to harness the reading of fiction to disciplinary or reformatory social programmes.

the Arnoldian construction of literature as a 'humanizing' or
'civilizing' subject which underwrote the rise of English studies
in higher education at the end of the century;[20] indeed, an article
in *Punch* in 1895 satirizing the introduction of modern fiction
studies at Yale confirms James's sense that the novel was still
regarded, intellectually, as 'only a joke' (*LC* i. 45).[21] Victorian
schools tended to follow either classical or utilitarian educational
programmes, neither of which esteemed novels.[22] When fiction
did feature in Victorian discussions of education, the popularity
of novel-reading was almost invariably seen as a force not to be
exploited for intellectual or ideological ends, but curbed. This is
clearly seen in the campaigns to ban fiction from philanthropic-
ally or publicly funded libraries, on the grounds that the presence
of novels was either irrelevant or positively detrimental to educational enterprises.[23]

These campaigns reflect the enormous cultural energy channelled by the Victorians into attempts to control the harmful
effects of novel-reading. The question at issue in the debates
centred on Mechanics' Institutes libraries in the 1840s and public
libraries in the 1890s—the question of the relation, or lack of
one, between novel-reading and education—was part of the
much larger 'fiction question' that, with its roots in the old
evangelical and utilitarian hostility to the novel, surfaced again
and again in various forms throughout the nineteenth century.
Despite the range of concerns it embraced and the variety of
occasions which prompted it, the debate about fiction remained
essentially the same: how was novel-reading to be kept safe, and
prevented from levying grave personal, domestic, and social costs
through the immoral and subversive forces it constantly threatened to unleash? Richard Altick has presented the 'fiction question'
as largely a matter of middle-class anxiety over working-class
reading, and he demonstrates the political fears behind the desire

---

[20] Victorian fiction is conspicuously absent from Chris Baldick's discussion of
the Arnoldian project in *The Social Mission of English Criticism 1848–1932*
(Oxford: Clarendon Press, 1983).
[21] 'A Novel Education', *Punch*, 109 (1895), 255.
[22] See the discussion of Victorian philosophies of education in Richard D.
Altick, *The English Common Reader: A Social History of the Mass Reading
Public 1800–1900* (Chicago: University of Chicago Press, 1957), 141–87.
[23] Ibid. 195–8, 231–3; Peter Keating, *The Haunted Study: A Social History of
the English Novel 1875–1914* (London: Secker & Warburg, 1989), 414.

to keep that reading 'safe'.[24] However, as I wish to show, these issues were part of a much broader network of concerns about the reading of fiction which also involved gender politics, domestic authority, social ideology, and personal morality, and which affected all social classes and all levels of literary culture.

The fiction question focused on various centres of debate. The question of the desirability of allowing free circulation of novels throughout society was at the heart of discussions about the control of access to fiction by libraries or by law. Advocates of some form of censorship were particularly concerned with the representation of violence and sexuality in fiction, and this concern was expressed in discussion of the 'penny dreadfuls' produced for a working-class audience (and held to be especially dangerous for the young), the sensation novels popular with middle-class readers in the 1860s (to the effects of which women were considered especially vulnerable), the feminist 'New Woman' fiction of the 1890s, and, more generally, the 'realism' of subject matter associated with French fiction and English experimental novelists. Through all these debates a similarity of concern is evident, which reflects the old fear of the novel as a destabilizing social force. Penny fiction was blamed for inciting its readers to criminal or at least anti-social behaviour; even in its less violent forms it was held to promote subversive attitudes and a lack of respect for authority.[25] The sensation novel, similarly, was accused of encouraging crime and sympathy with crime, and of generally producing 'an impatience of old restraints, and a craving for some fundamental change in the working of society', for it 'willingly and designedly draws a picture of life which shall make reality insipid and the routine of ordinary existence intolerable to the imagination'.[26] The sexuality implied in sensation novels was explicitly expressed in feminist and avantgarde fiction of the 1890s, provoking anxieties about sexual subversion which were linked to political fears. An article written

[24] Altick, *English Common Reader*, 64–5, 76.
[25] [Francis Hitchman], 'Penny Fiction', *Quarterly Review*, 171 (1890), 152–3, 170; Hugh Chisholm, 'How to Counteract the "Penny Dreadful" ', *Fortnightly Review*, NS 58 (1895), 765; A. Strahan, 'Bad Literature for the Young', *Contemporary Review*, 26 (1875), 985–6.
[26] 'Our Female Sensation Novelists', *Christian Remembrancer*, NS 46 (1863), 210.

by Hugh Stutfield in 1895 addresses problems of modernity in
terms of traditional fears about fiction: 'Along with its diseased
imaginings—its passion for the abnormal, the morbid, and the
unnatural—the anarchical spirit broods over all literature of the
decadent and "revolting" type. It is rebellion all along the line.'[27]

The continuity of concern between Victorian debates on fiction
and the evangelical tradition of hostility to the novel was reinforced by a continuity of rhetoric. The Victorian discourse on
novels drew on traditional imagery of fiction as confectionery,
narcotic, or poison, which presented the effects of novel-reading
in terms of bodily health or disease. The idea of the 'morbidity'
of the novel-reader, always a favourite charge of anti-fiction
rhetoricians, was placed on a supposedly scientific basis at the
end of the century by Max Nordau's influential analysis of cultural degeneration.[28] The traditional *exempla* and *topoi* of anti-
fiction rhetoric—the stories of seduced maidens and disobedient
daughters, the images of domestic work left undone by wives and
servants buried in novels—were recycled for new purposes: as
Altick observes, the tales of the evil effects of fiction used at the
end of the century to discredit public libraries were 'well established in national legend' and could easily have dated from the
1830s or even the 1790s.[29]

Victorian debates on fiction did not engage in wholesale de-
nunciations of all fiction, but attacked particular kinds of novels
in the hands of particular kinds of readers—most often, sensational, politically subversive, avant-garde, or foreign fiction in
the hands of women, the working class, or the young. Constructions of the vulnerability of readers in terms of class or gender
could be used as a means of social control, allowing the manipulation of certain sections of society by controlling their access
to fiction.[30] Such constructions were also part of the way in

[27] Hugh E. M. Stutfield, 'Tommyrotics', *Blackwood's Magazine*, 157 (1895),
837–8.
[28] Max Nordau, *Degeneration*, trans. from the 2nd German edn. (London:
Heinemann, 1895).
[29] Altick, *English Common Reader*, 232.
[30] See ibid. 65 and Anne T. Margolis, *Henry James and the Problem of Audience: An International Act* (Ann Arbor, Mich.: UMI Research Press, 1985), 70.
As Kate Flint comments about the 'New Woman' fiction of the 1890s, 'the
contemporary debate *about* the woman reader sets up, above all, the figure of
the anxious and threatened *male* reader'; 'Reading the New Woman', *Browning
Society Notes*, 17 (1987–8), 62.

which Victorian culture constantly displaced its anxiety about its most important literary form on to various defined groups of readers and writers of fiction; the 'unsafe' nature of fiction could thereby be marginalized and controlled. The threat of fiction was often presented as in some sense external to 'mainstream' English culture: the idea of an unknown mass public and its potentially dangerous reading practices drew on fears of a working class dangerously empowered by literacy to threaten middle-class culture,[31] while the belief that dangerous theories were being imported via French realist and naturalist works played on English insularity and xenophobia, which had led to the conventional inscription of French fiction as the immoral 'other' to the English novel in critical rhetoric.[32] The 'fiction question' was thus continually being exported to the margins of culture—either the subliterary or the avant-garde—and was focused on groups of readers considered to be educationally or physiologically disabled from dealing with the dangers of fiction. Studies (carried out by figures of cultural authority) of what was read by the young, or by women or the working class, emphasized the otherness of these reading cultures and presupposed a norm of 'safe' reading practices against which their deviations might be measured.[33] This established a distinction between responsible and irresponsible readers (those who could determine their own consumption, and those whose consumption needed to be controlled from above) which tended to correlate with a distinction not only between the safe and the unsafe, but between the highbrow and lowbrow in fiction. This was evident in the debates on

[31] As Keating, *Haunted Study*, points out (401–4), writers such as Wilkie Collins and James Payn saw the 'unknown public' as a huge potential book-buying market, and believed the gulf between mainstream novelists and mass consumers could be bridged either by educating the taste of readers (Collins) or by learning to meet their demands (Payn). However, articles on penny fiction such as those by Strahan and Hitchman present the unknown public as the source not of commercial hopes but of grave political fears.

[32] See e.g. the views of Mrs Blake in Lee's 'Dialogue'.

[33] An assumption of otherness underwrites Edward Salmon's analyses of separate reading cultures, 'What the Working Classes Read', *Nineteenth Century*, 20 (1886), 108–17 and 'What Girls Read', *Nineteenth Century*, 20 (1886), 515–29. In 'What Do the Masses Read?', *Economic Review*, 14 (1904), 166–77, John Garrett Leigh emphasizes the difficulty of finding out about reading that is 'of a class which rarely or indeed never comes under the notice of the person of average culture' (166).

fiction in education and public libraries, in which the distinction was increasingly made between 'good literature' and 'trash'.[34]

However, attempts to displace anxiety about fiction onto the margins of culture were constantly undermined by a sense of shared reading practices throughout society. The sensation literature read by the middle classes was often acknowledged to be a refinement of the fiction provided for the working class in penny dreadfuls, and many critics in the 1860s and 1870s expressed alarm at the movement up the social scale of fictional modes designed for the masses.[35] Later in the century, Hugh Chisholm did not assign origins, but noted parallel developments at either pole of society, linking public interest in the effects of the penny dreadful on working-class readers with 'the exposure of the abominable immoralities of an accomplished producer of non-moral literature for the upper circles of the reading world', an allusion to the trial of Oscar Wilde.[36] In 1898 a critic in *Blackwood's Magazine* went further, arguing that:

The penny stories are wretched things enough, absolutely speaking. But it is infinitely better that the wives and sisters and daughters of our shopmen and our mechanics should spend their spare coppers upon them than that, like their 'betters', they should dabble in, and profess to admire, the pedantic obscenities of an Ibsen, the unintelligible nonsense of a Maeterlinck, or the dubious rodomontade of a Ruskin.[37]

This attitude corroborated Max Nordau's argument, received with much interest in England in 1895, that corruption was spreading downwards through society having originated in the culture of the upper classes.[38] The same anxieties about fiction embraced the subliterary culture of 'the unknown public' and 'the upper circles of the reading world', producing an anti-fiction discourse which affected all aspects of literary culture. For most of the century, the Victorians' suspicion of their most important literary form was, to use James's term, 'dissimulated' as a localized concern about particular kinds of novels and readers. But

[34] Keating, *Haunted Study*, 418–19.
[35] [H. L. Mansel], 'Sensation Novels', *Quarterly Review*, 113 (1863), 505–6; [W. F. Rae], 'Sensation Novelists: Miss Braddon', *North British Review*, 43 (1865), 204; Strahan, 'Bad Literature for the Young', 986.
[36] Chisholm, 'How to Counteract the "Penny Dreadful" ', 765.
[37] [J. H. Millar], 'Penny Fiction', *Blackwood's Magazine*, 164 (1898), 811.
[38] Nordau, *Degeneration*, 7; see also Stutfield, 'Tommyrotics', 844.

behind these local debates lay a much more general fear of fiction.

Only a deep anxiety about the novel can account for the formidable apparatus of literary surveillance and censorship that pervaded all aspects of Victorian literary culture. In its most public and visible aspect, this system could be enforced by law, and the prosecution of Henry Vizetelly in 1888–9 for publishing translations of Zola's works, like the Wilde trial of 1895 (indirectly a literary trial), was the focus of intense public debate about the role of the law in defining and mediating between public morality and literary value.[39] But the periodic eruptions of anxiety about fiction into legal prosecutions were only the more obvious expressions of the fact that fiction was always on trial in the nineteenth-century culture that produced, distributed, consumed, and criticized it, even in the institutions and discourses most closely allied with it. The principle of 'selection' exercised by the great circulating libraries of Edwin Mudie and W. H. Smith (which effectively controlled production and consumption of novels through most of the Victorian period) was an important form of censorship and showed how powerfully evangelical and philistine prejudices against fiction could operate even in the service of a system which had done much to extend the 'tyranny' of the novel over the lives and minds of the British

[39] The Vizetelly case and its effects on English fiction are discussed in Keating, *Haunted Study*, 241–84. In the debates on censorship that followed the trial, defences of the status quo were made by Walter Besant in 'Candour in English Fiction', *New Review*, 2 (1890), 6–9, and George Saintsbury in his preface to *Essays on French Novelists* (London: Percival, 1891), pp. ix–x. The case for greater tolerance for 'realism' and the need to curb the censoring powers of the circulating libraries, which had been made by George Moore in *Literature at Nurse or Circulating Morals* (London: Vizetelly, 1885), was taken up in the articles by E. Lynn Linton and Thomas Hardy on 'Candour in English Fiction', *New Review*, 2 (1890), 10–21. The development of the controversy is surveyed in William C. Frierson, 'The English Controversy over Realism in Fiction 1885–1895', *PMLA*, 43 (1928), 533–50. In *Oscar Wilde* (London: Hamish Hamilton, 1987), 414–25, Richard Ellmann shows how art and morality were both put on trial with Wilde. The Wilde trial features with varying degrees of explicitness in several analyses of fiction published in 1895, which were also influenced by the English publication of Nordau's *Degeneration* in the same year: see Stutfield, 'Tommyrotics'; Janet E. Hogarth, 'Literary Degenerates', *Fortnightly Review*, NS 57 (1895), 586–92; James Ashcroft Noble, 'The Fiction of Sexuality', *Contemporary Review*, 67 (1895), 490–8; and Harry Quilter, 'The Gospel of Intensity', *Contemporary Review*, 67 (1895), 761–82.

public.[40] Censorship at a domestic level was also encouraged: in 1863 a reviewer urged fathers and husbands 'to look about them and scrutinize the parcel that arrives from Mudie's' before the female members of their household could learn to contrast their lives with the excitements of sensation fiction,[41] while in 1890 'the locked bookcase' was advocated as a means of protecting young people from the unwholesome influence of modern fiction.[42] Journal articles and conduct manuals advised readers of all classes on the choice of books, encouraging an internalization of the principle of censorship through readerly self-regulation. Operating at a more subtle level were the censoring powers of cultural convention (which identified the English novel, as opposed to the French, with 'reticence') and, finally, the regulatory power of critical judgement.

Attacking the flagships of this system of censorship, George Moore condemned the circulating libraries for producing 'a literature of bandboxes' and, displacing the function of 'authorship' from the creative individual to the controlling institution, wrote: 'I judge Messrs. Mudie and Smith by what they have produced; for they, not the ladies and gentlemen who place their names on the title pages, are the authors of our fiction.'[43] Moore's image of a literature 'authored' by a system of censorship is applicable, not just to the effects of the circulating libraries, but to the impact of the whole range of regulatory forces discussed above. The 'fiction question' was the permanent background to the writing of novels in the nineteenth century, and moral and sociological debate about reading was intimately connected with the development of novel criticism and theories of fiction. The sustained debate at all cultural levels about the value

[40] For an extended discussion of Mudie's influence on Victorian fiction, see Guinevere L. Griest, *Mudie's Circulating Library and the Victorian Novel* (Bloomington: Indiana University Press, 1970).

[41] 'Our Female Sensation Novelists', 234.

[42] Linton, 'Candour in English Fiction', 14.

[43] George Moore, preface to *Piping Hot! (Pot-Bouille): A Realistic Novel*, by Émile Zola, trans. from the 63rd French edn. (London: Vizetelly, 1885), p. xvi. Moore's notion of 'authorship' suggests Foucault's interrogation of the 'author function' in our culture, whereby the question 'Who really spoke?' is replaced by 'What are the modes of existence of this discourse? Where has it been used, how can it circulate, and who can appropriate it for himself?' See 'What is an Author?', trans. Josué V. Harari, in *The Foucault Reader*, ed. Paul Rabinow (Harmondsworth: Penguin, 1984), 119–20.

and dangers of fiction affected the ways in which authors conducted and perceived their profession, influencing both the kinds
of novels written and the kinds of things said about them. Despite the attempts of many writers to get away from moralistic
criticism, commentary on fiction in the nineteenth century was
saturated with a concern with the effects of books on readers or,
conversely, with the effects of readers on books. In the debates
on realism and cultural degeneracy in the 1880s and 1890s, the
literary productions of high culture were discussed in the same
terms as the fictions of popular culture, as potential agents of
subversion or demoralization. It is impossible to separate the
nineteenth century's critical discourse on novels from its moral
and sociological discourse on fiction: the two were continuous,
'authored' by the same concern with censorship that controlled
Victorian literary institutions. Chris Baldick has argued that literary criticism, with its metaphors of judgement and evaluation,
has always been linked to censorship,[44] and this link is particularly striking in the case of Victorian novel criticism.

Criticism operated most effectively in the cause of censorship
through its manipulation of the terms 'true' and 'false' as a
means of judging the value of novels. In the second half of the
century, condemnation of the novel simply because of its fictional
status was rare, although Trollope still felt the need to refute
charges on this count in 1870.[45] However, although the novel
was rarely attacked for its fictionality *per se*, its fictionality made
it susceptible to censorious criticism, because it allowed critics
to disguise ideological objections as epistemological objections.
This tactic is very clearly displayed in a well-known review by
W. F. Rae of Braddon's sensational novels in 1865. Rae argues:

A novel is a picture of life, and as such ought to be faithful. The fault of
these novels is that they contain pictures of daily life, wherein there are
scenes so grossly untrue to nature, that we can hardly pardon the author-
ess if she drew them in ignorance, and cannot condemn her too strongly
if, knowing their falseness, she introduced them for the sake of effect.

Because of Braddon's infidelity to nature, Rae argues, 'the impartial critic is compelled, as it were, to unite with the moralist'
in condemning her fiction as 'one of the abominations of the

---

[44] Baldick, *Social Mission*, 9.   [45] Trollope, 'Prose Fiction', 112–13.

age'.[46] But the problem with Braddon's pictures of women's sexuality and subversive energy, to which Rae objects, is not that
they are 'untrue to nature' but that they are untrue to a middle-
class ideology of gender: in suggesting dissatisfactions and corruptions at the heart of Victorian domesticity, Braddon has not
been unfaithful to life, but exposed an unacknowledged reality.
The reviewer is able to present this as an affront to the real by
conflating outrages to nature with outrages to social convention.
Criticism thus paid lip-service to the idea that novels 'ought to
be faithful' to life, but in practice worked with ideological constructions of the true and the false. The same critical manœuvre
used to discredit sensation fiction in the 1860s was used to
discredit realist and naturalist works in the 1880s and 1890s.
Writing in 1890 to support the present system of censorship,
Walter Besant argued that ungoverned passion must inevitably
lead to social breakdown, and that to represent the first without
the second was to depict an impossibility; censorship was demanded, therefore, not by 'Average Opinion, but by Art herself,
who will not allow the creation of impossible figures moving in
an unnatural atmosphere'.[47] Similarly, in 1895 James Ashcroft
Noble attacked the modern 'fiction of sexuality' by testing it
against a 'mirror' theory of representation; the novels to which
he objected failed this test because they laid disproportionate
emphasis on one appetite, and were therefore not 'convincing'.[48]

The late nineteenth-century battle over the novelist's right to
represent life was an ideological battle fought in epistemological
terms. In condemning novels which were politically or socially
threatening, conservative critics were able to draw on the terms
of an established tradition of opposition to fiction as a false
mode of knowledge about the world, and could apply this epistemological objection not only when fiction proposed dangerous alternatives to the status quo, but also when it exposed
uncomfortable realities. Conservative criticism thus appeared to
base its verdicts on the analogy with history loosely inscribed in
nineteenth-century novel theory. But in fact, such criticism did
not speak in the name of history; rather, it appealed to social

---

[46] [Rae], 'Sensation Novelists', 203.
[47] Besant, 'Candour in English Fiction', 9.
[48] Noble, 'The Fiction of Sexuality', 493.

constructions of what was 'natural' or 'true'. In effecting a censorship of 'the real' by an appeal to 'the true', conservative
criticism was actually drawing on the epistemology of the pre-
novelistic romance, in which the theory of 'vraisemblance' authorized a displacement of physical or circumstantial fact by an
idealized 'truth'.[49] This disjunction between 'truth' and 'reality'
was contested in the censorship debates of the 1880s and 1890s
by novelists who pleaded their right to represent the real in terms
of the 'candour' of their enterprise. For James, the realignment
of 'truth' with 'reality' was to be achieved by appealing to the
cultural prestige of modern historiography. Novelists had always
sought to obviate distrust of fiction by appropriating the good
name of the historian, but now a more precise alignment with
the historian's rights and duties presented itself as a way of
freeing the novel from the forces of censorship. But this was only
made possible by an important shift in understanding, during the
nineteenth century, of what was meant by the term 'history'.

THE HISTORIOGRAPHICAL MODEL

In 1842 Philip Harwood wrote: 'We know now how much it
takes to make a written or printed book a *history*—a true and
full picture of what men have been and done—a genuine transcript of an era or event.'[50] Harwood's article on 'The Modern
Art and Science of History' is filled with this sense of a radical
break with earlier historiographical standards, as he enthuses
about the process of 'historical reform', based on a closer attention to facts, which pointed the way to a new ideal of history as
a science.[51] Half a century later, Harwood's language of reform

---

[49] Barthes writes: 'The whole of classical culture was for centuries nourished
by the idea that there could be no contamination of the "vraisemblable" by the
real. . . . what is "vraisemblable" is never other than the thinkable: it is entirely
subject to (public) opinion'; see 'The Reality Effect' in *French Literary Theory
Today: A Reader*, ed. Tzvetan Todorov, trans. R. Carter (Cambridge: Cambridge
University Press, 1982), 15. Lennard J. Davis discusses the romance epistemology
of 'vraisemblance' as a 'censoring device' in *Factual Fictions: The Origins of
the English Novel* (New York: Columbia University Press, 1983), 33.

[50] [Philip Harwood], 'The Modern Art and Science of History', *Westminster
Review*, 38 (1842), 357.

[51] Ibid. 356.

was replaced by the language of revolution when Lord Acton, in his inaugural lecture as Professor of Modern History at Cambridge in 1895, summed up the changes in historiographical practice over the century. Judging that 'the accession of the critic' in place of the compiler, artist or advocate, 'amounts to a transfer of government, to a change of dynasty, in the historic realm', he declared that 'in the second quarter of this century, a new era began for historians'.[52]

This new era was based on a transfer of scientific methods to historiography,[53] which had three main aspects: a theory of epistemology, a theory of causation, and a theory of representation. First, the 'scientific' historian was committed to a new rigour in testing the grounds of knowledge, based on scientific and legal conceptions of evidence. 'We are better skilled than our fathers', wrote Harwood, 'in the science both of doubting and of believing.'[54] The old deference to documentary authorities was replaced by a new spirit of scepticism: the narratives of scientific historiography were to be produced not, as in earlier practice, by conflating different accounts, but by testing them against each other; not by merely amassing material, but by judging its value as evidence.[55] As Harwood saw, the faculty of doubt enhanced the faculty of belief: evidence which passed the test of criticism acquired a scientific authority, and the attitude of suspicion on which the new historiography was founded was also the basis of its epistemological confidence.

The project of scientific historiography aimed not only to establish a record of past events, but also to discover the laws of cause and effect governing those events. As W. S. Lilly noted in writing on 'The New Spirit in History' in 1895, whereas the ancient historians had 'no true philosophy of causation', the scientific model of knowledge adopted by modern historians demanded that they 'proceed from facts to laws' and examine

[52] John Emerich Edward Dalberg-Acton, 'Inaugural Lecture on the Study of History', *Lectures on Modern History*, ed. with introd. by John Neville Figgis and Reginald Vere Laurence, first pub. 1906 (London: Macmillan; New York: St Martin's Press, 1960), 15, 14.

[53] Ibid. 21; W. S. Lilly, 'The New Spirit in History', *Nineteenth Century*, 38 (1895), 621.

[54] [Harwood], 'The Modern Art and Science of History', 357.

[55] Dalberg-Acton, 'Inaugural Lecture', 15–16; J. H. Round, 'Historical Research', *Nineteenth Century*, 44 (1898), 1010–11.

the underlying causes of events.[56] Indeed, in 1857 the most enthusiastic and notorious advocate of a science of history, Henry Thomas Buckle, had suggested the possibility of gaining so complete an understanding of the laws governing historical experience that historians would be able to predict and control future events.[57] This theory was attacked, as much for the anti-theological bias of its determinism as for the sheer impossibility of amassing the necessary quantities of evidence,[58] but in fact Buckle merely represented an extreme version of the widespread commitment to inductive reasoning in nineteenth-century historiography which was one of its most important debts to scientific method. The inductive model of knowledge, which required a reasoning from effects to causes, was linked to an interest in new kinds of evidence, as historians no longer relied merely on political documents for information, but engaged in minute 'circumstantial researches' based on physical, statistical, and literary evidence, in order to trace not only the psychological, but the social, economic, institutional, and geographical causes of events.[59]

The third 'scientific' element of the new historiography was its theory of representation, based on the impartiality and, as far as possible, the effacement of the narrator. The ideal was embodied in Ranke, as described by Acton: 'He decided effectually to repress the poet, the patriot, the religious or political partisan, to sustain no cause, to banish himself from his books, and to write nothing that would gratify his own feelings or disclose his private convictions.'[60] By suppressing the personality of the narrator, scientific historiography sought to create the illusion that events were somehow speaking for themselves. Acton approvingly

---

[56] Lilly, 'The New Spirit in History', 620.

[57] Henry Thomas Buckle, 'General Introduction', *History of Civilization in England*, 2nd edn., vol. i (London: Parker, 1858), 17–18.

[58] See William T. Thornton, 'History, and its Scientific Pretensions', *Macmillan's Magazine*, 8 (1863), 25–35; and James Anthony Froude, 'The Science of History', *Short Studies on Great Subjects*, vol. i (London: Longmans, Green, 1867), 1–36.

[59] Buckle, 'General Introduction', 2.

[60] Dalberg-Acton, 'Inaugural Lecture', 19. In *The Clothing of Clio: A Study of the Representation of History in Nineteenth-Century Britain and France* (Cambridge: Cambridge University Press, 1984), 13, Stephen Bann points out that English historians ignored the poetic and dramatic elements in Ranke's writing in order to make a connection between a supposedly plain style and a faithful representation of facts.

quoted the historian de Coulanges, who told his audience: 'Do not imagine you are listening to me; it is history itself that speaks.'[61] The use of a plain style helped to render the narrator invisible, and to give the impression of a reality unmediated by discursive elements, untainted by the traces of fiction historians were expected to detect and expose in their sources. The effacement of the apparatus of narration helped to hide the historian's ideological investment in the particular narrative mode or perspective adopted, and enhanced the idea that history worked in the interests, not of the historian, but of truth itself.

By the end of the century, the project of scientific historiography had become the academic orthodoxy in England—an orthodoxy as yet largely untouched by the crisis in historiographical practice gathering in Europe. However, popular conceptions of history rarely matched specialist ones, and even within the profession competition between scientific history and the older idea of literary history persisted throughout the century.[62] It is therefore impossible to generalize about the extent to which changes in historiographical theory and practice affected the use of the term 'history' in other cultural fields such as literary theory and criticism: the meaning of each usage depends on the writer's level of exposure to and sympathy with the changes in historiography.

That James was aware of and interested in new trends in historiography is evident from his scathing judgements of two of the most eminent exponents of 'literary' history, Froude and Kingsley, in which he clearly aligned himself with the cause of scientific historiography (*LC* i. 1014–17, 1103–4). In his 1867 review of Manning's historical novels he named Niebuhr, Mommsen, Guizot, and Buckle—'writers of a purely scientific turn of mind' (*LC* i. 1154)—as the great historians of the day, and it was to these writers that he looked for a narrative model for the modern novelist. Comparing his list of scientific histor-

[61] Dalberg-Acton, 'Inaugural Lecture', 12.
[62] The competition between 'literary' and 'scientific' history, which was often between amateur and increasingly professional historians, is discussed by Rosemary Jann in *The Art and Science of Victorian History* (Columbus: Ohio State University Press, 1985). Within the profession, the question was epitomized by the competing conceptions of the historian's role offered by Freeman and Froude; see Herbert A. L. Fisher, 'Modern Historians and their Methods', *Fortnightly Review*, NS 56 (1894), 805–9.

ians with a popular novelist, Trollope, James admitted: 'It is hard to imagine minds of these dissimilar types uniting their forces; or, rather, it is hard to imagine a mind in which their distinctive elements and sympathies should be combined' (i. 1154). But it is precisely this sense of the modern difficulty of uniting the interests of novelist and historian that animates James's idea of the novel as history, and distinguishes it from earlier conceptions which drew on a very different model of historical discourse. Fielding, for example, had referred his decision to call *Tom Jones* a history rather than a romance to a desire to evade

that universal Contempt, which the World, who always denominate the Whole from the Majority, have cast on all historical Writers, who do not draw their Materials from Records. And it is the Apprehension of this Contempt, that hath made us so cautiously avoid the Term Romance, a Name with which we might otherwise have been well enough contented.[63]

For Fielding, the choice of generic label has a cultural, but not a technical, significance; at a time when historiography was practised largely as an exercise in rhetoric, more concerned with conceptual frameworks than factual reconstruction, appropriation of the name 'history' did not bind the novelist to any very precise or alien set of technical practices.[64] In the second half of the nineteenth century, however, James was aware that the tasks of the novelist and the historian had greatly diverged since Walter Scott wrote his great historical novels: 'Both history and romance are so much more disinterested at the present moment than they were during Scott's lifetime, that it will take a strong hand to force either of them to look upon the other with the cold glance of the speculator' (*LC* i. 1154).

Nineteenth-century historiography, increasingly defining itself through its opposition to rhetoric and fiction, had made Fielding's cavalier interchange of generic labels impossible. In attempting to revitalize the idea of the 'historical novel' (meaning

[63] Henry Fielding, *The History of Tom Jones, a Foundling*, first pub. 1749, ed. Fredson Bowers with introd. by Martin Battestin, 2 vols. (Oxford: Clarendon Press, 1974), i. 489.
[64] Davis, *Factual Fictions*, 31; Leo Braudy, *Narrative Form in History and Fiction: Hume, Fielding and Gibbon* (Princeton, NJ: Princeton University Press, 1970), 8–10.

not just 'works of fiction which deal exclusively with the past' but the idea of the novelist as 'historian of contemporary manners', historian of 'the *moment*' (i. 1155)), James was aware of bringing together disparate things, crossing what had become a significant gap. The distinct streams of fiction and history had now to be 'forced into confluence' (i. 1154), and James's repeated use of the language of force conveys both the aggressive nature of this project and his sense of its difficulty.

In essays and reviews of the 1860s to the 1880s, James suggested ways in which the technical attributes of historical narrative could be used to enhance the realism and cultural standing of fiction. The question of evidence was central to nineteenth-century historiography, and James placed it at the heart of his comparison of the roles of novelist and historian in 'The Art of Fiction':

> To represent and illustrate the past, the actions of men, is the task of either writer, and the only difference that I can see is, in proportion as he succeeds, to the honour of the novelist, consisting as it does in his having more difficulty in collecting his evidence, which is so far from being purely literary. (*LC* i. 47)

The new historiography prided itself on what Acton called its 'heroic study of records'; tales of the enormous quantities of original research undertaken by historians such as Ranke became matter for professional legend, evincing a moral as well as intellectual commitment to the extension of knowledge.[65] In a bold move, James argued that the work of the novelist in collecting evidence is even more difficult, and therefore deserves even greater cultural 'honour'. However, his claim that this increased difficulty is 'the only difference' between novelist and historian is rather disingenuous: a more fundamental difference is that while a novel may refer to things in the world outside it, it also refers to a great many imaginary things, and these imagined characters, objects, and events are generated by the act of narration, whereas in historical narrative the act of narration comes after the things to which it refers. James's effort in delineating the task of the novelist as historian (and indeed, the

---

[65] Dalberg-Acton, 'Inaugural Lecture', 7. In partially reclaiming Froude for the scientific tradition, Fisher emphasized his massive work of original documentary research ('Modern Historians and their Methods', 806).

effort of realism in general) is to make the relation between story and narrative appear to follow the same order in fiction as it does in history—to reverse it, making the fictional narrative appear to be reporting events that have already taken place. Rhetorically, this can be achieved by manipulating historio- graphical codes of practice for the handling of evidence; by professing a commitment to these codes, James is able to create the illusion that the 'evidence' with which he deals is real, found not made.

Novelists had always imitated the historian's documentary ap- paratus as a way of enhancing the effect of realism; now the growing interest of historians in circumstantial evidence streng- thened the epistemological authority of the novel's traditional circumstantial mode of narration. In 1888 James observed: 'The effort of our time has been, as we know, to disinter the details of history, to see the celebrities of the past, and even the obscure persons, in the small facts as well as in the big facts of their lives' (*LC* ii. 422). As Harwood wrote in 1842, 'nothing is too lowly to furnish data for historic science', for 'Modern history knows the historical value of the little facts that make the common life of little men.'[66] A similar capacity to use the evidence of 'small facts' could give a work of fiction historical authority. According to James, it is Stevenson's 'talent for seeing the familiar in the heroic, and reducing the extravagant to plausible detail' that allows some passages in *Kidnapped* to 'read like a series of inspired footnotes on some historic page' (*LC* i. 1254), while on the other hand, the 'historical colouring' of Hawthorne's *The Scarlet Letter* is weak because it offers 'little elaboration of detail, of the modern realism of research' (*LC* i. 404). In the novel, 'small facts' play a dual role, acting not just as significant details which provide evidence of character or circumstance within the novel, but also as 'evidence' of the novel's referen- tiality. James described Turgenev's tales as 'a magazine of small facts, of anecdotes, of descriptive traits, taken, as the phrase is, *sur le vif*' (*LC* ii. 969). Of one of Turgenev's delineations of character, James wrote: 'These lines seem to carry a kind of historical weight. It is the Princess R—— and no one else. We feel as if the author could show us documents and relics; as if he had

[66] [Harwood], 'The Modern Art and Science of History', 365, 366.

her portrait, a dozen letters, some of her old trinkets' (ii. 970). Turgenev's use of significant detail not only adds depth to the characterization of the Princess R——, but acts as circumstantial evidence for the claim that the author is reporting on a real person. The denser the tissue of 'small facts' provided, the greater the impression that the narrative is referring to objects external to, and independent of, itself. In 'The Art of Fiction', James equates 'the air of reality' with 'solidity of specification' (*LC* i. 53), and this formulation may be traced to his admiration for Balzac's use of density of detail. 'Balzac is always definite; you can say Yes or No to him as you go on; the story bristles with references that must be verified' (*LC* ii. 38). James explains that this is one reason why Balzac's novels can never be classed as 'light literature'; demanding from the reader the kind of serious attention usually given to history rather than novels, the multiplicity of references makes Balzac's works sometimes 'as hard reading in the way of entertainment as Hallam or Guizot' (ii. 38).

The cultural value attached to 'hard reading' helps to promote Balzac to the rank of historian, but his constant appeal to the reader to verify references also operates in a more complex way to confer on his novels the status of history. By putting into his narratives a great many 'small facts' such as descriptions of material objects and details of quotidian existence, which appeal to and satisfy the reader's power of verification, Balzac creates in the reader a readiness to accept as 'true' other larger 'facts' on which the narrative depends—the fictional assertions about characters and events, which cannot possibly be verified because they have no existence outside the text. James felt that Balzac sometimes 'sins by extravagance' in giving too many material details: 'He has his necessary houses and his superfluous houses: often when in a story the action is running thin he stops up your mouth against complaint, as it were, by a choking dose of brick and mortar' (*LC* ii. 50). However, more importantly than simply filling out lulls in the action, this surplus of 'small facts' acts as a guarantee for the major assertions of the novel. Barthes has demonstrated the function of excessive denotation and apparently useless details as 'reality effects' in narrative, arguing that the model for this is history, with its assumption that 'the *having-been-there* of things is a sufficient reason for speaking of them'.[67] In fiction, a surplus of references to things which exist in the world creates a surplus of goodwill on the part of the reader to accept the reality of things which do not exist outside the language of the novel. Balzac's 'superfluous houses' create an 'air of reality' through which we view his fictional characters and events.

The use of circumstantial evidence was associated with the inductive methods at the heart of the historian's new 'scientific' philosophy of causation—a philosophy which James urged the novelist to adopt. In his review of Manning's historical novels James noted that the novelist begins with a cause, which he may trace to whatever effects he chooses, while the historian begins with an effect, the 'final manifestations of conduct', beyond which his imagination must not go; all his effort is devoted to a search for causes and relations beneath the 'vast fabric of im-penetrable fact [that] is stretched over his head' (*LC* i. 1154). The images of the novelist and historian used here conform to cultural stereotypes of 'light' and 'heavy' literature (i. 1153): over the novelist 'spreads the unobstructed sky, with nothing to hinder the flight of fancy', whereas the historian is associated with hard labour: 'He works in the dark, with a contracted forehead and downcast eyes, on his hands and knees, as men work in coal-mines' (i. 1154). But there is no reason, James argues,

why the novelist should not subject himself, as regards the treatment of his subject, to certain of the obligations of the historian; why he should not imprison his imagination, for the time, in a circle of incidents from which there is no arbitrary issue, and apply his ingenuity to the study of a problem to which there is but a single solution. (i. 1155)

According to this model, given certain premises (such as psycho-logical data about the characters), the story must unfold as these premises dictate, and must not be affected by external constraints such as the reader's expectations, the author's sentimental allegi-ances, or the exigencies of the production process. In assuming the constraints that bind the historian, the novelist also gains the historian's freedom, because adherence to a historical standard of causation demands that the novelist defy the forces of censorship.

[67] Barthes, 'The Reality Effect', 15.

Submission to certain 'obligations of the historian' is thus one
way of casting off the burden of being 'light' literature which, as
James noted in 'The Art of Fiction', purchased the novel's freedom of fancy at the price of its freedom to write seriously about
life, and was thus 'only an attempt to stifle it disguised in the
form of generosity' (*LC* i. 45).

James's idea of the novelist as historian also attempted to defy
censorship by drawing on historiographical standards of representation, particularly the idea of full and impartial disclosure
associated with 'scientific' history. In his 1867 review of Froude,
James criticized this famous practitioner of 'literary' history for
his lack of proper objectivity, accusing him of a 'readiness to
make vague moral epithets stand in lieu of real psychological
facts' (*LC* i. 1015) and of a tendency to grow maudlin over some
characters, 'a kind of psychological exercise which is essentially
at variance with the true historical and critical spirit' (i. 1017).
James believed that moral judgements distort historical accounts
because history does not teach moral lessons—'What strikes an
attentive student of the past is the indifference of events to man's
moral worth or worthlessness' (i. 1014–15)—and he criticized
Kingsley and Carlyle, as well as Froude, for attempting to read
moral patterns into history (i. 1113). Froude's attempts to shape
his histories according to his own moral prejudices led not only
to personal intrusions upon the narrative, but to a decision to
suppress evidence that was 'too bad to print'; such censorship of
the historical record affronted James's scientific conception of
the historian's obligation to 'effect a dispassionate logical synthesis of the material at hand' (i. 1017). In keeping with this
historiographical model, James found the 'poetic reticence' practised by Scott inappropriate to the modern historical novelist,
whose task was 'not to invest, but to divest the past' (i. 1203).
Scientific historiography demanded a record of the past divested,
not only of inaccuracies and pruderies, but of unnecessary rhetorical elaborations, and James used this austere standard of
representation to criticize Hardy's 'verbose and redundant style'
in *Far from the Madding Crowd*, reminding him that 'a novelist
is after all but a historian, thoroughly possessed of certain facts,
and bound in some way or other to impart them' (i. 1045). In
this case, James draws upon a historiographical model of representation primarily to call attention to the virtues of compression,

but his comment also suggests, again, his wish to place the novelist beyond the reach of censorship by claiming the responsibilities of the historian: whereas the novelist was constantly required to withhold information, the historian was morally 'bound . . . to impart' all he knew. At the same time, this appeal to the obligations of the historian helps to construct the very referential illusion on which the claim of historical status rests. The image of the historian used here is a Rankean one, and James's remark that the novelist is 'but a historian' is reminiscent of Ranke's famous statement that he wished 'only' to represent the past 'as it really was'. In both cases, the apparent modesty of the statement (a disclaimer of higher analytical or rhetorical aims) masks the enormity of the claim being made: in the historian's case, the claim that the facts really can be recovered and represented just as they happened,[68] and in the novelist's case, the even greater claim that he is dealing with real 'facts' at all.

James's early novel theory constantly borrowed from historiographical practice in order to maintain this illusion that the novel is a report on independent, pre-existing data. In an early review he recommended the novelist Harriet Prescott to study the method of Balzac, who 'set down things in black and white, . . . in prose, scientifically, as they stood'. James stressed the word '*scientifically*' as the key to the lesson, suggesting the historiographical enterprise which was also based on an ability to 'transcribe facts' in their original order (*LC* i. 609). Nearly twenty years later, James made the same point in 'The Art of Fiction':

Catching the very note and trick, the strange irregular rhythm of life, that is the attempt whose strenuous force keeps Fiction upon her feet. In proportion as in what she offers us we see life *without* rearrangement do we feel that we are touching the truth; in proportion as we see it *with* rearrangement do we feel that we are being put off with a substitute, a compromise and convention. (*LC* i. 58)

Turgenev's work satisfied this condition of historical veracity: ' "It is life itself," we murmur as we read, "and not this or that or the other story-teller's more or less clever 'arrangement' of life" ' (*LC* ii. 976). Such injunctions against 'rearrangement'

---

[68] Bann's gloss on Ranke's dictum (*The Clothing of Clio*, 8–14) reveals the slipperiness of the historian's apparently straightforward language and 'the daring of the (understated) claim' (11).

make sense only when the idea has already been established that
the author is reporting a reality that preceded his own narrative.
To some extent, of course, he may do so, for example by including historical events in his narrative, or giving topographical
descriptions of real places; however, when discussing the events
of a fictional story (which have had no existence outside their
arrangement in the text), critical statements contrasting 'truth to
life' with 'rearrangement' do not make literal sense. Rather, their
rhetoric, borrowed from historiography, both depends on and
helps to establish the fiction that the story preceded the narrative made about it: stressing the importance of keeping the
narrative true to the story helps to create the belief that the story
itself is true. This was achieved in Balzac's works, as James
realized: 'At bottom, his incidents and character [*sic*] were as
fictitious as those of Spenser's "Fairy Queen;" yet he was as
averse from taking liberties with them as we are bound to conceive Mr. Motley, for instance, to be from taking liberties with
the history of Holland' (*LC* i. 1155).

James's interpretation of Balzac's narrative technique shows
how complex was his notion of the novel as history: the events
of Balzac's narratives are known to be fictitious, yet assumed to
be real. This response on the part of a reader is achieved by a
repertoire of formal devices which work to turn modes of attention into forms of belief: verifiable facts stand guarantee for
unverifiable fictional assertions; the impartiality of the narrator
underwrites the truth of his reports; the fidelity of the narrative
to the story presupposes—or constructs—the reality of the story
itself. All these techniques suggest the referentiality of the narrative, but ultimately the idea of fiction as history is a matter of
contract between author and reader. In drawing an analogy between Balzac, the model of the novelist as historian, and the
actors Garrick and Kemble (*LC* i. 1343), James reveals that the
notion of historical narrative is an artificial, constructed thing.
He knew that we cannot read 'history', only 'histories' (*LC* i.
1015)—our access to the historical real is always discursively
mediated, always plural. But the rules of the genre mean that we
are 'bound to conceive' of the historian as committed to the
truth; similarly, when an author such as Balzac engages to behave
like a historian, respecting the integrity of his material and keeping it free from external manipulation and arbitrary intervention,

the reader in turn must behave like a reader of history, and credit the story with reality. By establishing a consensus about the conventions borrowed from the writing and reading of history, a contract is established between author and reader which enables the idea of the novel as history to operate.

When he sees this contract being fulfilled, as in Balzac's case, James provides a sophisticated analysis of its technical basis; it is when he sees (as he believes) the contract broken—as in the case of Trollope—that the insecurities and contradictions in his own theoretical position become apparent. This is the effect of his famous attack on Trollope in 'The Art of Fiction':

> In a digression, a parenthesis or an aside, he concedes to the reader that he and this trusting friend are only 'making believe.' He admits that the events he narrates have not really happened, and that he can give his narrative any turn the reader may like best. Such a betrayal of a sacred office seems to me, I confess, a terrible crime; it is what I mean by the attitude of apology, and it shocks me every whit as much in Trollope as it would have shocked me in Gibbon or Macaulay. (*LC* i. 46)

Similarly, in his 1883 essay on Trollope he wrote of the novelist's 'suicidal satisfaction in reminding the reader that the story he was telling was only, after all, a make-believe' and declared that 'when Trollope suddenly winks at us and reminds us that he is telling us an arbitrary thing, we are startled and shocked in quite the same way as if Macaulay or Motley were to drop the historic mask and intimate that William of Orange was a myth or the Duke of Alva an invention' (*LC* i. 1343). Trollope's breaking of the fictional frame is presented as an affront to historiographical practice, betraying an 'ambiguity of mind as to what constitutes evidence' (i. 1343). Many twentieth-century critics have accused James of misreading the effects of Trollope's intrusions,[69] but

---

[69] Several accusations that James misrepresented Trollope are cited by Vivien Jones in 'James and Trollope', *Review of English Studies*, NS 33 (1982), 278–94. Jones argues that James's 'inappropriate reaction' (294) to Trollope's intrusions reveals his own uncertainties about his relation to his audience and about the basis of the realist illusion. In *The Theoretical Dimensions of Henry James* (London: Methuen, 1984), 58–83, John Carlos Rowe argues that an 'anxiety of influence' leads James to construct a version of Trollope which minimizes his contributions to the kind of realism James himself wanted to pioneer. Defending the narrative tradition of 'telling' against the privilege accorded to 'showing' by such theorists as Percy Lubbock, Wayne Booth maintains in *The Rhetoric of Fiction* (Chicago: University of Chicago Press, 1961) that Trollope's intrusions

James's verdict is in keeping with the widely held principle in nineteenth-century criticism that any authorial commentary, not just intrusions which specifically admitted the fictional nature of the work, diminished the realism of a novel.[70] However, the important question is not whether James was right to construe Trollope's comments as a confession of fictionality, but why the idea of a novelist revealing the fictionality of his enterprise disturbed him so deeply and provoked so violent a response. The answer lies, of course, in the continuing force of hostility to fiction, which James's model of the 'historical novel' was designed to obviate. But in attacking Trollope for breaking the historian's contract with the reader, James expresses exactly those negative attitudes towards fiction that the historical model for the novel was designed to overcome.

There is a deep contradiction in James's response to Trollope. Trollope's 'terrible crime' is that he fails to disclaim the fictionality of his work, and therefore fails to take his work as seriously as it deserves; it seems that in order to take fiction seriously, it is necessary to deny that it is fiction.[71] In admitting that his work is 'only "making believe" ', Trollope is, according to James, guilty of an 'attitude of apology' towards his work. But James's warning that the novel must not 'give itself away' itself expresses an 'attitude of apology' towards the whole enterprise of novel-writing (*LC* i. 46). Calling the failure to deny fictionality a 'crime' is a displaced expression of the old attitude, 'as explicit as it was narrow' (i. 45), that labelled fiction itself a crime. James called 'The Art of Fiction' 'simply a plea for liberty' (*Letters* iii. 58), and his appeal to a historiographical model for the novel is here, as elsewhere in his early theory and criticism, part of an

suggest only his control over how events are narrated, not over the events themselves (205–6). In his attack on Ian Watt's theory of authorial effacement, Mark Spilka claims that James's reading of Trollope has itself been misread to support arguments against intrusion: see 'Ian Watt on Intrusive Authors, or the Future of an Illusion', *Hebrew University Studies in Literature*, 1 (1973), 23.

[70] Stang, *Theory of the Novel*, 91–107; Kenneth Graham, *English Criticism of the Novel 1865–1900* (Oxford: Clarendon Press, 1965), 121–8. A reviewer of *Barchester Towers* in 1858 anticipated James's criticism of Trollope's intrusions; see [Percy Greg], 'Mr. Trollope's Novels', 425. Trollope himself made a similar criticism of Thackeray's intrusions: see *Thackeray* (London: Macmillan, 1879), 201.

[71] J. Hillis Miller makes this point in 'Narrative and History', *Journal of English Literary History*, 41 (1974), 457.

attempt to free the novelist from the cultural distrust of fiction expressed in both institutional censorship and prescriptive criticism. However, this technical manœuvre fails to move outside the terms of a critical discourse imbued with prejudices against fiction. In choosing to defend the novel on the grounds of truth rather than value, James ties his theorizing to the primitive epistemology of evangelical and utilitarian hostility to fiction, an epistemology which recognized only history and lies, failing to acknowledge that fiction is intentionally and effectively distinct from either. Ideas that transcend the fixed categories of true and false—jokes, games of self-conscious make-believe, the paradox of truth reached through lies—are erased from the critical discussion. In James's most extreme statements, such as his criticism of Trollope, history comprehensively displaces fiction—fiction on its own terms has not 'the smallest *locus standi*', and the 'narrator of fictitious events' is 'nowhere' (*LC* i. 1343). Censoring not only some aspect of the content of fiction, but its very fictionality, James's theory shows itself to be produced by and complicit with the culture of censorship he deplored. To use James's terms, 'traces (dissimulated though they may be)' (*LC* i. 46) of suspicion of fiction lie at the very heart of his defence of the novel as history, turning 'The Art of Fiction' into a self-contradictory document, expressive of the very attitudes against which it rebels.

This fundamental contradiction in James's thinking about fiction and history is reinforced by other conflicts arising from his attempts to promote incompatible novelistic values. As his reviews of Goncourt's *La Fille Elisa* and Eliot's *Middlemarch* show, the lack of selection exercised in French naturalism and English realism raised problems of subject-matter and form respectively, which the early James could confront only by arguing against the value of the historiographical model he advocated so strenuously elsewhere (*LC* ii. 404, i. 965–6). More significant for his later development was the difficulty of reconciling a historiographical model with his strengthening belief that 'A novel is in its broadest definition a personal, a direct impression of life' (*LC* i. 50). Impressionism is, of course, a form of realism, and a shift in concern from objectively defined to subjectively defined notions of experience is not incompatible with an idea of the novelist as historian; after all, it was through the figure of James as 'the historian of fine consciences' that Conrad made a direct link between the nineteenth-century project of fiction as history and the modernist project of exploring the subjectivity of experience.[72] However, James's recognition of the subjectivity of experience was incompatible with the particular narrative model provided by nineteenth-century scientific historiography, which sought to produce a purely objective record. In his 1883 essay on Daudet James asserted that 'the main object of the novel is to represent life', but proceeded to qualify this, saying: 'I am perfectly aware that to say the object of a novel is to represent life does not bring the question to a point so fine as to be uncomfortable for any one. . . . For, after all, may not people differ infinitely as to what constitutes life—what constitutes representation?' (*LC* ii. 242). Scientific historiography was based on the assumption that people would not 'differ infinitely' about what constituted reality or its representation, assuming that both would be objectively or, at least, consensually defined.[73] In contrast, James's critical writings of the 1880s constantly interrogate objective or consensual definitions of 'experience' or 'reality', destabilizing the fixed notions on which his historiographical model depended.[74]

It is a short step from 'a personal, a direct impression of life' which calls into question objective definitions of experience, to the personal fiction which actively contests the collectively defined real. James's interest in the subjective nature of experience would lead him increasingly to explore the contestatory nature of the imagination, bringing him into even greater conflict with his own commitment to a historiographical model of narrative. The conflict is potentially already present in 'The Art of Fiction', in the ambiguity of James's statement that the novelist 'competes with life' (*LC* i. 53).[75] The phrase holds in tension two quite different conceptions of the novel as, on the one hand, a

---

[72] Joseph Conrad, 'The Historian of Fine Consciences' (1905), in *The Question of Henry James: A Collection of Critical Essays*, ed. F. W. Dupee (London: Allan Wingate, 1947), 62.

[73] See e.g. Fisher's assumption that 'the views of sensible men as to what is good evidence and what is bad, do not differ very appreciably', and that therefore 'As the evidence accumulates the margin of doubt contracts in history as well as in other branches of study' ('Modern Historians and their Methods', 811).

[74] James agreed with Maupassant that 'it is . . . absurd to say that there is, for the novelist's use, only one reality of things' (*LC* ii. 523); see also his comments in 'The Art of Fiction' on the subjectivity and plurality of experience (*LC* i. 51–2).

[75] The original version of 'The Art of Fiction' contained several more references

representational discourse, claiming to reproduce life in its intensity, variety, and totality, and on the other hand, an oppositional discourse offering new ways of imagining experience and formulating alternatives to the status quo. While the first meaning upholds the novel's claim to historical status, the second undermines it and suggests exactly the qualities feared by opponents of fiction—its subversive reformulations of experience, and its refusal to be governed by the authority of the socially constituted real. James's declaration that the novel must compete with life is intended to align it with the representational discourse of history, but also suggests (however undesignedly) its complicity with the oppositional discourses of jokes, lies, and romances.

The ambiguity of the phrase 'competes with life' epitomizes the multivalency of 'The Art of Fiction', in which the historical model coexists uneasily with other, incompatible ideas of fiction. Such conflicts were important in determining the plots and narrative methods of James's early fiction. In particular, I am interested in two theoretical stress-points in 'The Art of Fiction' which undermine the analogy between novel and history: the attack on Trollope, which shows that James can uphold the historiographical model only by collaborating with cultural forces hostile to fiction, and the idea of competition with life, in which the contestatory nature of fiction (neutralized by its alignment with history) is allowed to reveal itself. These theoretical tensions are expressed technically, structurally, and dramatically in the early novels, where romantic, idealistic, subjective, and oppositional forms of narrative compete with the model of history for the power to determine the events and form of the novel. From the energies of competition and contradiction in these works emerge new narrative techniques and new theories of fiction which lead the later novels into radical departures from James's early commitment to history.

to the idea of competing with life (see *Longman's Magazine*, 4 (1884), 503); James omitted these from the version printed in *Partial Portraits* in response to Robert Louis Stevenson's objections that art could not compete with the breadth and complexity of life ('A Humble Remonstrance', *Longman's Magazine* (Dec. 1884); reprinted in *Memories and Portraits* (London: Chatto & Windus, 1887), 281–3). The 'troublesome presence' of the idea of competition, suggesting more radical formulations of the relations between art and life that would emerge later in James's career, is discussed by Mark Spilka in 'Henry James and Walter Besant: "The Art of Fiction" Controversy', in *Towards a Poetics of Fiction*, ed. Spilka (Bloomington: Indiana University Press, 1977), 207.

2

Competing with Life: The Earlier Novels

THE NOVELS produced by James between 1870 and 1890 are narrated 'with the tone of the historian' (*LC* i. 46).[1] From the early melodramatic and romantic novels through to the later naturalistic works of this period, James's narrators are presented as historians sifting documents, weighing evidence, working from data which, as they disarmingly admit, is sometimes too abundant and sometimes too meagre for their purposes. Using 'small facts' and verifiable details, scrupulously distinguishing fact from speculation, recognizing the obligation to tell all, but no more, than the evidence warrants—in all these ways the narrators imitate the historian's code of practice, working to create the impression that the narrative is an impartial report on autonomous material. In thus producing the illusion of referentiality, 'the air of reality', the novelist, James wrote in 'The Art of Fiction', 'competes with life' (*LC* i. 53).

However, the dramatic energies of the novels arise from the attempts of the characters to create plots which, in a very different sense, compete with the life thus narrated—not by imitating it, but by offering alternatives to it. While developing the role of the narrator as objective historian, James created characters obsessed with the need to plot their lives for themselves, in opposition to received experience as recorded by that narrator. Like Christopher Newman in *The American*, James's heroes and heroines aim to achieve a 'victory over circumstances' (*TA* 37) by confronting them with an imagined counter-reality, a coherent and irresistible alternative vision. These fiction-making characters anticipate their author's later movement away from a

---

[1] The scope of this chapter follows James's statement that *The Tragic Muse* 'closes, to my mind, what I should call as regards my novels, my earlier period' (*Letters* iv. 367).

realist epistemology; more flexible formulations of the relations between art and life are dramatized through the actions of these characters long before they are fully theorized in James's later writings on the novel. Competing with life in very different ways, the narrators and the characters of the early novels are engaged in a struggle for narrative authority which has important consequences in undermining the model of the novel as history expounded in James's early theory and criticism.

The conflict between desire and circumstance that is at the heart of James's novels dramatizes a conflict between two kinds of narrative. The plots of the characters exhibit qualities exactly the opposite of the attributes of historical narrative already discussed. Historical narrative supposedly presents 'life *without* rearrangement' (*LC* i. 58), the narrative discourse being, ideally, an exact, transparent transcription of a pre-existing sequence of events. The characters' plots are versions of life '*with* rearrangement' (*LC* i. 58), which aim to serve the interests of the plotter by effecting a change in experience or the way in which it is perceived. History is tied to retrospective responsibilities, whereas plot opens up prospective opportunities. The relation between story and narrative discourse on which history is based is reversed in plot, where the discourse precedes the story, generating rather than recording a sequence of events.

While the novels themselves are offered as history, their action consists of the interplay of the various plots launched by the characters, which compete with each other for the power of shaping reality, and with the facts as given in the narrator's version of events for the status of history. In most of the novels of this period, the characters' plots are unable to make a lasting impression on reality, and in the end are defeated by the immutable facts and incontrovertible truths represented by the narrator's historical record. James's novels follow a recurrent pattern of aspiration and defeat, which has been commented upon by many critics. Philip Weinstein notes 'the essential Jamesian paradigm: inflation followed by deflation; *illusions* followed by *illusions perdues*'.[2] Sallie Sears finds the expression of a 'negative imagination' in the 'basic pattern of James's work': the

[2] Philip M. Weinstein, *Henry James and the Requirements of the Imagination* (Cambridge, Mass.: Harvard University Press, 1971), 9.

creation by his characters of imaginary worlds which are 'doomed to collapse when brought into conjunction with the "facts." The facts are always that things are different from what a given character had wanted.'[3] The unhappy endings that resulted from this 'paradigm' or 'pattern' were referred by James to a sense of what was likely to happen in real life, as is shown in his letter to W. D. Howells explaining the ending of *The American* (*Letters* ii. 104–5). It seems it is necessary for the characters to become disillusioned with their plots in order that the reader may not become disillusioned with the novel itself. James wanted to construct narratives in which the outcome was inevitable, as the working out of a situation from which there could be 'no arbitrary issue' (*LC* i. 1155); the plots of the characters are arbitrary, and must be defeated lest the narrator's story should also appear so. The novelist imitates the historian in pretending that a 'vast fabric of impenetrable fact is stretched over his head' (*LC* i. 1154); playing the part of history, his own narrative becomes the fabric of 'fact' which acts as a resistance to his characters' imaginations.

But in seeming to defer in this way to the historical nature of the novel, James was in fact constructing it. The appearance of truth or realism in a narrative may be heightened by making a contrast with another narrative which appears false or romantic. Drawing such a contrast made the novel's traditional disclaimer of fictionality more persuasive; narrators in the realist tradition commonly contrasted the kind of plot which would be possible in a novel or romance with the more painful or dull events which a commitment to 'reality' compelled them to narrate—the narrative's identity with history was implied by pointing out its difference from romance. Indeed, history itself is defined more by contrasting true and false discourses than by claiming direct links with reality. For Acton, modern historical method began with 'the art of exposing falsehood', and was best exemplified by Ranke who, he claimed, defined himself as a historian against the false discourse of fiction, 'determined' in his career by his early disillusionment with the historical value of Scott's novels.[4] Acton's anecdotal account of the origins of modern historical

---

[3] Sallie Sears, *The Negative Imagination: Form and Perspective in the Novels of Henry James* (Ithaca, NY: Cornell University Press, 1968), 127.

[4] Dalberg-Acton, 'Inaugural Lecture', 5, 19.

study accords with Michel de Certeau's observation that history and fiction operate through a 'reciprocal determination': 'the technical discourse capable of determining the errors characteristic of fiction has come to be authorized to speak in the name of the "real" '; history is constituted through a system of contrasts, 'enforcing belief in something real through a denunciation of the false'.[5] In James's early works, such a contrast is built into the structure of the novels, as our sense of the truth of the narrator's version of events is strengthened by the fact that its ability to describe reality is superior to that of the more romantic plots which compete with it.

As a means of heightening realism, the defeat of plot by history encodes an implicit disclaimer of fictionality into the structure of the novel. This formal device helping to construct the narrative's status as history at the same time expresses the suspicion of fiction also manifested in James's theory of the novel as history. Indeed, the dramatic structure has close affinities with the *exempla* used by anti-fiction rhetoricians to illustrate the harmful effects of reading novels. The propensity of James's characters to rebel against the given constraints of their lives, and their desire to plot their own futures, are exactly the kinds of attitudes which were commonly attributed to excessive novel-reading. In 1893 an article in the *Nineteenth Century* 'deprecating excessive devotion to fiction' pointed out that reading a good novel is like visiting a wealthy friend who has disposed everything for your entertainment—on returning home you are apt to be annoyed that everything is not so well endowed and arranged; therefore 'it is not safe to tarry too long with this phantom company, or we shall find ourselves out of tune with real men and women; unbraced for the stern difficulties, the dark perplexity which, at one time or another, we all have to encounter'.[6] This late nineteenth-century warning is continuous with the old evangelical argument that novels not only engendered dissatisfaction with the common circumstances of life, but were responsible for a dangerous excitement of the imaginative faculty. An article on novel-reading

---

[5] Michel de Certeau, 'History: Science and Fiction', *Heterologies: Discourse on the Other*, trans. Brian Massumi (Manchester: Manchester University Press, 1986), 201.
[6] Herbert Maxwell, 'The Craving for Fiction', *Nineteenth Century*, 33 (1893), 1060, 1058, 1057.

in the *Methodist Magazine* in 1819 asserts that 'if, unhappily, a mind naturally strong and active has been led into this course of reading, it is very often engaging in aerial pursuits, spining [*sic*] out fictions of its own'.[7] In 1815 a concerned commentator on novel-reading warned against the influence of the imagination, 'whose province it is to forecast and combine ideal expectations with apparent realities; to divest the future of all those pangs which yet we must endure when we pass through this future', for, when the imagination rules, 'it increases that tendency of the mind to look forward, to forecast its own lot, and so to provide for its own continual disappointment and misery'.[8]

Anti-fiction diatribes sought to prove that attempts to speculate against given circumstances and to forecast one's own lot always did end in disappointment, and to support this argument offered moral tales in which the novel-fed, deceived imagination was corrected by a harsh reality. The exemplary stories of anti-fiction rhetoric provide the basic structure of novels in the tradition of *Don Quixote*, in which the exposure of the follies of imagination by mundane circumstances is designed to illustrate the dangerous consequences of a belief that reality may imitate romance. A character such as Lavinia Penniman in *Washington Square* is taken directly from this literary tradition, and belongs to a long line of deluded female readers including Arabella in Charlotte Lennox's *The Female Quixote*, Lydia Languish in Sheridan's *The Rivals*, Laura and Sophia in Austen's *Love and Freindship* [*sic*] and Catherine Morland in *Northanger Abbey*, Flaubert's Emma Bovary, and Isabel Gilbert in Mary Elizabeth Braddon's *The Doctor's Wife*.[9] However, James's characters usually represent more complex versions of the corrupted reader and corrupting writer presented in anti-fiction literature. Ad-

---

[7] G. Birley, 'Thoughts on Reading Novels', *Methodist Magazine*, 42 (1819), 608.

[8] 'A.A.', 'On the Practice of Novel-Reading', 515, 514.

[9] For further examples of the genre, see Robert A. Colby, ' "Rational Amusement": Fiction vs. Useful Knowledge in the Nineteenth Century', in *Victorian Literature and Society: Essays Presented to Richard D. Altick*, ed. James R. Kincaid and Albert J. Kuhn (Columbus: Ohio State University Press, 1983), 50–1; Gallaway, 'The Conservative Attitude toward Fiction', 1045–7, 1053; Winfield H. Rogers, 'The Reaction against Melodramatic Sentimentalism in the English Novel, 1796–1830', *PMLA*, 49 (1934),98–122; and Taylor, *Early Opposition*, 69–71.

dicted, if not to reading novels, then to reading experience in a novelistic way, James's heroes and heroines combine interpretative and compositional skills to become dangerous imitators of the novelist's task. When they declare a lack of interest in reading novels, it is to profess all the more strongly their predilection for what was the feared result of excessive novel-reading—the desire to write, novelistically, one's life for oneself; expressions of disdain for novels only emphasize their confidence that they can outdo novelists in creating counter-realities. 'Young persons', James had written in an early review, 'however they may outgrow the tendency in later life, are often more or less romancers on their own account. While the tendency lasts, they are very critical in the matter of fictions' (*LC* i. 1197). In *Roderick Hudson*, Christina Light protests: 'No novels, please! I am tired of novels. I can imagine better stories for myself than any I read' (*RH* ii. 58). Miriam Rooth declares in *The Tragic Muse*, 'Of course I'm not so fond of reading; I go in for the book of life' (*TM* i. 151), a book she wants to help to write, as well as read. In most cases, James's characters find that the book of life has already been written for them, and that they are not empowered to revise it. As in anti-fiction *exempla* or in the anti-romance tradition, pretensions to plot one's own experience lead to error and delusion, or simply meet the superior force of an irresistible reality. The narrator's role is thus a corrective one, providing an ironic commentary on the characters' plots and communicating the truth that finally defeats them. Renunciation (which often seems so perverse and unnecessary) is imposed on the characters by a narrative structure which reinforces the sense of the novel as history, at the expense of any concessions to the value of fiction.

The defeat of plot by history creates a narrative structure which meets the demand made in 'The Art of Fiction', that the novel should differentiate itself from the kind of morally and epistemologically questionable fictions which had attracted a tradition of hostility to the genre. However, in practice the model may have the opposite effect of revealing similarities between the characters' and the author's activity, which the interpolated figure of the narrator-historian cannot disguise. The characters' plots embody many of the qualities of fiction which the model of the novel as history aims to hide—its prospective energies, its

romanticism, its subjectivity, its arbitrariness or contingency—
and James's obsession with these characters may be seen as a
displacement not only of anxiety, but of energy, allowing novelistic expression to values irreconcilable with the historiographical model that dominated his theory of fiction. As the characters,
making fictions and sending them out into the world, replicate
the work of an author, the analysis of their activity reveals a
desire to work out, again and again, the problem of the relationship of fiction to life. The narrative tension generated by the
conflict between history and plot has a reflexive dimension,
expressing a contest between different conceptions of the novelist's role. Peter Brooks defines plot as 'a concerted plan for the
accomplishment of some purpose which goes against the ostensible and dominant legalities of the fictional world, the realization of a blocked and resisted desire'.[10] In James's novels, the
characters' plots not only resist the given circumstances of the
fictional worlds they inhabit, but also contest the 'dominant
legalities' which define how those worlds are written and read
about, specifically the idea that the novel should masquerade as
history. As these plots seek to realize the particular ambitions of
the characters, they also give expression to another 'blocked and
resisted desire'—the wish to explore what fiction is, and what it
can do, when it is allowed to operate on its own terms, rather
than on terms set by another discourse.

This desire is indulged or resisted to different degrees in various
works from this period. Some novels, such as *The Portrait of a
Lady* and *The Princess Casamassima*, fall firmly within the anti-
romance tradition, in which the fictive imagination is defeated
by an overwhelming and antipathetic reality; these works may
test, and at times blur, the boundary between truth and fiction,
but the structural dominance of history over plot controls their
action and meaning. However, James's early period also includes
novels which question the foundations of the anti-romance tradition; in *The Europeans* and *The Tragic Muse* characters are more
successful, if not in overthrowing the power of history, at least
in articulating a theory of fiction which overcomes the fixed
binary opposition of truth and falsehood. These differences in

[10] Peter Brooks, *Reading for the Plot: Design and Intention in Narrative*
(Oxford: Clarendon Press, 1984), 12.

approach may be linked to the cultural politics of the fiction debate, for the two strands in James's early fiction stand in significantly different relations to defensive Victorian discourses on novels. The characterizations of Isabel Archer and Hyacinth Robinson are very much the products of the discourses on women's and working-class reading into which Victorian culture channelled much of its anxiety about fiction, and these characters' futures are tragically foreclosed by the distrust of the imagination expressed in those discourses. But when it came to the cultural stereotyping of foreign and avant-garde figures, James could more easily see through the manœuvres through which nineteenth-century English culture managed its residual fear of fiction by directing it towards alien and marginal groups. In *The Europeans* and *The Tragic Muse*, Eugenia and Miriam are brought into comic conflict with the cultures hostile to them, and these novels offer a detached and ironic commentary on Victorian culture's anxieties about foreign and avant-garde fiction.

THE ANTI-ROMANCES: *WASHINGTON SQUARE*, *THE AMERICAN*, *THE PORTRAIT OF A LADY*, *THE PRINCESS CASAMASSIMA*

One of James's most straightforward uses of the character—a stock figure of anti-fiction literature and anti-romances—whose morals and grip on reality have been perverted by reading novels, is Lavinia Penniman in *Washington Square*. Corrupted by her 'taste for light literature' (*WS* i. 13), Mrs Penniman indulges in the dangerous habit of trying to fashion her own life and the lives of others according to the plots of romantic novels. When a potential 'hero' for such a plot appears in the person of the opportunistic Morris Townsend (i. 64), she tries, as her brother, Dr Sloper, says, 'to get up a romance' (i. 39) between him and her plain, shy niece, Catherine Sloper. Morris is only too willing to fall in with Mrs Penniman's romance in the hope of gaining Catherine's fortune; he tries to present his courtship in terms of the traditional comic situation of young lovers conspiring against parental opposition, but in fact he is enacting the cruder melodramatic plot of the fortune-hunter or false lover. Catherine, on the other hand, lacks both the perspicacity to see through the plots of others, and the imagination to plot effectively for what she sees as her own happiness. This is the source of her vulnerability throughout the novel but also, finally, of her survival. The moral weight of the novel rests with Catherine, who does not plot, and passively accepts the narrow circumstances of her life. Although she does not intend to be ironic, there is much 'effective sarcasm' (ii. 50) in her refusal to engage imaginatively in the plots of others, and the judgement passed by her naturalness and innocence on the plots of her aunt and lover is aligned with the narrator-historian's more knowing condemnation of them.

The anti-romantic perspective shared by Catherine and the narrator has the moral and epistemological authority of history. However, an instability in the novel's formulation of 'history' is suggested in the description of an object in Dr Sloper's house in Washington Square. Between two windows in the drawing-room is a long mirror, at the base of which a bracket supports 'a backgammon board folded together in the shape of two volumes, two shining folios inscribed in letters of greenish gilt, *History of England*' (i. 93). The description of this object by the narrator is a piece of excessive denotation such as James had observed in Balzac's work, which helps to support the illusion of the novel's referentiality, but it is also an exercise in reflexive irony, which destabilizes the idea of the novel as history. The mirror reflects, not only Morris as he acts out his plot against Catherine, but an image of the novel itself which, like James's other works of this period, is presented as history. But the *History of England* is a fake, a toy, a playful attempt to pass off as serious and educational something frivolous which, as a game, involves an element of the arbitrary. Narrated as a history, *Washington Square* was also presented to the English public in two volumes, and so the superfluous description of the game masquerading as a two-volume history in the Slopers' drawing-room creates for the reader an instant of arrest, in which the idea of the historical nature of the narrative is momentarily subverted, before the novel resumes its apparently inevitable chronicle of the triumph of circumstances over plots.

The idea that what passes for history may be the outcome of a game or a gamble is explored more extensively in *The American*, although in this earlier novel moral value also resides in the renunciation of plots rather than in their execution. The American, Christopher Newman, has come to Europe in search of a new cultural and emotional life, having turned away from the single-minded pursuit of money that has hitherto been his reason for existence. However, he conducts his private life, particularly his plan to marry Claire de Cintré, with the same aggressive energy that had characterized his business life. When Claire's family conspires against him, Newman responds by attempting to use their unsavoury history as a means of blackmailing them. But this plot requires an audience for his tale-telling, and in his failure to find one he loses the aggressive impetus necessary for forcing on others his perception of the past and plan for the future. At the end of the novel he is no longer 'a man with a plot in his head' (*TA* 347) for he realizes that 'such things were really not his game' (346): having failed to marry Claire and having renounced revenge, he gives up his attempt to rewrite his experience and instead tries 'to read the moral of his strange misadventure' (340).

In a letter to W. D. Howells, who was dissatisfied with this gloomy outcome, James justified his decision to prevent Newman's marriage in terms of its 'correspondence' with real life (*Letters* ii. 105), and called upon Howells to acknowledge 'the inevitability of the American *dénouement*' (*Letters* ii. 104):

No, the interest of the subject was, for me, (without my being at all a pessimist) its exemplification of one of those insuperable difficulties which present themselves in people's lives and from which the only issue is by forfeiture—by losing something. (*Letters* ii. 105)

This explanation accords with James's exhortation to the novelist to imitate the historian and 'imprison his imagination, for the time, in a circle of incidents from which there is no arbitrary issue, and apply his ingenuity to the study of a problem to which there is but a single solution' (*LC* i. 1155). In Newman's case, the 'single solution' is renunciation and solitude, for, as James wrote to Howells: 'We are each the product of circumstances and there are tall stone walls which fatally divide us' (*Letters* ii. 105). The wall of circumstances, like the wall of the convent in which Claire is immured, remains unscaled by Newman at the end of the novel (*TA* 348), and for the author the inviolability of these walls serves the purpose of the 'fabric of impenetrable fact' stretched over the head of the historian, which prevents the flight of his imagination into the realm of romance (*LC* i. 1154). The fact that the 'single solution' possible represents the victory of circumstances over desire means that a prejudice against the hero's attempt to rework experience imaginatively has also been served; the author's history triumphs at the expense of the character's plot. James's explanation of the ending of *The American* illustrates how the model of historical narrative expresses a hostility towards fiction, for in the necessity for Newman's 'forfeiture', technical and ideological imperatives coincide.

However, there was a flaw in this structure which James analysed in his preface to *The American*, written thirty years later. Here he acknowledged that his preconceived idea that Newman should be ill-used led him into an 'affront to verisimilitude' (*LC* ii. 1067), for the Bellegarde family would, 'given the circumstances, given the *whole* of the ground, have comported itself in a manner as different as possible from the manner to which [the] narrative commits it' (*LC* ii. 1065). Far from being constrained by irresistible facts, in *The American* James's imagination enjoyed, as he later realized, an unhindered flight, 'uncontrolled by our general sense of "the way things happen" ' (*LC* ii. 1065). In the novel the narrator's realism and the characters' reality are increasingly taken over by romance and, moreover, by a romance plot accurately predicted by Newman, whose melodramatic ideas about the Bellegardes (162) prove to anticipate remarkably accurately the secrets he later discovers about them; as Peter Brooks suggests, 'Newman's imagination here generates the novel to come'.[11] Newman's prediction of the Bellegardes' history according to a fictional formula before he discovers it as a documented fact confuses the distinction between history and plot. Moreover, the 'reality' to which he finally surrenders is not a fabric of immutable circumstances, but a fabrication—the Bellegardes' lie about their past: in short, another plot. Newman's failure to carry out his plot endorses a sense of the objective power of history, but the Bellegardes' success in carrying out theirs suggests that 'history' is a much more subjective and arbitrary construction.

[11] Brooks, 'The Turn of *The American*', in *New Essays on* The American, ed. Martha Banta (Cambridge: Cambridge University Press, 1987), 61.

The final paragraphs of the novel are concerned with the contractual dynamics of constructing history—the elements of bluff and confidence, the need for an audience without which historical assertions cannot stand. The Bellegardes' superior command of history is their superior command of an audience, while it is only Newman's good nature that has led him to give up his attempt to engage public belief in his tale about them, and to destroy his evidence of their crime. The arbitrariness of this ending is suggested by the last sentence of the novel, in which Newman momentarily wonders if his evidence may be retrieved and therefore his revenge plot revived;[12] history has been fixed only because of a personal decision and the mistiming of a possible wish to revoke it, not because of any innate inevitability in the course of events.

The overriding impression produced by *The American* is one of personal defeat, as it is in the later and more complex novel, *The Portrait of a Lady*. James's description of Isabel Archer as a heroine 'affronting her destiny' (*LC* ii. 1076) encapsulates the conflict between imaginative self-making and incontrovertible fact which determines the course of the narrative and is finally resolved as a disciplining of fiction by history. Early in the novel we encounter an instance of the kind of adverse commentary on fiction conventionally included in novels as a means of suggesting, by contrast, their own realism. Newly arrived in the old world, Isabel confesses to her uncle that her expectations of English life and manners derive from 'the novels'. Mr Touchett replies:

I believe the novels have a great deal of ability, but I don't suppose they are very accurate. We once had a lady who wrote novels staying here . . . She was very positive, very positive; but she was not the sort of person that you could depend on her testimony. Too much imagination—I suppose, that was it. (*PL* i. 69)

This distrust of fiction is authorized by Mr Touchett's moral standing in the novel as a man of wisdom and experience, and his remarks function as a commentary on the way in which the narrative of *The Portrait of a Lady* begins by defining itself through the criticism and rejection of fictional formulae. For Isabel, life in England almost immediately seems to follow such a

[12] This is omitted from the 1907 edn. of the novel. For a discussion of the various endings of the novel, see Martha Banta's 'Introduction' in ibid. 33–6.

formula. 'Oh, I hoped there would be a lord,' she says on first
meeting Lord Warburton; 'it's just like a novel!' (i. 17). For Lord
Warburton too, meeting Isabel is like something from a novel:
he claims that he fell in love with her 'at first sight, as the novels
say; I know now that is not a fancy-phrase, and I shall think
better of novels for evermore' (i. 133–4). Isabel, however, is
less willing to entrust her experience to the improbable yet conventional patterns of fiction, and she refuses to complete the
novelistic plot by marrying Lord Warburton. The first fourteen
chapters of the novel are spent outlining and then rejecting a
romantic plot—the fairytale marriage of a penniless American
orphan to an English lord—which sets a boundary to the movement of the rest of the novel. Isabel's life and James's narrative
are to be defined, negatively, against this rejected plot-line: each
gains in realism by heeding Mr Touchett's warning that the
'testimony' of novels is not to be relied on as an accurate model
for experience or history.

Curiosity about Isabel is now narrowed from the novel's
general question about its heroine—'Well, what will she *do*?' (*LC*
ii. 1081)—to the more specific interest anticipated by Ralph, 'the
entertainment of seeing what a young lady does who won't marry
Lord Warburton' (*PL* i. 192). In Ralph's formulation, Isabel is
now defined by her rejection of romance. But in fact, as her
subsequent career shows, Isabel has not rejected romance outright, but has merely substituted one kind of romance for another. Isabel rejects the obviously novelistic option of marrying
Lord Warburton, not because it embodies expectations which life
is unlikely to fulfil, but because it falls short of her sense of her
own worth, which demands a more original, but no less romantic, means of expression. Marriage to Osmond (against family
opposition) satisfies her desire for originality, but Isabel's pride
in having avoided the conventionally romantic blinds her to the
romanticism of her attitude towards her marriage. This is
brought out more fully in the *New York Edition*, where Isabel's
sense of herself as one who has both rejected Lord Warburton
and been proposed to by Osmond involves 'drinking deep, in
secret, of romance', a 'rare volume' which she is unwilling to
close (*NYE* iv. 34). The bookishness of this image reminds us
that although Isabel exchanges the obvious attractions of conventional romance for the subtler satisfactions of an original,

personal romance, her approach to experience is nonetheless
literary. As Edward Said has observed, nineteenth-century fiction
presents a strong line of characters 'hungry for the distinction
of more and more originality' who engage in a process of self-
making based on a desperate pursuit of novelty, often at the
cost of their own happiness.[13] 'Isabel's originality was that she
gave one an impression of having intentions of her own' (i. 78),
distinct not only from conventional romance plots, but from the
conventional social plot demanding that women should wait 'in
attitudes more or less gracefully passive, for a man to come that
way and furnish them with a destiny' (i. 78). Isabel is engaged
in a constant quest for ways of expressing her intentions of
originality; 'she was very observant, as we know, of what was
good for her, and her effort was constantly to find something
that was good enough' (ii. 151). In 'always planning out her own
development, desiring her own perfection, observing her own progress' (i. 65) she is, as Richard Poirier says, 'a kind of novelist
of her own experience',[14] perpetually engaged in acts of imaginative self-creation. The close link between the literature she consumes and the self she produces is suggested by the fact that the
decisive turning-points of her life almost invariably occur as
interruptions to her reading. Her acceptance of Mrs Touchett's
invitation to go to Europe, her receipt of Caspar Goodwood's
importunate letter followed by her refusal of Lord Warburton at
Gardencourt, her rejection of Goodwood at Pratt's hotel, her
acceptance in Rome of Osmond's declaration of love, and her
final rejection of Goodwood at Gardencourt—all these decisive
events take place when Isabel has been reading, or trying to read.
This suggests a continuity between reading and acting which, as
several critics have noted, places Isabel in the anti-romance tradition of female readers who confuse life and literature.[15]

[13] Edward W. Said, *Beginnings: Intention and Method*, first pub. 1975 (New
York: Columbia University Press, 1985), 143.
[14] Richard Poirier, *The Comic Sense of Henry James: A Study of the Early
Novels* (London: Chatto & Windus, 1960), 224.
[15] See Juliet McMaster, 'The Portrait of Isabel Archer', *American Literature*,
45 (1973), 56–7; Elizabeth Sabiston, 'Isabel Archer: The Architecture of Consciousness and the International Theme', *Henry James Review*, 7 (1986), 29; and
Margolis, *Henry James and the Problem of Audience*, 49. In *The Book World of
Henry James: Appropriating the Classics* (Ann Arbor, Mich.: UMI Research Press,
1987), 216–21, Adeline R. Tintner points out specific similarities between Isabel
and Emma Bovary as heroines 'romantically determined'.

Isabel's position in the female-quixotic line of heroines seals her fate: she is destined for disillusionment. The story of *The Portrait of a Lady* after Isabel's marriage traces the chastening and disciplining of her romantic imagination by the forces of history. The prospective interest of the question 'what will Isabel do with her life?' is replaced by the retrospective interest of the question 'what has happened in the past to control her fate?', and *The Portrait of a Lady* exchanges the narrative form of the thriller for that of the detective story. This change in narrative emphasis is reinforced by the structure of the novel, which falls into two distinct halves separated by a narrative ellipsis of three years. Although the narrator has from the beginning called his work a 'history' (i. 1), it is in the second half of the novel that he clearly displays his commitment to the historian's methods. To use the terms defined by James in his review of Anne Manning, in the first half of the novel the narrator works as 'story-tellers' do, beginning with a cause (Isabel's personality) and following this to its effects (the original plot she chooses for her life); in the second half of the novel, he operates as a historian who takes as his starting-point an unalterable effect (the ruin of Isabel's happiness) and traces it to its causes in past events (*LC* i. 1154). Detection displaces imagination as the epistemological mode governing the narrative.[16] The imagery used in the review is also appropriate to the change of mood and imagery in *The Portrait of a Lady*: the image of the story-teller's 'unobstructed sky' expresses the sense of limitless opportunity embodied in Isabel when she first appears in the novel, while James's claustrophobic image of the historian working 'as men work in coal-mines' (*LC* i. 1154) is strikingly similar to the imagery of enclosure and suffocation associated with Isabel at the end of the novel as, her imagination led 'downward and earthward' (iii. 32),

---

[16] James's explanation of the modes of causality engaging 'story-tellers' and 'historians' accords with Tzvetan Todorov's distinction between the thriller (stimulating 'suspense' which follows a cause to its effects) and the detective story (provoking 'curiosity' which traces an effect to its cause); see *The Poetics of Prose*, trans. Richard Howard (Oxford: Blackwell, 1977), 47. David Lodge uses Todorov's formulations of the thriller and detective story as examples of the prospective and retrospective reading processes stimulated by Barthes's 'proairetic' and 'hermeneutic' narrative codes: see *Working with Structuralism: Essays and Reviews on Nineteenth- and Twentieth-Century Literature* (London: Routledge & Kegan Paul, 1981), 19.

she struggles to understand the causes of her own unhappiness. These causes are complex, but centre on two historical facts revealed to Isabel in the final chapters of the novel: that Madame Merle is her husband's former lover and the mother of Pansy, and so her interest in Isabel's life has been part of a conspiracy to make use of her for her own ends; and that her cousin Ralph engineered his father's legacy for her as part of an attempt to direct the course of her life. The second of these facts is already known to the reader, but the first must be worked out from clues in the text. In both cases there is an ironic distance between the narrator's knowledge and Isabel's discovery: the historian's view, to which the reader is invited to aspire and which indeed he or she must accept, omnisciently, ironically transcends the heroine's limited power to plot and interpret.

Isabel's discovery that the course of her life has been determined, not by her own imagination, but by historical forces embodied in the past actions of others, is linked to her attaining in the final chapters of the novel a larger historical perspective. Walking in the Campagna, she gains an 'objective' sense of her own suffering, for 'in a world of ruins the ruin of her happiness seemed a less unnatural catastrophe' (iii. 152), and she draws on a 'historic sense' of evil and treachery to describe her awareness of Madame Merle's duplicity (iii. 153). As she asks herself whether 'the great historical epithet of *wicked* were to be applied' to her friend (iii. 153), the adjective 'historical' works as an intensifier of feeling and understanding, and her need to find expression for her experience in 'historic' terms signals the replacement of her romancer's desire for originality of experience with the humbler sense of being placed within a common history of human suffering. No longer seeking to plot her life in defiance of social and historical scripts, Isabel now has a 'haunting sense of the continuity of the human lot' (iii. 152). The desire for originality that drove Isabel's novelistic approach to life is replaced by the historian's recognition of common experience, and this recognition has a moral significance, as it allows Isabel to experience imaginative sympathy for her enemy, 'Poor Madame Merle!' (iii. 155).

Isabel's humbling sense of herself as the product of history is the ironic answer to the question she asked herself when she rejected Lord Warburton's proposal: 'What view of life, what design upon fate, what conception of happiness, had she that pretended to be larger than this large occasion?' (i. 141). The word 'pretended' suggests not only aspiration and ambition, but artificial self-creation: Isabel's pretensions compete with the author's right to create her and her destiny, and it is perhaps this hubris, rather than her purely personal egotism, which is 'ruined' at the end of the novel. Isabel is reduced to the position of passive, accepting readership rather than active, defiant authorship of her life. 'Now that she was in the secret, ... the truth of things, their mutual relations, their meaning, and for the most part their horror, rose before her with a kind of architectural vastness' (iii. 207–8), just as the novel rises before us in its ' "architectural" ' quality as a 'literary monument' (*LC* ii. 1080) and we too are told 'the truth of things, their mutual relations, their meaning' (iii. 208). Like Christopher Newman, Isabel is forced to renounce her plot and instead read the moral of her misadventure, which is summed up by Ralph: 'You wanted to look at life for yourself—but you were not allowed; you were punished for your wish. You were ground in the very mill of the conventional!' (iii. 230). Ralph's use of the passive voice leaves the agent of punishment unspecified: the 'mill of the conventional' is operated by Osmond and Madame Merle at Isabel's expense, and perhaps Ralph means that her individualism is punished by the forces of social convention which they represent. But the right to look at life for herself, which she claimed when she rejected Lord Warburton (i. 151), is also taken away from her by the constraints of a narrative which defines its realism through the disillusionment of its characters.

Both the morality and the realism of *The Portrait of a Lady* are based on a disciplining of the fictive imagination by historical fact: the defeat of Isabel's attempt to plot her own life is presented as a moral lesson for the heroine, which also reinforces the narrative's claim to historical status. But in fact the distinction between history and plot on which this project depends is far from stable in the novel. The 'history' that defeats Isabel consists of the plots of other characters: Ralph's well-intentioned but disastrous attempt to liberate his cousin through the gift of his father's fortune, and the predatory plot launched by Madame Merle and Osmond to appropriate that fortune for their own ends. Moral and epistemological distinctions between the narrator's work and these plots are constantly undermined as the plotters reveal an imaginative sense of their activity which closely resembles the novelist's enterprise. Madame Merle, who plots constantly not just for material gain, but for things which 'satisfied the imagination' (iii. 149), resembles the author as described in the preface to the novel, who cannot resist 'the intensity of suggestion that may reside in the stray figure, the unattached character, the image *en disponibilité*' (*LC* ii. 1073). Like the realist author, Madame Merle takes the guise of a disinterested spectator, but in fact competes with life; she tells Isabel, 'I want to see what life makes of you' (*PL* i. 243), but it is she herself who takes on the role of fate, Providence, author, directing Isabel's movements in the light of her overall plan. Ralph too harbours authorial designs on Isabel behind the façade (convincing even to himself) of mere passive spectatorship of an independent action. Arranging for Isabel to inherit a fortune which will enable her 'to gratify her imagination' (ii. 185), Ralph turns his cousin into a *disponible* figure able to be employed in gratifying the imagination of others, not least his own. Like the author committed to 'organising an ado about Isabel Archer' (*LC* ii. 1077) so that she will have opportunities to display her character to the fullest, Ralph engineers Isabel's legacy in order to prove his theory that she will be 'as good as her best opportunities' (*PL* i. 239). However, this act of liberation reveals itself to be an act of appropriation, as Ralph later admits to Isabel: 'I had a sort of vision of your future ... I amused myself with planning out a kind of destiny for you' (ii. 180–1). The authorial nature of Ralph's interest in Isabel has already been suggested by Henrietta Stackpole who, when he jokingly calls himself a Caliban to her Ariel, more seriously replies: 'You were Prospero enough to make [Isabel] what she has become' (i. 153). Prospero is the type, not of the historian, but of the fabulist, with the power to initiate, direct, and end fictions. It is a suggestive image, especially in the light of Henrietta's attempt to correct Ralph's too literary point of view: 'But I am not talking about imaginary characters; I am talking about Isabel. Isabel is intensely real' (i. 153). In a sense this is Henrietta's plea for freedom, for the right of the 'intensely real' individual not to be subject to the plots of others. But her disapprobation of Ralph's role also contains a plea from author to reader to accept that 'Isabel is intensely real':

once again, the historical status of the narrative is affirmed by decrying the propensity of the characters to play author. However, the plea for our belief in Isabel's reality is strangely undermined by the mention of Prospero, reminding us that fictions are intensely artificial plots, not direct transcripts of the 'intensely real', and that realism itself is simply 'intensity of illusion' (*LC* ii. 168).

The history that defeats Isabel's fictions is constituted by plots which are presented as both morally reprehensible and self-consciously fictive. The content of history is thus seen to stand in a close alliance with the fictive imagination; it is also suggested that historical narrative may be complicit with fictions and falsehood. Isabel's disillusionment is caused by her discovery of a piece of historical information concerning an event that preceded all the plots with which the novel deals—the earlier liaison between her husband and Madame Merle. This fact is presented as the key to her whole experience, essential knowledge, 'the eclipse of which had made life resemble an attempt to play whist with an imperfect pack of cards' (iii. 208). Historical knowledge is privileged as the only means of explaining why Isabel's attempts at self-determination have failed; 'the truth of things' (iii. 208), which gives significance to the whole novel, is encapsulated in a bundle of immutable historical facts. The disclosure of these to Isabel by Osmond's sister, the Countess Gemini, is the climax of the novel in terms of narrative structure, for it reveals the relation between plots and histories that has propelled the whole action. The Countess names outright the 'something detected' (iii. 10) which has hitherto only been hinted at and which, above the characters' colliding and collapsing plots, has now become the major interest of the novel. Yet we may wonder why the Countess Gemini—a minor and unreliable character, her very name suggesting duplicity—should be given the privileged function of revealing to Isabel the information which pre-existed all plots and which has placed the omniscient narrator and the attentive reader at a superior and ironic distance from the heroine. Isabel, having accepted the information, perversely considers that 'the very frailty of the vessel in which it had been offered her only gave [it] an intrinsic price' (iii. 196). Yet the value of the information is compromised by its retailer's notorious unreliability: the Countess 'very often lied' (iii. 41), and it is possible that her tale is to be counted amongst 'her little fibs, her frivolity' (iii. 124). The Countess's only evidence that she is not lying is her own word: 'It's not a lie, you know; it's exactly as I say' (iii. 184). The narrator's comments do not lend her any authority, and, most mystifying of all, when Isabel asks her sister-in-law, 'How do you know all this?', she replies with a 'bold stare': 'Let us assume that I have invented it!' (iii. 190).

Has the Countess decked out a plot in the guise of history? Of course, subsequent events rule out the possibility that one should reject her story: Isabel accepts it and acts upon it, and if the Countess's status as a witness is unreliable, later discoveries act as 'vivid proof' (iii. 193) of her account.[17] Moreover, the Countess's story confirms, rather than competes with, all the hints placed by the narrator throughout the text suggesting that Osmond and Madame Merle were connected in the past and in their present activities, these hints culminating in Isabel's sense of 'something detected' (iii. 10) in the discovery of the two 'grouped unconsciously and familiarly' in her house (iii. 45). There is thus no reason to doubt the truth of the Countess's story and to do so would demolish the carefully constructed relation between history and plot in this novel, and would confound the relationship of trust and privilege between author and reader. Yet, we may still ask why such important information is entrusted to such an unreliable witness, and why our attention is drawn so pointedly to 'the very frailty of the vessel' (iii. 196).

The Portrait of a Lady follows the model of the novel as history, narrated with an authority which defeats the subversive pretensions of the characters to launch counter-realities against it. Yet James's fascination with characters who attempt to launch such plots, and his exploration of their activity in terms which strikingly resemble those he uses for his own enterprise, leads to a confusion of the difference between plot and history, and an obsession with the points at which they meet. While in general he maintains the authority of realism by regarding with suspicion

[17] This is expressed more forcefully in the *New York Edition*, where, for Isabel, the sight of Madame Merle at Pansy's convent has 'the character of ugly evidence, of handwritings, of profaned relics, of grim things produced in court' (*NYE* iv. 375). This language imparts a menacing quality to the standard of historical representation found by James in Turgenev's work, the authority of 'documents and relics' (*LC* ii. 970).

the characters' plots, and keeping them contained within and dominated by the historical framework of the narrator, the Countess Gemini's role in _The Portrait of a Lady_ subverts this system: she takes over the role of the narrator in being the custodian of the historical information that will override the plots of Isabel and her friends and enemies. When this information is presented as, possibly, a 'lie', the status of the narrator as historian and the narrative as history is radically undermined. Even if the Countess is not lying, the way in which the narrator presents her story in a sense 'gives the lie' to the idea of fiction as history. If the narrator must not 'give [himself] away' (_LC_ i. 46), the Countess almost does it for him. While she dares Isabel not to believe her, we are dared not to accept this frail vessel of historical truth as adequate to the conception of veracity and authority in realism which has been built up throughout the novel.

The Countess's story, the climactic revelation that gives to the reader the sense-making retrospection which the novel's careful ironies and hints have anticipated, is likened to a gypsy's 'bale of fantastic wares' (iii. 187). This is reminiscent of Madame de Bellegarde's comment to Christopher Newman when he comes to her with his story, that he is 'like a peddler with something to sell' (_TA_ 317). The similarities between the two situations are striking: both Newman and the Countess are using the past to try to force an issue. Yet, while Newman has documentary evidence for his story (the letter written by Claire's father before he died, corroborating Mrs Bread's story that he was murdered by his wife), he fails to find an audience for his tale and so fails to have its historical status recognized. The Countess, on the other hand, provides no such evidence for her version of events, and yet because she persuades Isabel to believe her story, she succeeds in gaining for it the power of history. The arbitrariness of these outcomes radically unsettles the epistemological status of history, and blurs the boundary between history and the plots which contest it.

Exploring this boundary is the central concern of _The Princess Casamassima_, a novel in which attempts to rewrite personal experience are viewed in relation, not only to existing circumstances, but to the powerful plots constituted by revolutionary interpretations of and interventions in history. Individual and

social discontent are linked, and collective plots to re-form society offer both a metaphor, and a possible channel, for personal
rebellion. Revolutionary activity expresses, or exploits, the impulse (shared by so many of James's characters) to counterplot
experience in the interests of self-determination, and to trans-
form an imaginative vision from a state of 'mere sharp, tantalis-
ing desirableness into that of irresistible reality' (*PC* ii. 70). The
drama of the hero of *The Princess Casamassima*, Hyacinth Robinson, resides in his need, and inability, to choose whether to
enact his personal rebellion through the plots offered by his
anarchist co-conspirators, or through other ideological and formal structures.

Revolutionary plots are the most extreme expression of the
subversive impulses which many analysts of the 'fiction question'
believed could be associated with the influence of novels on
readers. Opponents of fiction had always warned that reading
novels could fuel social as well as personal discontent and rebellion, and concerns about making reading 'safe' had a political as
well as a moral component. Expressions of anxiety about the
social and political influence of fiction in encouraging imaginative dissent from, or practical opposition to, the *status quo*, are
to be found in commentaries on sensation novels, decadent literature, and penny fiction in the later nineteenth century. In 1863
a critic warned that sensational literature could undermine social
custom because it 'disturbs . . . the reader's sense of the stability
of things, and opens a new, untried vista of what may be'.[18] In
'Tommyrotics' (1895), Hugh Stutfield linked 'hysteria' in politics
and art, called decadent literature 'cultural anarchism', and
maintained: 'In these days the unbridled licentiousness of your
literary decadent has its counterpart in the violence of the political anarchist. Each is the *alter ego*-maniac of the other. The one
works with the quill, the other with the bomb; and the quill is
the more dangerous weapon of the two.'[19] For these writers,
anxieties about fiction and revolution involved sexual politics
and the fear of decay in the upper and intellectual classes. Meanwhile, the old concerns about the links between working-class
literacy and the spread of Jacobinism current at the end of the

[18] 'Our Female Sensation Novelists', 211.
[19] Stutfield, 'Tommyrotics', 841.

eighteenth century[20] revived in a new form in the later nineteenth century, as middle-class commentators surveyed the effects of the Board Schools in creating a new reading public whose tastes were catered for by the penny-fiction industry. Reports on working-class reading in the quarterly and monthly reviews expressed concern about the subversive nature of much penny fiction, which made heroes of criminals and reinforced ideas that 'the constituted authorities are both rogues and fools';[21] in 1890 one commentator warned that the popularity of such fiction could turn the newly literate working class into 'agents for the over-throw of society'.[22]

What emerges from these commentaries is a nexus of the reading of fiction (especially working-class fiction), personal discontent, and revolutionary activity, which is exemplified by the career of Hyacinth Robinson. The Princess sums up Hyacinth's sense that he deserves better than life has offered him: 'Fancy the strange, the bitter fate: to be constituted as you are constituted, to feel the capacity that you must feel, and yet to look at the good things of life only through the glass of the pastry-cook's window!' (ii. 149). The Princess's image recalls a much earlier picture we are given of Hyacinth as a child, habitually

planted in front of the little sweet-shop on the other side of the street, an establishment where periodical literature, as well as tough toffy and hard lollipops, was dispensed, and where song-books and pictorial sheets were attractively exhibited in the small-paned, dirty window. He used to stand there for half an hour at a time, spelling out the first page of the romances in the *Family Herald* and the *London Journal*, and admiring the obligatory illustration in which the noble characters (they were always of the highest birth) were presented to the carnal eye. (i. 4–5)

The image of the shop window is used in each case to represent Hyacinth's desire for, and exclusion from, 'the good things of

[20] Altick, *English Common Reader*, 76.

[21] [Hitchman], 'Penny Fiction', 153. In 1866, an article in *Macmillan's Magazine* had argued that a change in the character of penny publications in the previous twelve to fifteen years had rendered false the common belief that penny journals encouraged anti-social and subversive views ('Penny Novels', *Macmillan's Magazine*, 14 (1866), 97). However, the upsurge of concern about penny fiction in the 1880s and 1890s suggests either another change in the character of the journals, or increased anxiety in the middle and upper classes about working-class discontent.

[22] [Hitchman], 'Penny Fiction', 170.

life',[23] but the parallel images also have a more particular significance. The romances in the shop window are not just desirable
commodities, items in the list of 'good things' denied to Hyacinth,
but offer examples of plots through which these good things may be
achieved and enjoyed. The *London Journal*, with its trashy stories
and crude illustrations, and the more respectable *Family Herald*,
were two of the most popular journals providing cheap fiction for
the working classes in the second half of the nineteenth century,
and are the publications most frequently mentioned in articles on
penny fiction and working-class reading.[24] Analysts of this class
of publication found that it retailed two basic kinds of fiction to
its working-class readers: sentimental romances, and sensational
tales of seduction, crime, and revenge. These two kinds of fiction
present relations between the classes in different ways. The first
group specialized in tales of high life written 'from the point of
view of the servants' hall';[25] they might feature a nobleman kept
out of his rights who finally regains his place in the aristocracy[26]
or a virtuous plebeian promoted to the nobility—a favourite
ending was 'the marriage of young men and maidens belonging to
the opposite poles of society'.[27] With their fantasies of wish-
fulfilment and vicarious experience, these plots were fundamentally
conservative; as J. H. Millar noted in 1898, 'as long as to be
happily married and to "get on in the world" are the secret or
avowed ideals of . . . the working classes, so long will any dangerous and far-reaching scheme of communism remain an

---

[23] In *Person, Place, and Thing in Henry James's Novels* (Durham, NC: Duke
University Press, 1977) Charles R. Anderson notes that in *A Small Boy and Others*
James used a similar image to describe his own childish wish to be 'other' (127);
see *SBO* 184.

[24] These articles repeatedly testify to the superiority of the *Family Herald* to the
London Journal and other penny-fiction papers in terms of both literary and
moral inoffensiveness; see Salmon, 'What the Working Classes Read', 112; [Hitch-
man], 'Penny Fiction', 164. An important difference was that the *Family Herald*
did not have illustrations, and therefore achieved a higher tone by omitting the
kinds of crudely executed, sensational pictures employed by the *London Journal*
('Penny Novels', 101–2). (James was therefore wrong to imply that the 'obligatory
illustration' was a feature of both journals.) However, despite the obvious differences in quality between the two journals, commentary on them does not make
any absolute identification of one with sentimental, and the other with sensational, fiction.

[25] [Hitchman], 'Penny Fiction', 166.

[26] [Millar], 'Penny Fiction', 805.

[27] 'Penny Novels', 104–5.

impossibility'.[28] On the other hand, as we have seen, penny fiction could also proffer politically subversive plots. Discussing penny novelettes in 1886 (the year *The Princess Casamassima* was published), Edward Salmon wrote:

It is hardly surprising that there should exist in the impressionable minds of the masses an aversion more or less deep to the upper classes. If one of their own order, man or woman, appears in the pages of these unwholesome prints, it is only as a paragon of virtue, who is probably ruined, or at any rate wronged, by that incarnation of evil, the sensuous aristocrat . . . Throughout the story the keynote struck is highborn scoundrelism. . . . the influence exercised over the feminine reader, often unenlightened by any close contact with the classes whom the novelist pretends to portray, crystallises into an irremovable dislike of the upper strata of society.[29]

Salmon's comments show that the penny novelettes generally associated with female readers could be just as politically subversive as the more blatantly anti-social 'penny dreadfuls', and the romantic but subversive plots he describes closely resemble the tale passed on to Hyacinth, and fundamental to his sense of identity, of his working-class mother who died in prison, where she had been sent for murdering his father, the decadent aristocrat who seduced and abandoned her. As the identity of Hyacinth's father is not proved, this story is, possibly, a fiction; certainly it follows a standard sensational plot such as was found in the penny journals. Indeed, when Hyacinth's friend Millicent hears the story of his parentage, it produces in her 'a generous agitation—something the same in kind as the impressions she had occasionally derived from the perusal of the *Family Herald*' (iii. 161). Millicent is moved by the suffering of Hyacinth's mother, but wonders that he has not gained more by his aristocratic association, and this reaction epitomizes the two paths of response open to Hyacinth: to enter sympathetically into his mother's wrong, and seek revenge against the social system responsible for it, or to exploit—at least imaginatively—his aristocratic inheritance, and try to gain by the social system as it stands. In effect, this is a choice between the revolutionary and conservative plots familiar to Hyacinth from the penny romances

[28] [Millar], 'Penny Fiction', 811.
[29] Salmon, 'What the Working Classes Read', 112–13.

he read as a child. Because of his mixed parentage and ambiguous social position, it is possible for Hyacinth to interpret his role in these plots in a number of ways, and therefore to open up for himself choices of action which he is tragically unable to resolve.

The stories about Hyacinth's aristocratic relations 'set into spasmodic circulation' (iii. 161) by his guardian, Pinnie, are the kind of wish-fulfilment fantasies associated with conservative romance plots; indeed, the word 'circulation' suggests the affinity between such gossip and periodical literature. Pinnie's ideas about Hyacinth's noble parentage are based on an acquaintance with novels rather than with facts (i. 10), and she is another of James's uses of the figure of the habitual novel-reader, whose approach to reality has been compromised by her immersion in fiction. Pinnie's belief that the Lord Frederick murdered by Hyacinth's mother was in fact his father is the foundation of 'a certain tall imaginative structure which she had been piling up for years' (i. 8); the dream of Hyacinth stepping into his rightful place in society is the conventional penny-fiction plot of the nobleman debarred from, but finally restored to, his rights. Like Mrs Penniman in *Washington Square*, Pinnie is a woman of 'furious imagination' (i. 20) who 'told fibs as freely as she invented trimmings' (i. 10). She 'had placed at [Hyacinth's] disposal . . . a passionate idealism which, employed in some case where it could have consequences, might have been termed profligate, and which never cost her a scruple or a compunction' (i. 147). But Pinnie's romancing has consequences she has not foreseen: a belief in his father's aristocratic status gives a political edge to Hyacinth's sense of his mother's wrongs, and places at his disposal, or rather disposes of him within, a sensational revenge plot which he elects to enact through revolutionary activity. 'His miserable mother's embrace seemed to furnish him with an inexhaustible fund of motive' (i. 167), and Hyacinth commits himself to working for the overthrow of the social arrangements that made her plight possible. In engaging in such action he is both re-enacting and completing her story: if he were to carry out his revolutionary assignment of shooting the Duke, he would replicate his mother's action in killing Lord Frederick, and at the same time provide the act of revenge against the upper classes which would complete her sensational story.

However, Hyacinth does not carry out this plot, because he ceases to believe in it. From the moment he pledges himself to an active role in the great Hoffendahl's plot, by undertaking to assassinate the Duke, he loses all imaginative faith in the interpretation of history and society from which that plot springs. At the same time, the 'legend' of the account to be settled on his mother's behalf, which makes his personal history explicable and meaningful by its consonance with a general code of class history, becomes increasingly untenable. There had always been 'times when it wavered and faded, when it ceased to console him and he ceased to trust it' (i. 105), but now the explanations and motives supplied by his mother's history have more than ever to compete with the inclinations and allegiances arising from that of his putative father. In the second half of the novel it is the things of his father's world that attract Hyacinth, as his old instinct that privileged institutions are the 'most fascinating' (and therefore most compensatory) things in 'a world of suffering and injustice' (i. 238) grows into a full-scale defence of the achievements of the surface skin of civilization which stretches over that abyss of misery. Having lost faith in Hoffendahl's plot, he finds he can believe in 'the splendid accumulations of the happier few' (ii. 229) as things 'thanks to which . . . the world is less impracticable and life more tolerable' (ii. 230). It is an interesting choice of words: revolutionary conspiracies may make the world resistible, but the higher products of civilization make it practicable, and Hyacinth's sympathies lie increasingly with the latter path. He is content to surrender his imagination to the world as it is, with its sensual surface and social antics, and the plots, both personal and political, which he derived from his mother's story succumb to the power of the given circumstances of 'the beautiful, horrible world' (ii. 211).

Hyacinth's acceptance of the status quo is not really an acceptance of his own lowly place in society: in celebrating 'the splendid accumulations of the happier few' (ii. 229), he projects himself imaginatively into his father's world, just as he tries actually to maintain access to the world of the Princess Casamassima. The social rebellion inspired by his mother's story gives way to the social aspirations inspired by his father's, and his falling in love with the world of privilege is linked to his falling in love with the Princess. Hyacinth's ambiguous social status allows him to imagine himself enacting two conservative plots from penny fiction: as (possibly) the illegitimate son of an aristocrat, he can fantasize about regaining his rightful inheritance, and as the artisan living in poverty and obscurity, he can dream about gaining the love of a princess. Although Hyacinth is never so deluded as to believe that the Princess is in love with him, his relationship with her constitutes a kind of wish-fulfilment, not disconnected from Pinnie's fantasy that 'a princess might look at [him] and be none the worse!' (i. 147). But Hyacinth fails in his desire to enjoy, even in a displaced or imaginative sense, his inheritance from his father. Staying with the Princess in a country house he enjoys 'novel scenes' (ii. 180) which are, indeed, like a chapter of romance in his life, but after a few days is recalled to reality by Pinnie's illness and death. By the end of the novel, the Princess has more or less abandoned him and his oath to Hoffendahl requires him to act against the very social institutions in which he now believes. Caught between opposed allegiances derived from his mixed parentage, Hyacinth sees no solution but suicide.

Hyacinth's career illustrates the moral James found in Turgenev's work: 'that there is no effective plotting for happiness' (*LC* ii. 982). Hyacinth ceases to believe in the Princess's habit of living 'on high hopes and bold plans and far-reaching combinations':

These things, from his own point of view, ministered less to happiness, and to be mixed up with them was perhaps not so much greater a sign that one had not lived for nothing, than the grim arrangement [ie. suicide] which, in the interest of peace, he had just arrived at with himself. (iii. 213)

In the extreme pessimism of this novel, all plans, plots, arrangements, and combinations are reduced to devices for attempting to ensure that one has not lived for nothing, and all are condemned to failure anyway. The 'grim arrangement' of Hyacinth's life—determined by the author so that the mixed forces of heredity form an irresolvable and paralysing conflict of loyalties—offers a critique of both the revolutionary and wish-fulfilment plots of popular fiction, while satisfying the demand for the defeat of the characters' plots built into James's model of historical narrative. However, *The Princess Casamassima* differs importantly from *The Portrait of a Lady* in that these plots collapse without being replaced by the superior power of history.

No corrective, omniscient vision overrides the characters' mistaken views or takes over their failed attempts to read and write their own experience. The climax of *The Portrait of a Lady* is the discovery of a secret which makes sense of all that has gone before. In *The Princess Casamassima* history is not privileged in this way as a mode of explanation.

At the heart of the novel is the unresolved mystery of Hyacinth's parentage, a secret of the same importance in this novel as the information about Pansy's parentage in *The Portrait of a Lady*, 'the eclipse of which', like that other secret, 'made life resemble an attempt to play whist with an imperfect pack of cards' (*PL* iii. 208). In *The Princess Casamassima*, in contrast to the earlier novel, the information remains in eclipse. The unanswered question of Hyacinth's origins provides a focus for a much more comprehensive sense of uncertainty in the novel. The characters are constantly forced to confess their ignorance of matters which concern them. Discussing Hyacinth's mother's claims about the identity of his father, Mr Vetch says, 'Yes, indeed, what does any one know? what did she know herself?' (i. 27), to which Pinnie adds her belief that 'the truth never is found out' (i. 30). Of the Princess's reasons for taking him up, Hyacinth can only say, 'Of course I don't know what you thought', to which she replies 'No; how should you?' (ii. 116). Hyacinth is tormented by not knowing what relationship the Princess and Paul Muniment share; of where he and the Princess finally stand in relation to each other, and to the anarchist movement, he admits, 'I don't know—I don't understand' (iii. 157); concerning the change in his friendship with Paul, he concedes, 'I can't make it out' (iii. 162), while of his origins he can still only say, 'It's all darkness' (iii. 158).

Hyacinth 'had a high ambition: he wanted neither more nor less than to get hold of the truth and wear it in his heart' (iii. 85). This ambition is constantly confounded, as the 'truth', both as to the facts of his parentage, and as to how he should best interpret and respond to this, is never obtained. This obsession with the impossibility of knowledge casts a curious light on the historical pretensions of the novel. While writing *The Princess Casamassima*, James wrote to his friend Thomas Sergeant Perry: 'I have been all the morning at Millbank prison (horrible place) collecting notes for a fiction scene. You see I am quite the Naturalist'

(*Letters* iii. 61). As such, he launched his novel under 'the rich principle of the Note' (*LC* ii. 1101), exemplifying the naturalist's belief that accurate observation could establish a correct record of the world. Yet in the preface James found himself forced to defend the 'sketchiness and vagueness and dimness' of his novel by declaring that it was designed to produce the effect 'of our not knowing, of society's not knowing, but only guessing and suspecting and trying to ignore' (*LC* ii. 1102). When the narrator holds back, with Hyacinth, from accompanying the Princess on her excursions with Lady Aurora into the London slums and with Paul Muniment into the heart of anarchism, we feel that these things are not told because they are not known.[30] Certain regions of social experience are designated as impossible to discover, and so, in spite of the many 'small facts' (*LC* ii. 422) and concrete details in which the novel abounds, the texture of knowledge provided remains extremely uneven, with dense notation followed by glaring absences of information, while historical representation is intermittently displaced into self-reflexive fictionality. Such features of the narrative are exemplified in the account given by the Prince Casamassima to Madame Grandoni of his attempt to track his wife through the streets of London as she accompanies Paul Muniment to a revolutionary meeting:

The street is small and black, but it is like all the streets. It has no importance; it is at the end of an endless imbroglio. They drove for twenty minutes; then they stopped their cab and got out. They went together on foot some minutes more. There were many turns; they seemed to know them well. . . . Chiffinch Street, N.E.—that was the name, . . . and the house is number 32—I looked at that after they went in. (iii. 127–8)

---

[30] Critics have disagreed about the accuracy of the social and political information in *The Princess Casamassima*. Lionel Trilling defends the novel as 'a brilliantly precise representation of social actuality', 'confirmed by multitudinous records' ('*The Princess Casamassima*', *The Liberal Imagination: Essays on Literature and Society* (London: Secker & Warburg, 1951), 74, 68), but John Lucas maintains that the 'ignorance of the characters too often suggests the ignorance of their creator': see 'Conservatism and Revolution in the 1880s', in *Literature and Politics in the Nineteenth Century*, ed. Lucas (London: Methuen, 1971), 208. Similarly, in 'Words and Deeds in *The Princess Casamassima*', *Journal of English Literary History*, 37 (1970), 112, Taylor Stoehr argues that James did not have authentic information about anarchism, and questions the accuracy of the newspaper reports on which he must largely have relied.

The detail given by the Prince conforms to a naturalist standard of 'solidity of specification'—referentiality seems to be promised, and verification invited, locating the experience in the concrete entity of the city of London. However, the Prince's use of detail desperately circles around the absence of any real knowledge of what is most important to him, to his interlocutor, and to the reader: what happens, personally and politically, when the Princess and Paul Muniment go into the house. This parallels the way in which James's detailed descriptions of the city, especially the life of the shops and the streets, fail to penetrate to the real misery of the slums or the real centres of revolutionary activity. The heart of conspiracy, always tantalizingly absent from the text, is hidden within a house 'at the end of an endless imbroglio' (iii. 127); this alternative form of the address erases 32 Chiffinch Street N.E. from all possible maps, as there is, simply, no end to the endless. As well as undoing the illusion of historical referentiality, the Prince's formulation of the position of the house dissolves the notion of plot; the house is the place where plots originate, but these origins are buried at the end of the endless. This topological 'imbroglio' suggests the 'imbroglio' (*LC* ii. 1089) which is the subject of the novel itself. The representation of the city, 'vague and blurred, inarticulate, blunt and dim' (*PC* ii. 209) with its 'baffled lamplight' (iii. 87), images the characters' and reader's—and perhaps author's—groping for knowledge in the novel, and the city takes on a topological significance which is a map of the novel's narrative discomforts.

The Prince's account of his pursuit of the Princess and Muniment to the conspirators' house both sets up and undercuts expectations of the precise information associated with naturalist reporting. A more extended parody of this kind of reporting is given in chapter 44, when one of the conspirators, Schinkel, gives Hyacinth the letter that calls him to fulfil his vow to the revolutionary organization. Hyacinth's curiosity about 'whatever the mysterious document was' (iii. 190) focuses all the curiosity expressed throughout the novel—about the state of society and the workings of revolutionaries, about his origins and his personal relationships—on the single, withheld document that contains the secret information which will, as it turns out, bring about the end of Hyacinth's life and the end of the novel. The sense of unsatisfied curiosity, formerly centred largely on origins, has suddenly become urgently end-directed, and Hyacinth's unbearable suspense is drawn out by Schinkel's slow, meticulous method of narrating to him the history of his reception of the letter in all its circumstantial detail. Schinkel's speech is a parody of naturalism, with its dispassionate recounting of material facts, and of personal information as if it were merely an aggregate of such facts:

It took Schinkel a long time to tell this story—his calm and conscientious thoroughness made no allowance for any painful acuteness of curiosity that Hyacinth might feel. He went from step to step, and treated his different points with friendly explicitness, as if each would have exactly the same interest for his companion. (iii. 196)

Like a scientific historian, Schinkel gives 'a dispassionate logical synthesis of the material at hand' (*LC* i. 1017) and presents his material '*without* rearrangement' (*LC* i. 58), either chronological or rhetorical, impervious to the effect it is having on his listener. The 'mysterious document' being delivered is, presumably, a tersely worded and purely factual counterpart to Schinkel's speech; Paul Muniment later says that he believes it contains 'minute instructions' (iii. 228). However, the message of those who 'know everything—everything' (iii. 198) is never transcribed into the text, and although we later learn of its content, at this point in the narrative its omission functions in the same way as our exclusion (with the Prince) from the house visited by the Princess and Muniment: each is a lacuna around which irrelevant details helplessly cluster, exposing the incapacity of the scientifically historical narrative to carry the most important information we require. The omission of the letter, while Schinkel's narrative is reported in full, creates an imbalance which throws the latter into the position of stylistic parody, for Schinkel tells us 'everything—everything' except the most important thing, whether this really is the call to action which Hyacinth has been dreading.

In the end, those who 'know everything' are denied the satisfaction of seeing their plot fulfilled, for Hyacinth is able to rewrite his fate, if only to the extent of redirecting to his own heart the bullet that 'would certainly have served much better for the Duke' (iii. 242). This last reflection is again Schinkel's, who is also the one to report Hyacinth's death to his landlady: 'Mr. Robinson has shot himself through the heart. He must have done it while you were fetching the milk' (iii. 242). The facts are clear, and Schinkel's only conjecture does not delve into motives or meanings, but deals purely with time and logistics. The two sentences make up a 'veracious history' (i. 95) of a single event, Hyacinth's death, reminding us of the kind of record which the novel, with its lacunae and unresolved mysteries, is not able to provide of his life.

It is appropriate that naturalistic reporting, despite its earlier parodic status, should have the last word in this novel. Schinkel's bald statement of the facts of Hyacinth's death expresses the sense in which this outcome is not, and never has been, negotiable through imaginative counterplottings. Hyacinth asserts control over his life to the extent of choosing the manner of his death, but his suicide is determined by the initial data of his characterization—the opposed, and fatally balanced, hereditary influences working through his mixed parentage. Against this, the power of revolutionary plots to make reality resistible, or of conservative plots to make it 'less impracticable' (ii. 230), have no force: Hyacinth is merely 'a detached, irresponsible witness of the evolution of his fate' (iii. 181). Yet the fact that the identity of his father is never proved diminishes the authority of history to adjudicate over his plots, for the deterministic model devised by James depends on the same belief about Hyacinth's parentage as Pinnie's fantasy or Hyacinth's own legend of the motive provided by his mother's story. This means that these plots cannot be placed in the light of delusions, to be corrected by superior historical knowledge, for the characters' and the author's plots rest on the same questionable basis. It is therefore impossible for Hyacinth to imitate Christopher Newman or Isabel Archer and 'to read the moral of his strange misadventure' (*TA* 340) in the light of a superior knowledge of history; such knowledge remains in eclipse throughout the novel. The 'grim arrangement' (iii. 213) that ensures Hyacinth's defeat belies the impression of life '*without* rearrangement' (*LC* i. 58) which the inexorable unfolding of his fate is intended to produce. The factitiousness of Hyacinth's fate is suggested in a discussion with the Princess about his vow before he receives his call to action. The Princess expresses her belief that it 'will never come to anything': 'It's too absurd, it's too vague. It's like some silly humbug in a novel.' Hyacinth replies 'theatrically', '*Vous me rendez la vie!*' (iii. 95). However, the Princess's insistence that such an outcome is too novelistic to be believed does not give Hyacinth's life back to him; her comments do not function as a trope reinforcing the novel's realism by pointing to the implausibility of a discarded plot, but rather act as reflexive irony, highlighting the artificiality of the novel's plot, as Hyacinth's life remains forfeit to the exigencies of 'some silly humbug in a novel'. There is no chance that his life may be returned into his own hands, because he has been controlled from the beginning by an authorially determined plot masquerading as the inexorable evolution of impersonal history. In *The Princess Casamassima*, history does not seem to have earned its authority, which it wields rather wilfully, to end the hero's plots, nor does it fulfil the function of enlightenment and explanation associated with its triumph in novels such as *The American* and *The Portrait of a Lady*.

CHALLENGING HISTORY: *RODERICK HUDSON*, *THE EUROPEANS*, *THE TRAGIC MUSE*

Despite—or because of—the emptiness at the heart of its view of history, *The Princess Casamassima* is the bleakest of anti-romances, epitomizing the obsession of James's early novels with the defeat of the imagination. However, another, quite different strand of thinking about fiction is also to be found in James's early works, and may be glimpsed even in *The Princess Casamassima* itself. One of the questions Hyacinth repeatedly asks himself, and to which he receives no answer, is whether the Princess is sincere:

To ask himself whether she were in earnest was now an old story to him, and, indeed, the conviction he might arrive at on this head had ceased to have any practical relevancy. It was just as she was, superficial or profound, that she held him, and she was, at any rate, sufficiently animated by a purpose for her doings to have consequences, actual and possible. (*PC* iii. 81–2)

The keynote to the Princess's character is her constant playacting, and in her earlier appearance as Christina Light in *Roderick Hudson*, this is also the case. The young Christina uses her narrative imagination as a means of self-definition, infinitely mutable, and as an escape from or counter to the attempts of others to plot her life:

She had a fictitious history in which she believed much more fondly than in her real one, and an infinite capacity for extemporised reminiscence adapted to the mood of the hour. She liked to idealise herself, to take interesting and picturesque attitudes to her own imagination; and the vivacity and spontaneity of her character gave her really a starting-point in experience, so that the many-coloured flowers of fiction which blossomed in her talk were not so much perversions as sympathetic exaggerations of fact. (*RH* ii. 160–1)

Christina's imaginative excesses utterly seduce the unstable Roderick Hudson, but the potential for truth in her fictions also attracts the sterner Rowland Mallet. Rowland feels that 'whatever she said of herself might have been, under the imagined circumstances' (ii. 161), and is partially drawn by Christina into a willingness to renegotiate the relation between self and circumstance on the basis of an imagination which is not 'absolutely historical' (ii. 160). However, although he can, theoretically, find ways of understanding her 'want of veracity' (ii. 160), in practice he is incapable of offering her the kind of prospective trust she craves, or of ceasing to judge her except according to a strict code of literal truthfulness. When Christina does finally manage to make Rowland believe in one of her most cherished fictions—that she is capable of disinterested and highminded action—by breaking off her engagement to the Prince Casamassima, she is prevented from realizing this sense of herself by her mother's insistence that she marry the Prince. Mrs Light's coercive power is, of course, her control over historical information—in this case, the fact of Christina's illegitimacy, a 'secret card' (iii. 87) which makes the establishment both of the publicly accepted version of the past, and the limits of future action, a power game similar to that played between Newman and the Bellegardes in *The American*.

Christina's challenge to the value of literal truthfulness in regulating human relations is extended in *The Europeans* through the figure of Eugenia, the Baroness Münster. Eugenia's European manners throw into confusion the moral values of her New England cousins and their friends. Like Christina, she is 'a woman who will lie' (*TE* ii. 194), who covers herself with fictions which are simultaneously protective and exploratory, ways of negotiating her relationship to the world, of counter-plotting what she sees as adversity; her lies, her neither 'wholly true' nor 'wholly untrue' (i. 147) versions of events, are trial revisions of unsatisfactory realities.[31] 'There were several ways of understanding her: there was what she said, and there was what she meant, and there was something, between the two, that was neither' (ii. 148–9). This third element may be the contribution of the listener to the communicative process, for Eugenia's statements stand or fall, not by their correspondence with an established reality, but by the responses of those who receive them. Her lies are intended, not to deceive, but to elicit the enlightened engagement of others in realizing the new perspectives they suggest. When she tells her brother Felix that Robert Acton wants to marry her, the statement is untrue; at least, Acton has not proposed. The statement is a way of trying out an idea and testing responses to it: what would Felix think about her marrying Acton? Her lie also attempts to do more than this, as the narrator explains: 'It is probable that, in the last analysis, what she meant was that Felix should spare her the necessity of stating the case more exactly and should hold himself commissioned to assist her by all honourable means to marry the best fellow in the world' (ii. 149).

Such lies are an invitation to the listener to help realize the arbitrarily missing circumstances which as yet prevent them from being true; as Rowland Mallet observed of Christina Light's fictions, these lies are always potentially true, and their unsettling power comes from the fact that it is impossible to condemn them utterly. 'Unfortunately' for Acton, he may say that 'she is not honest', but he is 'unable to say it finally, definitively', and at times 'it seemed to matter wonderfully little' (ii. 194). However, although he is in love with Eugenia, Acton cannot overcome the fear that she is untrustworthy; he toys with the idea that 'a finer degree of confidence in this charming woman would be its

---

[31] My understanding of Eugenia's character owes much to Richard Poirier's chapter on *The Europeans* in *The Comic Sense of Henry James*, 95–144. Poirier maintains: 'Her adoption of different roles and her capacity to say things which she knows she does not mean are attempts to take advantage of as many opportunities as possible. Behind the protection of her elaborate manners she can freely consult her own responses to these opportunities. Her deception of others is a way of being honest with herself' (104). I wish to extend this reading of Eugenia's character to suggest that Eugenia also invites others to enter into her fictions, offering them, as well as herself, an opportunity to test their feelings and explore new ideas.

own reward' (ii. 108), but finally rejects it. Although imaginatively capable of this response, he refuses to take the moral risk of entering into Eugenia's view of one's relation to history as negotiable through fiction. He never asks Eugenia to marry him, and she is therefore excluded from the happy ending of the novel, in which the pressure to 'consent!' sweeps up most of the characters in a train of marriages (ii. 248). In failing to persuade Acton to consent to her fictions, Eugenia fails to elicit the comic 'yes' which resounds through the last pages of this novel, and instead enacts a more typically Jamesian dénouement of forfeiture. Renouncing her designs on Acton and on the New England community, Eugenia sails for Europe having threatened, but not changed, the truth-telling values of her American relatives. Her failure to engage others (particularly Acton) in a contractual relationship which will realize her fictions leaves these in the position of lies and errors, out of keeping with the values of recognition and enlightenment on which the resolution of the other love affairs rests.

It is Miriam Rooth in *The Tragic Muse* who, much more systematically and successfully than Christina or Eugenia, challenges the authority of a historical epistemology over experience. Miriam's development of a 'special language' (*TM* iii. 124) which operates outside the categories of true and false is explored in relation to her career as an actress. In this, and in the parallel story of Nick Dormer's decision to give up politics for painting, the novel engages in debates about the value of artistic professions in the face of the hostile forces of British philistinism. As James suggested in 'The Art of Fiction' and showed in 'The Author of Beltraffio', the philistine's moral and social antipathy to art was often allied to the old evangelical distrust of the imagination and its influence on the perception and conduct of life. When Miriam's theatrical fictions threaten to spill over the boundaries of professional practice and intervene directly in experience, they pose a challenge to established values similar to Eugenia's challenge to the New England community. *The Tragic Muse* forms a companion piece to *The Europeans*, the one addressing the philistine strand, the other the puritan strand, of what was essentially the same tradition of hostility to fiction.

The careers of Nick and Miriam are both encouraged by Gabriel Nash, who constantly asserts the value of art, not only as a

profession, but as a mode of living. Nash is the only literary artist
in the novel, but he has given up the art of literature for 'the art
of life' (i. 31), and he explains what it means to 'work in such a
difficult material' (i. 144):

What we contribute is our treatment of the material, our rendering of the
text, our style. A sense of the qualities of a style is so rare that many
persons should doubtless be forgiven for not being able to read, or at all
events to enjoy us; but is that a reason for giving it up—for not being, in
this other sphere, if one possibly can, a Macaulay, a Ruskin, a Renan? Ah,
we must write our best; it's the great thing we can do in the world, on the
right side. One has one's form, *que diable*, and a mighty good thing that
one has. I'm not afraid of putting all life into mine, without unduly
squeezing it. (i. 163)

Nash believes he can construct artistic forms complex and capa-
cious enough to contain all of life 'without unduly squeezing it',
and therefore that art may flourish, not to the detriment of life,
but to its benefit. His 'art of life' will, he hopes, be both personally and socially beneficial, doing good to others while also
working towards his own happiness. However, Nash's contention
that he goes about his business 'like any good citizen' (i. 167) is
an affront to the prejudices of Nick's family. Even to Nick's sister
Biddy, an ardent defender of the values of art, Nash's tone and
face seem to be 'the highest expression of irresponsibility' she has
ever seen (i. 25), and it is in connection with this impression that
she asks him, hesitantly, if he is 'an aesthete' (i. 30), loading the
word with a deep suspicion of the ways in which art may corrupt
life. Nash rejects such 'formulas' (i. 30), but Nick realizes that the
rest of his family would not hesitate to label his friend according
to philistine stereotyping of the aesthetic movement (iii. 221).
Nick himself cannot decide whether Nash is 'the greatest humbug
and charlatan on earth, or a genuine intelligence, one that has
sifted things for itself' (i. 160), and he is unsure what mode of
attention or belief is an appropriate response to Nash's outland-
ish utterances:

Nick Dormer had already become aware that he had two states of mind in
listening to Gabriel Nash: one of them in which he laughed, doubted,
sometimes even reprobated, and at any rate failed to follow or to accept;
the other in which this contemplative genius seemed to take the words out
of his mouth, to utter for him, better and more completely, the very things

he was on the point of saying. Nash's saying them at such moments appeared to make them true, to set them up in the world . . . (ii. 152)

Influenced by Nash, Nick decides to give up his promising parliamentary career to pursue the profession of portrait painter, thereby defying his mother's prejudices against the artistic life. Nick's report of Lady Agnes's views on art is very much like Mark Ambient's summary of his wife's beliefs in 'The Author of Beltraffio':

She has the darkest ideas about it—the wildest theories. I can't imagine where she gets them; partly, I think, from a general conviction that the 'aesthetic'—a horrible insidious foreign disease—is eating the healthy core out of English life (dear old English life!) and partly from the charming drawings in *Punch* and the clever satirical articles, pointing at mysterious depths of contamination, in the other weekly papers. (iii. 50)

This is an expression of the attitude of which James complained in 'The Art of Fiction', the Protestant idea that art 'is supposed in certain circles to have some vaguely injurious effect upon those who make it an important consideration, who let it weigh in the balance' (*LC* i. 47). In its use of the language of disease, Nick's report also prefigures the particular cast of anti-fiction rhetoric associated with the Wilde trial and the idea of Decadence which was current five years after the publication of *The Tragic Muse*. Peter Sherringham considers that Nick has misrepresented his mother's views, and that she is not subject to 'a horror, the old-fashioned horror, of the strange licenses taken by artists under pretext of being conscientious: the day for this was past' (iii. 64). However, as we shall see, Peter does not even recognize 'traces (dissimulated though they may be) of a suspicion' of art (*LC* i. 46) in his own mind, and so is perhaps disinclined to recognize the part such attitudes may continue to play in English society.

The battle between art and its opponents is played out in bold type between Nick and his mother, but takes a more complex and subtle form in the relationship between Miriam and Peter. Suspicion of the theatre is thoroughly 'dissimulated' in Peter Sherringham's behaviour, for he acts as Miriam's benefactor and mentor, contributing financial assistance, personal encouragement, and theoretical knowledge to the furthering of her career. Yet his personal relations with Miriam—his initial reluctance to consider her capable of entertaining sincere emotions, and then his desire to marry her only on condition that she gives up the theatre—reveal both his lack of respect for acting as a profession, and his fear of the uses of art in life.

Early in his relationship with Miriam, Peter explains that, following a rational profession by day, he keeps the theatre as 'a superstition'; 'it leaves a margin, like having a second horse to your brougham for night-work. The arts, the amusements, the aesthetic part of life are night-work, if I may say so without suggesting the nefarious' (i. 204). Of course, he cannot say so without suggesting 'the nefarious', or at least the frivolous. The attraction of the theatre, for him, is that it 'was not the region of responsibility' (ii. 48), and so he is shocked to find that he has become 'seriously entangled' in what he has never considered 'a serious field' (ii. 48). However, his entanglement is not with the art itself, but with Miriam, and when she rejects his proposal of marriage because she will not, as he demands, give up her acting career, his anger at 'this sudden offensive importunity of "art" ' (iii. 179) is 'as heavily charged with the genuine British mistrust of the bothersome principle' (iii. 180) as if he had never left England. Miriam reiterates her earlier challenge that if he were 'serious' he could become an actor himself (i. 211), and accuses Peter of a half-love of the profession which has placed him in a false position (iii. 175). There remain, in the end, the social prejudices against art which he cannot banish: 'Several acquired perceptions had struck a deep root in him, but there was an immemorial compact formation which lay deeper still' (iii. 180).

It is all the more surprising, then, that he has been able to find a path through the ethical and emotional traps set by Miriam's intensely theatrical personality. Miriam constantly transgresses the boundaries between world and stage: 'there were hours . . . in which she wore her world's face before the audience, just as there were hours when she wore her stage face in the world' (iii. 84), and, perpetually rehearsing and performing before her friends, she treats Peter to 'specimens of fictive emotion of various kinds' (ii. 235). This inspires the same mistrust that Christina Light evoked in Rowland Mallet, and Eugenia in Robert Acton:

It struck him abruptly that a woman whose only being was to 'make believe,' to make believe that she had any and every being that you liked, that would serve a purpose, produce a certain effect, and whose identity resided in the continuity of her personations, so that she had no moral privacy, as he phrased it to himself, but lived in a high wind of exhibition, of figuration—such a woman was a kind of monster, in whom of necessity there would be nothing to like, because there would be nothing to take hold of. (i. 179)

Later, he comes to a much more sophisticated understanding of her 'figuration':

her changing face affected this particular admirer at least not as a series of masks, but as a response to perceived differences, an intensity of sensibility, or still more as something cleverly constructive, like the shifting of the scene in a play or a room with many windows. Her incarnations were incalculable, but if her present denied her past and declined responsibility for her future, it made a good thing of the hour and kept the actual very actual. (iii. 47)

Reminding Peter of 'a room with many windows', Miriam reminds us also of the many-windowed 'house of fiction' later described by James in the preface to *The Portrait of a Lady* (*LC* ii. 1075), and indeed while Sherringham's first response is expressed in the language of hostility to fiction, his second foreshadows the terms in which fiction is discussed and the values with which it is invested in James's late novels and criticism. Like Eugenia, Miriam often says what she does not mean, but Peter, unlike Robert Acton, can accept these terms of communication, including the role that the listener must play in realizing her intentions: he understands that she 'speaks a special language; practically it isn't false, because it renders her thought, and those who know her understand it' (iii. 124). Miriam's use of a language which is neither literally, historically true, nor 'practically' false, foreshadows William James's ideas on pragmatism and Henry James's later exploration, in *The Ambassadors* and *The Golden Bowl*, of pragmatic fictions. She enacts the paradox of truth achieved through fiction; just as her private performances 'kept the actual very actual' (iii. 47), after one of her public performances Peter 'felt somehow recalled to reality by the very perfection of the representation' (iii. 255). Miriam therefore upsets the categories of the literal-minded who rigidly oppose truth and fiction, world and stage. After treating Nick to a private 'scene of comedy', and hearing her mother call her a '*Comédienne*!', she replies: 'It's rather cruel, isn't it . . . to deprive people of the luxury of calling one an actress as they'd call one a liar?

I represent, but I represent truly' (iii. 146). Personal and professional, technical and moral terms merge in this expression of triumph over limiting dichotomies. Miriam's 'special language', which is both make-believe and true representation, cannot be understood in terms of a historical model of referentiality. Just as she refuses to sacrifice her pride in her profession to Peter Sherringham's prejudices, she refuses to have her 'figuration' and 'personations' (i. 179) judged according to literal categories of true and false, or labelled as jokes or lies according to the rhetoric of the detractors of fiction.

If Miriam is a kind of muse for a theory of fiction which so uncompromisingly rejects the bases of the old hostility to the novel, the most remarkable thing about her is the stock from which she springs. For Miriam's mother is James's most direct use, since Mrs Penniman in *Washington Square*, of the stock figure from anti-romance of the woman reader addicted to fiction. Miriam explains how novels sustained her mother through years of poverty and insecurity:

They served her for food and drink. When she had nothing to eat she began a novel in ten volumes—the old-fashioned ones; they lasted longest. She knows every *cabinet de lecture* in every town; the little, cheap, shabby ones, I mean, in the back streets, where they have odd volumes and only ask a sou, and the books are so old that they smell bad. (i. 188–9)

Mrs Rooth is almost never seen without a novel: 'She had always a greasy volume tucked under her while her nose was bent upon the pages in hand' (i. 216). Prepared to haunt libraries carrying odd volumes (i. 189) and to reread books if she can get nothing new (i. 216), Mrs Rooth is a true fiction addict, and in Peter's eyes there is a certain stigma attached to her mania. She reads books 'as to which he had vaguely wondered to what class they were addressed' (i. 216), and there are hints of an aesthetic and moral, as well as domestic, fastidiousness in his irritation at the sight of her 'odd volumes from the circulating library (you could see what they were—the very covers told you—at a glance) tumbled about with cups or glasses on them' (iii. 45).

The effects on Mrs Rooth of all this novel-reading are very much those shown by Mrs Penniman, Pinnie, and the whole family of corrupted readers to which they belong. 'She delighted in novels, poems, perversions, misrepresentations and evasions, and had a capacity for smooth, superfluous falsification which made Sherringham think her sometimes an amusing and sometimes a tedious inventor' (i. 206). 'She moved altogether in a world of genteel fable and fancy', and Peter soon learns that he can always take what she says for 'untrue' (i. 207). At first he sees no connection between Mrs Rooth's 'facile genius' and Miriam's dramatic talents, for the mother 'never could have been accused of successful deceit, whereas success in this line was exactly what her clever child went in for' (i. 207–8). However, he later reflects that 'the evolution was after all natural: the figurative impulse in the mother had become conscious, and therefore higher, through finding an aim, which was beauty, in the daughter' (i. 208). Miriam had been wrong to say of her mother's reading that it was 'very well for her, but it doesn't feed me. I don't like a diet of dirty old novels' (i. 189). The mother's fictionalizing, derived from her reading, does in fact 'feed' Miriam's dramatic impulses, which develop into the profession which will feed them both. Miriam herself is 'on almost irreconcilable terms with the printed page' (i. 213), and Mrs Rooth does not understand the theatre, except as a source of publicity and income. Yet there is a symbiotic relation between Miriam's acting and her mother's reading, suggested in the depiction of Miriam practising drama with Peter while her mother is buried, as usual, in her novels (i. 216). Miriam professionalizes her mother's 'figurative impulse' (i. 208), and her private mode of relating to people through theatricality also owes much to this influence. Peter comes to realize of Mrs Rooth that it 'was harsh to call her a hypocrite, because you never could have resolved her back into her character: there was no reverse to her blazonry' (i. 206–7). He uses a similar figure to describe his sense that Miriam is 'always playing something; there are no intervals. It's the absence of intervals, of a *fond* or background, that I don't comprehend. You're an embroidery without a canvas' (i. 199). Without a 'background' against which to place her fictions, it is as useless to call Miriam dishonest as it is to call her mother a hypocrite, and Peter finds the language of mask and essence inappropriate for describing her infinitely various modes of self-presentation. Of course, the crucial difference between mother and daughter is that Miriam knows that her fictions are fictions, neither deluding herself nor seeking to deceive others through them. In this she foreshadows the terms of the fictional contract as James was later to develop it in *The Ambassadors*, for which the character of Madame de Vionnet—very much like Miriam in many ways—provides the inspiration.

The 'evolution' of Miriam from Mrs Rooth (i. 208) is an important development in James's work, because it makes a direct and explicit link between two different sets of female characters through which antithetical attitudes to fiction are expressed, and derives a positive value from a conventionally negative one. Mrs Rooth belongs to the family of foolish novel-readers, whose loss of the ability to discern fact from fiction is exhibited in their endless 'fibs' and stories. Mrs Penniman and Pinnie are versions of the same character, and one might also include in this category the Countess Gemini, whose corruption is not explicitly attributed to romance-reading, but who perpetually concocts romances for herself, and who has the same irresponsible attitude towards the truth. Such characters are the stock figures of anti-romances and anti-fiction rhetoric, where their dissatisfaction with mundane existence and proclivity for imaginatively reinventing the conditions of experience are punished by an assertion of the superior power of reality. As we have seen, this is a pattern for the process of illusion and disillusion through which James's heroes and heroines enact their more active and complex, but still doomed, resistance to circumstances. However, when the Countess Gemini is allowed to report, as a possible lie, the 'history' that defeats Isabel's plot of self-determination, and when Pinnie's romantic and possibly delusory belief in Hyacinth's aristocratic connections is found to be also the premise on which the author's deterministic thesis rests, such characters exhibit a power to disrupt the distinction between history and plot on which their own condemnation depends. This power is most fully conceded to Mrs Rooth, who cannot be condemned as a 'hypocrite' because she has so thoroughly confounded truth and fiction; indeed, James explicitly forgoes the chance of using her as an example of the corruption of fiction: 'she was not dangerous even if you believed her; she was not even a warning if you didn't' (i. 206). Moreover, when Miriam takes over her mother's 'figurative impulse', perfecting the uses of fictive assertion and dramatic self-presentation explored by

Christina and Eugenia, she provides a direct link between the set of romance-readers, to which her mother belongs, and the women of complex imaginative powers (foreshadowing Madame de Vionnet in *The Ambassadors*) who employ and articulate a theory of fiction which overcomes the fixed binary opposition of true and false. Whereas Christina is forced to submit to a cruelly coercive historical secret, and Eugenia is excluded from the otherwise comic resolution of *The Europeans*, in Miriam the fictive principle flourishes, both privately and professionally; if she is 'punished' for this by the loss of Peter Sherringham, it is her own choice, an outcome which she herself controls. Just as Mrs Rooth does not become the occasion for anti-fiction rhetoric, Miriam is not required to enact the typical Jamesian arc of illusion and disillusion, but is allowed an ascent of fortune which, it is suggested at the end of the novel, will only continue, for 'every one is agreed that both in public and in private she has a great deal more to show' (iii. 258).

Through Miriam, James explored ways in which the historical contract set out in his early criticism, but challenged by the behaviour of the characters in his early novels, could be replaced by a fictional contract resting on very different attitudes towards experience and the imagination. The terms of such a contract were to be explored more fully in the later novels *The Ambassadors* and *The Golden Bowl*. However, first, after a disastrous five-year experiment of writing for the theatre, James's career was to go through another phase in which a much more negative view of fiction is expressed. Miriam's fictions, like Strether's, depend on the collaboration of interlocutors or readers to make them intelligible and powerful, and such collaboration is lacking to James's fiction-makers of the late 1890s. Reflecting his growing sense of alienation from his audience, James's fiction of the period 1895–1901 explores a world where contracts of any kind between author and reader, or speaker and listener, are impossible, and the making of plots is therefore condemned to a realm of fantasy, delusion, and solipsism, fulfilling the worst judgements of the opponents of fiction as to its essential uselessness and immorality.

3

'The Old Superstition about Fiction being "Wicked"'

'WE SEE our lives from our own point of view; that is the privilege of the weakest and humblest of us; and I shall never be able to see mine in the manner you proposed' (*PL* i. 151). Isabel Archer's rejection of Lord Warburton's proposal of marriage in *The Portrait of a Lady* articulated a conviction about the supreme privilege of the individual point of view which increasingly became the site of epistemological and narrative interest in James's fiction. The years between his resumed commitment to writing fiction in 1895 (after the failure of his attempts to write for the theatre), and the writing of the major, late novels in the early 1900s, form a period of narrative experimentation distinguished by a particular concern with point of view. Whether in 'subjective' third-person narratives organized around limiting centres of consciousness, or in possibly unreliable first-person narratives, the characters' privilege of seeing their lives from their own perspectives displaces the authorial privilege of omniscience as the dominant mode of perception and narration. This experimentation with the ' "subjective" adventure' (*LC* ii. 1170) marks an interest in new kinds of realism, which leads to a profound change in the basis of the relation between fiction and the world in James's work.

In his review of Anne Manning in 1867, James had argued that the novelist should imitate the historian by constraining his imagination beneath a ceiling of impenetrable fact (*LC* i. 1154). In a letter to his sister, Alice James, in 1869, he employed a related image to describe the inevitable subjectivity of experience:

Wherever we go we carry with us this heavy burden of our personal consciousness and wherever we stop we open it out over our heads like a great baleful cotton umbrella, to obstruct the prospect and obscure the light of heaven. (*Letters* i. 145)

The umbrella of subjective consciousness, like the canopy of historical fact, could be used in the construction of a narrative as a means of disciplining the novelistic imagination: fidelity to the subjective nature of a character's experience, like fidelity to a consensus about the nature of external fact, could not only guarantee the internal coherence of a narrative, but anchor it to a law of correspondence with something independent of it, thus safeguarding against drifting into the 'arbitrary' region of authorial invention. The fictions of James's 'experimental' phase, which unfold beneath the umbrella of a particular dramatized consciousness, mark a shift from an objective to a subjective concept of realism, from a realism based on the model of history to one based on the ways in which individual characters plot their own stories. Yet the spectre of the first kind of realism continues to haunt the practice of the second, as the focus of the narrative interest and the reader's interpretative effort becomes the question of how far the subjective record conforms to the (absent or only implied) ideal of a historical record. The reading process is still based on the distinction of true from false narratives, through the judgement of the central character's perceptions and testimony as historical or otherwise.

The questions we must constantly ask of the narrators and centres of consciousness in these works—have they perceived the world accurately? have they reported experience faithfully?—are the same questions asked of authors in nineteenth-century realist criticism. Shifting responsibility for the way in which the world is reported to us from the author to the characters, these works dramatize the questions of the authority, truth-telling pretensions, and moral responsibility of fiction that dominated both formal criticism and sociological debate about the writing and reading of novels in the nineteenth century. The narrative form foregrounds the question of reliability of testimony, a concern borrowed from historiography and law which was implicit in the way Victorian fiction was conventionally read and judged.

All the narrative centres in the novels of James's experimental phase are readers of experience and producers of subjective versions of it, but I wish to discuss three works which have an even closer relation to the fiction debate. *In the Cage* engages explicitly with the readership debate in that its heroine's consumption of romantic fiction has direct effects on the ways in which she tries to plot her own experience. *The Turn of the Screw* and *The Sacred Fount*, as first-person narratives in which the characters have produced written, and not just mental, transcripts of their experience, are studies in authorship as well as readership. Once again based on the opposed concepts of history and plot (the idea of history no less forceful for being hidden or unattainable), the competition for narrative authority in each of these works also involves the politics of class and gender which informed the Victorian 'fiction question'.

More explicit discussion of social and economic aspects of the production of fiction in late Victorian England is to be found in the tales of the literary life that James produced in the 1880s and 1890s. It is here that one usually seeks evidence of James's opinions about the relations between producers and consumers of fiction in his society. The tales show a relationship seriously awry, defined by loss and sacrifice, driven by interests fundamentally opposed. They reflect James's growing sense of alienation from his audience, shown in the lack of demand for his novels in the late 1880s, the disastrous reception of his play *Guy Domville* in 1895, and his own expressions of contempt for the obtuseness and vulgarity of the public.[1] James's problem in attracting an audience reflected broader cultural trends at the end of the century, including the disintegration of the shared social values and literary conventions that had placed writers such as Dickens, Thackeray, and Trollope in open communication with their readers, and the increasing fragmentation of the reading public and concomitant hardening of the lines between highbrow and lowbrow fiction. This left writers such as Meredith, Hardy, Gissing, Moore, and Conrad, as well as James, unsure of whom they were addressing or how to address them in what John Goode

[1] The performance of *Guy Domville*, its reception, and James's response to this are described by Leon Edel in *The Life of Henry James*, 5 vols. (London: Hart-Davis, 1953–72), iv. 56–88. For James's sense of estrangement from the reading public, see *Letters* iii. 209, 511.

describes as an atmosphere of 'intensifying mutual hostility between writers and readers of fiction'.[2]

In James's tales of the literary life, the novelist is repeatedly
presented as the victim of the public, which consumes, not only
his works (in fact, often not his works at all) but his time, his
privacy, even his physical existence. In 'The Death of the Lion',
circulation of the author's person amongst his supposed admirers
replaces circulation of his books, and in the end both the author's
life and his new novel are lost; in 'John Delavoy', an author's
daughter and faithful disciple battle to save him from posthum-
ous sacrifice to a public which demands personal revelations
rather than critical insights and tries to neutralize the challenging
power of an author it professes to admire but actually fears; in
'The Next Time', a writer's hope of making a living is blocked by
a publishing and distribution system representing a vulgar public.
The tales clearly draw the lines between the custodians of culture
and the enemies of literature, all the more forcefully because they
frequently do so in terms of gender. Devoted, male readers try to
protect vulnerable, male writers who are 'heroes and martyrs of
the artistic ideal' (LC ii. 1180) from inimical forces which are
often cast in female form.[3] Although there are some sympathetic
female characters, women often represent artistic compromise or
outright hostility to literature. Mrs Highmore, the lady novelist
in 'The Next Time' who cannot distinguish literary from pecu-
niary motives, is complicit with the publishing and library system
that excludes the finer artist, Ray Limbert. Mrs St. George, in
'The Lesson of the Master', displays a similar economic philistinism which is the very spirit of Mudie's, and like Mudie is also a
moral censor, for she burns one of her husband's books which she
does not like. The reader of 'The Author of Beltraffio' may expect
Mrs Ambient to do likewise in the effort to protect her son from
the contaminating influence of his father's fiction, but is shocked

---

[2] John Goode, 'The Art of Fiction: Walter Besant and Henry James', in *Tradition and Tolerance in Nineteenth-Century Fiction: Critical Essays on Some English and American Novels*, ed. David Howard, John Lucas, and John Goode
(London: Routledge & Kegan Paul, 1966), 255. See also Allon White, *The Uses of
Obscurity: The Fiction of Early Modernism* (London: Routledge & Kegan Paul,
1981), 30–54.
[3] Margolis finds such a 'sexual bias' in the formulations of good and bad
readers and writers in James's earliest criticism; see *Henry James and the Problem
of Audience*, 7–10.

at the intense hostility to literature reflected in her decision to destroy, not the offending manuscript, but the potential victim himself. Neil Paraday is adopted by a literary hostess whose salon's utter lack of genuine interest in his work reminds the narrator of 'Gustave Flaubert's doleful refrain about the hatred of literature' (*CT* ix. 108). As narrator, Paraday's male disciple takes up this refrain, expressing the values of the literary avant-garde as he pleads the cause of art against the depredations of the public.[4]

However, *In the Cage* and *The Turn of the Screw* offer a very different perspective on the question of the relationship between fiction and readers at the end of the century. Whereas the tales of artists and writers are set amongst the middle and upper classes and deal with professional male critics and writers—who considered themselves exempt from sustaining or inflicting injury through fiction—the two novellas explore the experiences of women of low or ambiguous social status, whose class and gender mark them as the traditional subjects of corruption by fiction, most likely (according to Victorian sociologies of reading) to be endangered or made dangerous by what they read. At the same time, these female characters are, like James's writer-figures, 'supersubtle fry' (*LC* ii. 1229) who may be identified both with James as an author and with his conception of ideal readers. This confuses the 'sides' of the debate about authors and readers, and unsettles the defences of art made in the tales of the literary life, which depended on a scapegoating of the reading public (especially as represented by women) and a complete dissociation (strengthened by gender difference) of creative artists from destructive readers. The cultural pattern of pinning anxiety about fiction on to the reading behaviour of marginal groups is disrupted by the power of the telegraphist and the governess as masterly Jamesian artists. *The Sacred Fount*, with its male narrator, returns to the arena of cultural privilege, but in an atmosphere of decadence in which artistic and social values are highly unstable. In all three works, the main characters perpetrate irresponsible and dangerous acts of readership and authorship, in

---

[4] The extent of the tales' commitment to this modernist view of the artist is the subject of Sara S. Chapman's *Henry James's Portrait of the Writer as Hero* (Basingstoke: Macmillan, 1990).

which James's own enterprise is deeply implicated. In each, the rule of consumption, of the costs of art, set up in the tales of artists and writers, is reversed, as it is the author and his or her fiction, rather than the public, which is predatory. Thus all three works take a different view of the historical situation of the collapse of relations between authors and readers in late Victorian society from the seemingly definitive version presented in the earlier tales. Instead of defending art and lamenting the evils of the public, these works dramatize versions of the 'old superstition about fiction being "wicked" ' (*LC* i. 45). At the same time, they pursue formal interests which problematize the issue of communication between author and reader. The limitations of consciousness which define the narrative method lead to epistemological problems which mirror readerly difficulties of interpretation, and suspicion about the reliability of the narrators' testimonies can lead to a deep questioning of the narrative process itself, raising grave doubts about the value of imaginative narrative as a means of representing the world or communicating experience.

IN THE CAGE

In his 1908 preface to *In the Cage* James recalled his interest in the young telegraphists of London and 'what it might "mean," wherever the admirable service was installed, for confined and cramped and yet considerably tutored young officials of either sex to be made so free, intellectually, of a range of experience otherwise quite closed to them' (*LC* ii. 1168). Reflecting on the process of speculation necessary for the author to write the tale of an 'obscure little public servant' (*ITC* 14), the preface effectively asks what it also 'means' for the author to attempt to make himself 'free, intellectually, of a range of experience otherwise quite closed' to him. The answer it offers is that his attempt to enter imaginatively into the experience of the telegraphist, like her speculation about her upper-class customers, is an 'amusement' and an 'obsession' which may also be characterized as a 'barren trouble', 'a great occupation for idleness' for the 'morbid imagination' (itself an 'idle faculty'), and a possible 'vitiation' of the independence of others (*LC* ii. 1169). Such language recalls the complaints of opponents of fiction, that reading novels led to an unhealthy neglect of one's own affairs and an idle, voyeuristic interest in the affairs of others. We are faced with the puzzle that the preface to *In the Cage* describes the genesis of the tale by employing the rhetoric of the 'old evangelical hostility to the novel' (*LC* i. 45) against which James, in 'The Art of Fiction', had pitted his defence of the novelistic imagination. The language of the preface, which describes both author's and heroine's activities in terms of this anti-fiction rhetoric, suggests ways in which, in the tale, concerns with the sociology of reading and the morality of authorship collapse into each other, confusing the distinctions between female reader and male author, between mass consumption and high art, and, finally, between fiction and history, on which James's early fictional theory and practice had so heavily depended.

Like many of James's earlier novels, *In the Cage* explores the possibility of employing a narrative imagination to become 'a skilful counter-plotter to adversity' (*RH* i. 2). The young telegraphist is a person 'in whom the sense of the race for life was always acute' (40). In her struggle against economic adversity, her life is dominated by work, while a grocer, Mr Mudge, represents her 'contracted future' (4), the pun on the marriage contract suggesting her feeling that an even more reduced field of experience awaits her. Escape is offered by books 'from the place where she borrowed novels, very greasy, in fine print and all about fine folks, at a ha'penny a day' (6). But tales of 'fine folks' also pass before her all day, scrawled on the telegraph forms pushed to her through the bars of the cage which shuts her off from the world of Mayfair, and yet, by an irony of technology and economics, makes her 'so free, intellectually' (*LC* ii. 1168) of a world otherwise only available to her through cheap fiction. Reading is thus not limited to her lunch-time breaks with her 'ha'penny novels' (73), but is a constant activity: it is her job to read (counting the words) and translate (into the language of 'the sounder') the messages given to her; at the same time she pieces together the discontinuous narratives that these messages form and translates them into complete fictions which 'beat', not only life, but 'every novel in the shop' (70). The ladies and gentlemen coming into the shop were always in communication, 'and she

read into the immensity of their intercourse stories and meanings
without end' (31). Like novels, these stories are an 'extension
of her experience' (25); they offer 'more impressions to be
gathered and really—for it came to that—more life to be led'
(9). Instants of interpretative inspiration provide her with 'the
moments that made up' (9): the pun reveals the compensatory
nature of her imagination. This imagination is a form of resistance to reality, a defence against accepting the identity of 'the
very shopgirl . . . that she hugged the theory she was not' (89),
against the estimation of others (for it 'was at once one of
her most cherished complaints and most secret supports that
people didn't understand her' (7–8)), and against the facts of
material existence: 'She was perfectly aware that her imaginative
life was the life in which she spent most of her time; and she
would have been ready, had it been at all worth while, to contend
that, since her outward occupation didn't kill it, it must be strong
indeed' (8).

   The telegraphist's imaginative life is fed more richly than ever
before by the emerging story of two particularly handsome and
fascinating customers, Lady Bradeen and Captain Everard. From
their cryptic messages, with their mysterious aliases and lists of
numbers, the girl pieces together a sense of 'their high encounter
with life, their large and complicated game' (18) which satisfies
her appetite for romance; meanwhile, her attention, sympathy
and increasing knowledge as reader of their story form the basis
of what she persuades herself is a real relationship between the
Captain and herself. She comes to believe that she enjoys a special
relation with this dazzling member of the privileged classes; that
there is something 'between' them, 'something unusual and
good—something not a bit horrid or vulgar' (99–100). However,
a different perspective on the material she has interpreted and the
relation she has constructed comes from Captain Everard and
Lady Bradeen. There are hints that the pair's 'large and complicated game' is in some way illicit; thus the girl's attempt to write
herself into their story and, particularly, to secure the Captain's
attention by demonstrating 'my knowing, and that sort of thing'
(102) is misconstrued by the couple as an attempt at blackmail.
Unwilling to believe that the Captain would impute such a motive
to her, the girl invents supersubtle and unconvincing explanations
of his apparent attempts to pay her off: 'He wanted to pay her

because there was nothing to pay her for. He wanted to offer her
things that he knew she wouldn't take. He wanted to show her
how much he respected her by giving her the supreme chance to
show *him* she was respectable' (138–9).

Captain Everard's and the girl's conflicting interpretations of
events form a clash of two modes of reading which also occurs in
The Turn of the Screw and *The Sacred Fount*: the collision of
'literal, vulgar' (*TS* 7) readings with over-ingenious and supersubtle ones. The Captain's reading presumes that the telegraphist
is motivated by a desire for profit. The girl, although she is trying
to use her only asset of exchangeable value, her cleverness, to
gain some happiness, scorns the material motives of the grocer-
class (as represented by Mr Mudge) and defines the source of her
actions as a 'heroism of sympathy' (64). Each mode of reading
provides an ironic perspective on the other. The Captain's reading
has a better sense of social reality, but the girl's seems to be more
nobly motivated. However, her motives are more complex than
she admits. The telegraphist's circumstances give her good cause
to seek their imaginative overthrow. 'Real justice was not of this
world: she had had too often to come back to that; yet, strangely,
happiness was, and her traps had to be set for it in a manner to
keep them unperceived by Mr. Buckton and the counter-clerk',
her literal-minded and vulgar fellow workers (65). 'Real justice'
is meaningless as a factor in her imaginative calculations when
real injustice is so apparent and inescapable, but happiness may
be trapped in the snare of speculation that gives her access to the
world of those 'in whom all the conditions for happiness actually
met' (14) and allows her to realize, in her own terms at least, the
sense of an actual relation with Everard, who is himself 'the
happiest of the happy circumstances' (17). If all this is motivated
by a desire to create something 'unusual and good' (100), to
act out a 'heroism of sympathy' (64), may not her supersubtle
reading be defended, as James later defended his creation
of 'supersubtle fry' (*LC* ii. 1229), as an improvement on reality?
Yet the girl's actions have less admirable aspects. She has a
strong sense of fate—a romantic sense, picked up from or confirmed by her cheap novels, and similar to the irresponsible,
escapist romantic sensibility of Mrs Penniman in *Washington
Square*. This concept of fate is part of her romantic vision of
Captain Everard, 'in the strong grip of a dizzy, splendid fate' (70),

enslaved to and endangered by Lady Bradeen, 'the real mistress of his fate' (141). Fate also provides a convenient excuse for her own actions, such as walking past the Captain's chambers after work. She remarks to herself that she won't go, but she goes anyway, feeling

that one's remarks were as weak as straws, and that, however one might indulge in them at eight o'clock, one's fate infallibly declared itself in absolute indifference to them at about eight-fifteen. Remarks were remarks, and very well for that; but fate was fate . . . (85)

By calling her own choice fate, she can shrug off responsibility for her motives and actions. Later, when her confidence in the extent of her 'knowledge' has grown, she places herself in a different relation to fate, as when the Captain comes to her for help in recovering a lost telegram:

It came to her there, with her eyes on his face, that she held the whole thing in her hand, held it as she held her pencil, which might have broken at that instant in her tightened grip. This made her feel like the very fountain of fate . . . (150)

Not needing to recover the telegram because she can remember its contents, she does indeed figure as an omniscient power in the Captain's affairs. Her knowledge allows her to exult over those who make use of her to transmit their secrets as if she had 'no more feeling than a letter-box' (107). 'How little she knows, how little she knows!' the girl crows inwardly over Lady Bradeen, and 'How much *I* know—how much *I* know!' (77). Her involvement with their affairs grows almost to a belief that she is able to direct them. With a sense of herself as Everard's providence she assures him that his friend will respond to his 'imperative appeal', 'as if she could absolutely guarantee it' (146). Yet this extravagance is strangely paired with timidity. Her sense of the Captain's 'danger' has always been safely indefinite. 'There were twists and turns, there were places where the screw drew blood, that she couldn't guess. She was more and more glad she didn't want to' (155). So, too, her idea of their 'relation' is a thing she doesn't want tested in the world outside, and although she likes to think that 'he practically proposed supper every time he looked at her' (137), 'to be in the cage had suddenly become her safety, and she was literally afraid of the alternate self who might be waiting outside.

He might be waiting; it was he who was her alternate self, and of him she was afraid' (136). She can live vicariously through this 'alternate self', but she cannot go out to meet it; rather, retreating within the cage, she creates fictions which are consolatory and escapist, and her motives for this include a mixture of aggressiveness and defensiveness towards the world outside.

Although the tale is narrated with the girl as 'centre of consciousness' (that is, it presents only her experience as she sees it), we are not encouraged to accept her interpretation and valuation of her experience. There is an ironic note to the narrator's talk of the girl's 'rich experience' (19) and 'the immensity of her knowledge of the life of the world' (85), for he reveals that the 'ha'penny novels' are still the source of much of her information (73). Romantic or sensational fiction was notorious for confusing ranks and inaccurately representing the manners of the upper classes, and readers could be wildly misinformed by a 'self-taught and guess-work novelist'[5] with as little experience of upper-class life as themselves, whose aristocrats were 'the dressed-up milliners of courageous inexperience'.[6] Having reported the girl's banal conversations with Captain Everard in the shop, the narrator clearly mocks her belief 'that no form of intercourse so transcendent and distilled had ever been established on earth' (63). Thus, 'not feeling all that could be got out of the weather' he joins the 'cheaply sarcastic people' (65) who are out of sympathy with her supersubtle interpretations. The narrator's detachment from his heroine's activity becomes not only implicit and ironic, but explicit and didactic, when he departs from his strict shadowing of her consciousness to draw the reader's attention to her imaginative extravagance: 'What may not, we can only moralise, take place in the quickened, muffled perception of a girl of a certain kind of soul?' (73–4). Here the narrator blatantly breaks the conventions of his chosen narrative mode by stepping aside from the heroine's consciousness and addressing the reader with an explicit criticism of her. In coming forward to 'moralise' in this way, the narrator indicates a strong desire to separate his voice from the imaginative practices of the heroine.

[5] This epithet was used to describe Mrs Henry Wood in 'Our Female Sensation Novelists', 217.
[6] Ibid. 224; see also [Hitchman], 'Penny Fiction', 161.

This address to the reader makes explicit the gap between experiencing heroine and moralizing narrator that is the source of irony in the tale. It also makes clear that this is a story with a moral—the moral being the folly of the girl's regarding herself as 'the very fountain of fate' (150) when in reality 'Mr. Mudge was distinctly her fate' (117). Events at the end of the tale overthrow the heroine's definitions of fate—the romantic sense gained from her cheap novels and the megalomaniac sense derived from her own fictions. Behind the acceptance by her friend, Mrs Jordan, that her best chance of survival is in marrying a butler and giving up dreams of marrying into the aristocracy, lies an awareness that 'her fate was pressing her close' (162). In this the girl recognizes 'the common element in their fate' (177), for

> what our heroine saw and felt for in the whole business was the vivid reflection of her own dreams and delusions and her own return to reality. Reality, for the poor things they both were, could only be ugliness and obscurity, could never be the escape, the rise. (176–7)

Fate is economically and socially determined in ways that the imagination can never finally overthrow, and the story's events endorse the irresistible dominance of the literal and vulgar facts of material life over the oppositional power of fiction.

Despite the limited role of the narrator and the space given to the subjective nature of the girl's adventure, *In the Cage* still offers a version of the narrative structure familiar from James's early novels, where the plots of the characters are viewed from an ironic distance by the narrator and are finally defeated by incontrovertible historical facts. We experience the events of the tale through the protagonist's eyes, but we also see enough of other points of view (not only the opposed interpretation of Captain Everard, but the dissonant incomprehension of Mr Mudge, Mrs Jordan's competitive theories, and Mr Buckton's 'cheaply sarcastic' comments) to make us question the validity of the girl's perspective. Meanwhile, although we are restricted to the girl's limited access to and understanding of the facts of the situation concerning Captain Everard and Lady Bradeen (the nature of which remains uncertain), we are left in no doubt as to the facts of her own future, the fate which resists her attempts to overthrow it. The conflicting views of other characters and the tyranny of events combine with implicit irony and explicit moralizing from the narrator to construct a 'historical' narrative at odds with that which we see through the eyes of the protagonist, and finally triumphant over it.

This structure enacts the demands made in 'The Art of Fiction' that the novel, as history, should have a different status from fictions (such as the telegraphist's) which manipulate and misrepresent life. But the relation of *In the Cage* to both 'The Art of Fiction' and to the attitudes about fiction to which that essay responded is far more complex than this, and the tale glosses the multivalency of 'The Art of Fiction' itself. In enacting the defeat of plot by history, the tale enacts the defeat of supersubtle readings by 'literal, vulgar' (*TS* 7) ones. Yet, during these years around the turn of the century, James was painfully aware of, and frustrated by, the 'childishness' of the reading public (*Letters* iv. 250), and was peopling his fictions with 'supersubtle fry' (*LC* ii. 1229) who may be seen as surrogates for the attentive, imaginative, appropriative readers he wanted but lacked. Moreover, the telegraphist's reading and plotting of her circumstances dramatizes skills which James advocated for the writer in 'The Art of Fiction'. In fact, the enumeration of these skills in that essay grows out of a discussion of the validity of speculation across class boundaries, an activity in which both the heroine and the author of *In the Cage* are involved. In reply to Walter Besant's assertion that 'a writer whose friends and personal experiences belong to the lower middle-class should carefully avoid introducing his characters into society', James notes that the 'remark about the lower middle-class writer and his knowing his place is perhaps rather chilling' (*LC* i. 51), and to the pronouncement that 'a young lady brought up in a quiet country village should avoid descriptions of garrison life' (i. 51) he counters that the 'young lady living in a village has only to be a damsel upon whom nothing is lost to make it quite unfair (as it seems to me) to declare to her that she shall have nothing to say about the military' (i. 52). He goes on to cite the case of a novelist whose much-commended picture of French Protestant youth was put together, not from 'peculiar opportunities' but from a glimpsed 'direct personal impression' (i. 52) combined with her own general experience of life:

she converted these ideas into a concrete image and produced a reality. Above all, however, she was blessed with the faculty which when you give

it an inch takes an ell, and which for the artist is a much greater source of
strength than any accident of residence or of place in the social scale.
(i. 52–3)

The telegraphist of *In the Cage* is, likewise, 'a damsel upon whom
nothing is lost', with an imagination 'which when you give it an
inch takes an ell'—exactly the kind of imagination which James,
in the preface to *The Princess Casamassima*, portrayed himself as
exercising in his speculative pursuit of the lower classes of London (*LC* ii. 1101). With her direct personal impressions of the
customers in the shop, and her 'power to guess the unseen from
the seen, to trace the implication of things', does she not also
have 'this cluster of gifts' which 'may almost be said to constitute
experience' (*LC* i. 53)?

   The tale rejects any such idea, demonstrating that the girl's gifts
cannot constitute, or produce, experience for her, and suggesting
that she will do less harm to herself and others if she simply
accepts the field of experience dictated to her by the accidents of
birth and residence. Although the girl's self-conscious artistry
brings her close to the author, she is also the very type of the
young girl corrupted by her infatuation with novels, one of
James's most direct uses of this conventional figure from anti-
fiction diatribes and parodic anti-novels. Discussions of penny
fiction and public libraries at the end of the century often employed versions of this character, and the associated enquiries by
male writers in positions of cultural authority into the reading
habits of working-class and lower middle-class women—a project similar to, and fraught with some of the same problems as,
James's writing of *In the Cage*—often produced this stereotype.[7]
The character of the telegraphist dramatizes what had become a
classic male construction of the woman reader, and her story
might be an *exemplum* based on the general fear of the effects on
women of romantic reading and a romantic imagination which
was a constant theme of discussions of the social influence of
fiction. More specifically, the narrative the telegraphist constructs, in which she imaginatively writes herself into a novel 'all
about fine folks' (*ITC* 6), reflects particular aspects of the reading
of 'the masses' which worried analysts: working-class news-

[7] See the discussion of this in Chapter 1.

papers and novelettes often showed contempt for the upper classes,[8] combined with envy of and desire to share in the ease of their position—a mixture of aggression and voyeurism.[9] Like Hyacinth Robinson, the telegraphist is offered two kinds of plots through which to define her relationship to the upper classes, and between which she finds it difficult to choose. She loves Captain Everard but likes to 'loathe' the rich (56), and her version of events where she helps him by offering a 'heroism of sympathy' (64) but at the same time gains power over his class by becoming 'the very fountain of fate' (150) combines fantasies of marrying an aristocratic husband and of gaining revenge over an aristocratic seducer or oppressor, which were common themes of the penny novelette:[10]

> She quite thrilled herself with thinking what, with such a lot of material, a bad girl would do. It would be a scene better than many in her ha'penny novels, this going to him in the dusk of evening at Park Chambers and letting him at last have it. 'I know too much about a certain person now not to put it to you—excuse my being so lurid—that it's quite worth your while to buy me off. Come, therefore; buy me!' (68)

As she is not 'a bad girl', and cannot, moreover, decide on 'the purchasing medium' (68) that would define their relation, she lets the idea drop, but the same complex of emotions, familiar from her 'ha'penny novels' (73), generates her continued efforts to involve herself in the Captain's affairs.

Reading *In the Cage* in relation to 'The Art of Fiction' and its cultural context, several contradictions emerge. The telegraphist is a good practitioner of the plotting skills outlined in 'The Art of Fiction', but in keeping with that essay's demand that the novel, as history, should be made superior to what is 'only a "make-believe" ' (*LC* i. 45), her imaginary narrative is denied validity and her skills dismissed as dangerous. Meanwhile, the girl is also representative of the reader whose view of life is distorted by novels, and thus *In the Cage* is a morality tale exposing the evils of fiction, expressing the very values against which 'The Art of Fiction' reacted. Such contradictions in the tale expose the

[8] Salmon, 'What the Working Classes Read', 114; see also the discussion of *The Princess Casamassima* in Chapter 2.
[9] Leigh, 'What do the Masses Read?', 172
[10] Ibid.

contradiction in 'The Art of Fiction' itself as a response to hostility to the novel. The structure which opposes veracious history to unreliable plot (and thus distinguishes the novel from dishonest or frivolous fictions) is a technique for heightening the realism of the text by implying that a narrative opposed to a false narrative must be a true one. This tactic has the effect of endorsing, not only the puritan's absolute distinction between false and true narratives, but a specifically puritanical attitude towards the imagination. The formal structure of *In the Cage*, dependent on—or, rather, trying to create the illusion of—a strict differentiation of false and true narratives, once again entails a moral understanding that 'there is no effective plotting for happiness' (*LC* ii. 982). Formally, *In the Cage* endorses the epistemological categories of the detractors of fiction. In arranging that the qualities of the imagination advocated in 'The Art of Fiction' should be defeated by the literal, vulgar facts of a historical inevitability also advocated in 'The Art of Fiction', it endorses a puritan morality which parallels an aesthetic philistinism. The telegraphist is made to learn that life is life, as 'a novel is a novel, as a pudding is a pudding, and that our only business with it could be to swallow it' (*LC* i. 44).

In the Cage thus reinforces the very attitudes towards fiction—moral and aesthetic—that 'The Art of Fiction' had set out to combat, and so the condemnation of the heroine's fiction-making programme comes dangerously close to condemning that of the author. To escape the implications of this, it may be argued that the 'moral' of the story is really that living and story-telling involve very different arts, and that it is dangerous to try to cross the boundary between them, to try to live by fictions. *In the Cage* may be illustrating a question of propriety, demonstrating that rules and dispensations appropriate to the author do not apply to his characters, and maintaining that an author has a professional immunity from the doubts and criticisms attached to a heroine.[11] Perhaps we are to accept that when the author makes himself 'so

---

[11] Trollope acknowledges that such distinctions are rarely absolute when he reveals how his profession of novel-writing grew out of a habit of daydreaming: 'There can, I imagine, hardly be a more dangerous mental practice; but I have often doubted whether, had it not been my practice, I should ever have written a novel' (*Autobiography* i. 58). The very important difference that, in his professional practice, he was able to lay aside his own identity as hero of the fiction,

free, intellectually' (*LC* ii. 1168) of a range of experience about
which he can only speculate, and becomes 'the very fountain of
fate' (*ITC* 150) in directing and judging it, this results in a fiction
with the status of history, accurate and morally responsible, but
when the girl does the same thing, she produces merely a plot,
and only harms herself and interferes with the lives of others if
she tries to act as if it were history. On the other hand, the
exposure of the girl's narrative as false and morally questionable,
rather than intensifying the reader's faith in the narrator's version
of events, may, reflexively, have the effect of discrediting the
author's fiction-making activity too.[12]

The implication of the author in this negative definition of the
narrative enterprise is made clear in the retrospective preface to
the tale, written in 1908. The affinities between the indulgence of
his own 'wonderment' in writing the tale (*LC* ii. 1168) and the
'range of wonderment' he attributes to his heroine (ii. 1170) are
emphasized, and at times it is difficult to determine to which of
them his judgements apply. In discussing how the questions posed
by 'the morbid imagination' provide 'a great occupation for
idleness', James states:

To the fantastic scale on which this last-named state may, in favouring
conditions, organise itself, to the activities it may practise when the
favouring conditions happen to crop up in Mayfair or in Kensington, our
portrayal of the caged telegraphist may well appear a proper little monument. (ii. 1169)

Does this mean that the tale is a monument to 'the fantastic scale'
of his own or his heroine's idle speculation? It is unclear whether

nevertheless indicates only a relative, not an absolute, disinterestedness on the part
of an author (compared with a daydreamer); even without the gratifications of
casting oneself as hero, the making of fictions allows for a re-ordering of the
conditions of experience which may operate as a form of escapism or wish-fulfilment. Concerning the connection between omnivorous novel-reading and authorship, we may remember that the young James was, according to his father, 'a
devourer of libraries'; see F. O. Matthiessen, *The James Family: Including Selections from the Writings of Henry James, Senior, William, Henry, and Alice James*
(New York: Alfred A. Knopf, 1947), 88.

[12] I do not accept Jean Frantz Blackall's contention in 'James's *In the Cage*: An
Approach through the Figurative Language', *University of Toronto Quarterly*, 31
(1962), 179, that 'the "novels" theme' in *In the Cage* simply confirms James's
ironic distance from the telegraphist and is used only to pursue 'the humorous
implications of a point of view so uninformed let loose on a world so unfamiliar'.

the 'moral' to be extracted from 'the vice of reading rank sub-
tleties into simple souls and reckless expenditure into thrifty
ones' is the moral of the story itself or of 'the story of its growth'
(ii. 1169), whether it concerns the telegraphist's or the novelist's
activity. Certainly, it is the same moral that the author, in his
'immoral' interest in the minds of others, might draw from his
'danger' of 'imputing to too many others, right and left, the
critical impulse and the acuter vision' (ii. 1169). This retrospective judgement is even extended to Hyacinth Robinson in
The Princess Casamassima. Hyacinth and the telegraphist share a
habit of wondering (ii. 1170) about what is beyond the field of
experience dictated by their class, but whereas in the preface to
The Princess Casamassima Hyacinth is simply a 'small obscure
but ardent observer' (ii. 1096), in drawing him into the imaginative
world of *In the Cage* James presents him as 'tainted to the core'
with the habit, not only of observation, but of speculation: 'He
collapses, poor Hyacinth, like a thief at night, overcharged with
treasures of reflexion and spoils of passion of which he can give,
in his poverty and obscurity, no honest account' (ii. 1170). How
then is the author to give an 'honest account' of his own 'treasures
of reflexion', his fictions? He has no better warrant for his
speculative overstepping of the range of his own experience than
his characters do; or rather, he has the warrant offered by 'The
Art of Fiction' (*LC* i. 51–3)—but if this is not enough to justify
the girl's activity, does it justify his own?

According to the preface, the author's fiction is only as defen-
sible (or indefensible) as the girl's; that is, we cannot make
distinctions between the proper spheres of art and life which
allow the author to escape the criticisms attached to fiction-making
in this tale. In the preface, the author implicates himself in his
criticisms of his heroine, which closely resemble the criticisms of
both written and lived fictions central to the English tradition of
hostility to the novel. But the corollary to this is that, with the
collapse of the rigid distinction between character's plot and
author's history on which the early novels and *In the Cage* itself
depend, the girl's fiction is made continuous with the authorial
achievements relentlessly analysed and interrogated, but also celebrated, in the prefaces.

THE TURN OF THE SCREW

The Turn of the Screw, published in the same year as *In the Cage*, also dramatizes aspects of the 'fiction question', adding further twists to James's complicated relationship to the detractors and defenders of fiction in nineteenth-century England. There are many similarities between the situations explored in the two tales. Like the telegraphist in *In the Cage*, the governess finds in reading fiction, and in her work which brings her into contact with the more fortunate classes, an escape from a troubled childhood and the prospect of a bleak future. Like the telegraphist, she finds herself faced with fragmented clues which may be pieced together to tell a story of high romance and danger in which she may be able to play a heroic part. Both women apply their readerly skills to life in order to uncover, or plot, such a narrative, and use their 'knowledge' as a means of interfering in the lives of others. In the governess's case this has more far-reaching effects than in the telegraphist's, as it leads to the death of one of her charges and the dispersion of the household to which she is attached. Yet, while most readers agree that the telegraphist's interpretation of her situation is inaccurate and self-delusive, no such consensus has been reached with regard to the governess's version of events at Bly.

The governess's perception of the ghosts at Bly, and the interpretation of the children's behaviour and of her own responsibilities towards them that she bases on this perception, are influenced by novel-reading and sustained by the exercise of a novelistic imagination. Her first sighting of Quint is clearly linked to desires fed by fiction—desires similar to those governing the imagination of the telegraphist in *In the Cage*, although in the governess's case finding expression through a much more complex series of displacements. During an afternoon stroll in the garden, she indulges in her customary wish-fulfilment fantasy: 'that it would be as charming as a charming story suddenly to meet someone' (*TS* 30). The 'someone' she has in mind is, of course, her handsome employer, the absent master of Bly, 'such a figure as had never risen, save in a dream or an old novel, before a fluttered, anxious girl out of a Hampshire vicarage' (9); the 'charming story' may be, specifically, the most famous of master-and-governess romances, *Jane Eyre*, but evokes more generally

the whole tradition of cross-class romance which flourished in
nineteenth-century working-class fiction, but which also, since
Richardson's *Pamela*, had a firm place in the mainstream novel.
Quint first appears, then, as a fiction materialized—'my imagination had, in a flash, turned real. He did stand there!' (30)—but
the trope of the story made real is instantly perceived to have
gone somehow wrong: whereas Gertrude Wentworth, in *The
Europeans*, looks up from her reading of the *Arabian Nights* to
find the Prince Camaralzaman perfectly embodied in her cousin
Felix (*TE* i. 62–3), the governess finds the hero of her 'charming
story' displaced by a threatening intruder. The relation between
fiction and reality is thus shown to be seriously awry, but the
governess nevertheless turns back to fiction for a means of explaining her disturbing experience: 'Was there a "secret" at Bly—
a mystery of Udolpho or an insane, an unmentionable relative
kept in unsuspected confinement?' (34). Radcliffe's classic Gothic
novel is coupled with an allusion to *Jane Eyre* which casts Quint
in the role of Bertha Mason as a terror to be braved, a rival to be
vanquished (or simply outlasted), and an impediment to be overcome before union with 'the master' is possible.[13] The Gothic
influences on the governess's imagination signal her willingness
to accept supernatural explanations of events, but an even more
important legacy of her novel-reading is her desire to see herself,
and be seen by others, as a heroine, heroic in adversity. This is
brought out more clearly in the second scene in which the governess's novel-reading is directly linked to her sighting of one of the
ghosts. The governess's third encounter with Quint occurs when
she has stayed up late alone, reading Fielding's *Amelia*. As a
heroine beset with troubles, and in particular besieged by villain-
ous males attempting to wreck the precarious domestic haven she
is trying, single-handedly, to protect, Amelia offers a role-model
to the governess in what she increasingly sees as her battle to save
the children from the ghosts of their former caretakers. And at
the interface between reading and acting is the governess's desire,
not only to behave heroically, but to be seen to do so: she remarks
that she laid down her book and went to meet the ghost 'with all

---

[13] See Alice Hall Petry, 'Jamesian Parody, *Jane Eyre*, and "The Turn of the
Screw" ', *Modern Language Studies*, 13 (1983), 61–78, for an extended discussion
of the governess's attempts to cast herself in the role of Jane Eyre.

the marks of a deliberation that must have seemed magnificent had there been anyone to admire it' (76).

The governess herself admits that this desire both to be heroic and to publish her heroism preceded the appearance of the ghosts at Bly: 'I dare say I fancied myself, in short, a remarkable young woman and took comfort in the faith that this would more publicly appear. Well, I needed to be remarkable to offer a front to the remarkable things that presently gave their first sign' (29). Causation gets blurred here between the governess's statements that she 'fancied' herself remarkable and that she 'needed' to be remarkable—is it rather that she needs to produce a remarkable situation in order to indulge her fancies about herself as a heroine? Later, she actually admits that the appearance of the ghosts at Bly provides 'a magnificent chance' (54) for her to be remarkable, a heroine, the centre of a story worth telling. Before this, an invitation to recount her history could only be an invitation 'to repeat afresh Goody Gosling's celebrated *mot* or to confirm the details already supplied as to the cleverness of the vicarage pony' (98); the appearance of the ghosts offers her the chance to create a narrative which is not the 'grey prose' (36) expected of a smothered vicarage girl turned governess, but something to rival the rich prose of the Radcliffe, Brontë, and Fielding novels that have formed her narrative imagination. The question arises whether these novels, which have presented the governess with models of heroines braving both worldly and Gothic dangers, have filled a need or produced one; whether they have helped her to become the heroine her situation requires her to be, or have led her to misread her situation in order to create for herself the heroine's role she craves. The threatened collapse into circularity of her reasoning about what she 'fancied' and what she 'needed' cannot simply be attributed to her feelings for, and possible 'designs' upon, her employer, for it is a danger which threatens any heroine who bases her attitude to her life on the idea that it will make a remarkable story, just as it threatens any reader who works from the premise that all narratives contain hidden meanings which require strenuous interpretation. Both run the risk of perceiving imaginary significances and thereby creating remarkable, but imaginary, narratives. *The Turn of the Screw* makes us ask whether the governess's novelistic approach to life has served her (and her charges) well or badly: has she read the situation aright? is the written record she produces a work of history or of fiction? The question has become, by the end of the tale, literally a matter of life and death.

On this desperate trial of readership James's own readers have, collectively, failed to reach a verdict, and critics have become increasingly aware that the irresolvability of the tale's ambiguity puts on trial their own readerly skills and assumptions about meaning in narrative. For the long-running opposition between 'ghostly' and 'psychological' readings masked the essential similarity of their aims. Whether affirming the reality of the ghosts or arguing that they are the products of the governess's imagination, whether confirming the story as apparent from her account or retelling it with a commentary, both groups of critics express the desire to establish 'what happens', to retrieve an authentic story of character and event.[14] Such criticism is based on the assumption that meaning in narrative resides at the level of 'story' rather than of 'discourse'. Those who accept the governess's testimony regard her discourse as merely a transparent window on an independent story. Those who do not accept her testimony locate narrative meaning in the distinction Leon Edel makes between *the story as told* and *the story to be deduced*; for such readers, the meaning of an obscure text is to be found by peeling away the layers of rhetoric and interpretation that make up the narrator's discourse, in order to reveal the pristine story beneath.[15] Critics attempting to fix the meaning of the tale at the level of story are, in effect, attempting to find or construct the missing historical perspective that will tell them how to read the governess's plot.

However, *The Turn of the Screw* is a true example of the 'fantastic': the mixture of objective and subjective evidence, hard facts, and utter blanks in the tale leaves its readers hesitating

---

[14] Edmund Wilson's 'The Ambiguity of Henry James', *Hound and Horn*, 7 (1934), 385–406, is the most famous interpretation of the tale as 'a study in morbid psychology' (390). A sampling of arguments for and against the governess's reliability may be found in Robert Kimbrough (ed.), The Turn of the Screw: *An Authoritative Text, Backgrounds and Sources, Essays in Criticism* (New York: Norton, 1966).

[15] Leon Edel, *The Psychological Novel 1900–1950* (London: Hart-Davis, 1955); reprinted in Kimbrough, The Turn of the Screw: *An Authoritative Text*, 234. Allon White proposes his reading of the uses of obscurity in early modernist fiction in opposition to such conditioning to look for 'an anterior message which has been muddled up in the telling' (*The Uses of Obscurity*, 22).

between supernatural and realistic explanations of events,[16] unable either to condemn utterly, or to accept without reservations,
the way the governess reads and composes her situation. It is
finally impossible to locate in the tale a position of interpretative
security which may be identified with 'history'. Indeed, the desire
to achieve such a perspective is mocked in the prologue to the
tale, a parodic historical 'frame' which wraps up the governess's
narrative in the trappings of historicity but fails to place it within
any secure epistemological system.

The prologue shows the activities of the two editors of the
governess's manuscript: Douglas, who encloses it in his own
commentary and performance, and the 'I' character who narrates
this and thereby edits the entire form in which the manuscript
and its marginalia are presented to us. The insistence on the
materiality of the text, the suspense stimulated by the delay in
procuring it from its hiding place, and finally its ritualistic presentation, all contribute to the sense of the manuscript as a potent
object of historical significance. We are reminded of James's
praise of Turgenev for writing lines of narrative which seem to be
backed by 'documents and relics' (LC ii. 970), and of his own
insistence in 'The Art of Fiction' that the subject matter of fiction,
like that of history, is stored in 'documents and records' (LC i.
46). However, in his review of Anne Manning James had mildly
mocked the documentary trappings used by the historical novelist
to create the illusion of authenticity (LC i. 1152). The device of
the 'found document' as a guarantee of veracity, combatting
distrust of imaginative narratives, had long ago lost its force to
command belief, and the prologue to The Turn of the Screw
parodies this unconvincing convention by failing to back an
insistence on documentation with an 'authorized' perspective on
the text.

The character reference that Douglas gives the governess might
be seen, at first, as offering such a perspective, endorsing her
presentation of herself and her story: 'She was the most agreeable
woman I've ever known in her position; she would have been
worthy of any whatever. . . . Oh yes; don't grin: I liked her
extremely and am glad to this day to think she liked me too' (6).

---

[16] See Tzvetan Todorov, The Fantastic: A Structural Approach to a Literary
Genre, trans. Richard Howard (Ithaca, NY: Cornell University Press, 1975), 33.

However, the fact that Douglas 'liked her extremely' is not a guarantee of the accuracy of her account, and in fact the suggestion that he was in love with her (7) raises the possibility that his judgement is clouded, or even that she may have invented her story to entice or repel him. Moreover, far from offering the reader a guide to the correct interpretation of the tale, Douglas maintains that the 'story *won't* tell, . . . not in any literal, vulgar way' (7). If not, this rules out equally the ghost story of 'sheer terror' (he 'seemed to say it was not so simple as that' (4)) and the psychological story of secret motives which one can 'easily judge' (6): at least, it rules out either as a definitive interpretation.

As well as failing to dispel the ambiguity about the reality of the ghosts and the reliability of the governess's account, the prologue makes the meaning of the tale even more elusive by proposing two entirely different modes of attention to it. Douglas seems to be presenting the governess's story as a serious moral problem, one of conduct and responsibility; in this case it would be important for the reader to try to determine whether the governess is faced with a supernatural or a psychological disturbance, whether her interpretation of it is true or false. Yet Douglas presents her story to a literal, vulgar audience seeking the obvious ghostly or psycho-sexual interest, who see his 'outbreak' as a 'tremendous occasion' (7) for 'a common thrill' (8), that is, as a piece of social entertainment. To them, it is a ghost story in competition with other ghost stories, to be judged by its ability to give a thrill of delicious dreadfulness. This audience recognizes horror not as part of a moral drama, but only as a performance-effect. We may wonder why Douglas chooses to expose the governess's precious manuscript to such an audience; it seems unlikely that he would betray her affection and trust for the sake of some amusement for idle holiday evenings. Perhaps his action is a challenge to the audience, an attempt to force them to recognize the human horror which is the real result of the ghostly horror they find so thrilling. Or perhaps it is a kind of joke played against the audience which simultaneously protects the meaning of the governess's mystery from their literal, vulgar apprehension; he presents the tale on their terms, while insisting that their terms are inadequate, for the meanings of the tale and the case of its author are more disturbing than they guess. Douglas's performance of the tale takes place shortly after Christmas, the season of uncanny tales in the Dickensian tradition; like these it is serialized, as its telling is spread over several nights. The timing also means that the tale is told within the twelve days of Christmas, season of misrule and narrative licentiousness. Other works which belong to this season, such as *Twelfth Night*, incorporate serious social or moral criticism within the misrule frame and offer epiphanies, revelations, new knowledge. *The Turn of the Screw* may belong to this tradition, but with the essential difference that it does not deliver any moment of revelation: we seek knowledge, but are never satisfied.

The puzzles of which mode of attention is appropriate to the text, and which is the right answer to its central question, are not resolved by the actions of the 'I' narrator, the editor and publisher of the manuscript. His decision to frame the manuscript with its textual and stage history, but not to include the other half of the frame, its reception history, means that readers of the whole text are given many clues that breed hesitation, but no information about 'right' or 'wrong' readings which could resolve it. The title he chooses is no help either: it could refer to the turn of the screw of human virtue (153), a moral dilemma, or the turn of the screw of horror (4), a performance-effect.

The prologue parodies the idea of a historical frame (such as that identified, in James's earlier works, with the narrator's point of view) which authorizes or corrects the characters' plots and stabilizes meaning in the text. The prologue's contradictory messages about how to read the tale, like the tale's contradictory messages about the reliability of its narrator, tease and baffle the reader's desire to fix the meaning of the tale by making a distinction between true and false narratives. The strength of this desire is evident in the intensity and longevity of the debate over the reality of the ghosts in *The Turn of the Screw*, but the tale's resistance to attempts to extract from it a stable meaning at the level of story has increasingly become the focus of critical attention. Since the late 1970s, many critics have identified the meaning of the tale, not with a particular version of events, but with the essential irresolvability of the reading problem offered by the text.[17]

---

[17] See e.g. Shlomith Rimmon, *The Concept of Ambiguity—The Example of James* (Chicago: University of Chicago Press, 1977), 116–66; Shoshana Felman,

The practical impossibility of proving the truth or falsity of the governess's narrative destabilizes various distinctions on which the Victorian 'fiction question', and James's early response to it, depended. The radical ambiguity of *The Turn of the Screw* leaves unresolved the question of whether the governess's novelistic imagination has enhanced or diminished her capacity to deal with life, and it is thus impossible to draw from this tale a clear moral (such as that offered by *In the Cage*) about the value or dangers of consuming and making fictions. Like the telegraphist, the governess confuses the distinction between history and plot by indulging in what may be a dangerous overexercise of the imagination, while at the same time employing the kinds of interpretative skills recommended to the novelist-historian in 'The Art of Fiction'. And finally, the way the tale provides 'evidence' for both the reliability and unreliability of the governess's narrative disrupts the epistemological categories essential both to the discourse of hostility to fiction, and to James's idea of 'historical' narrative.

The Turn of the Screw also stands in an ambiguous relation to a more specific feature of the 'old superstition about fiction being "wicked" ' (*LC* i. 45)—the fear of the exposure of children to corruption. The need to keep children's reading pure and safe was a major cause of puritan attacks on the novel, which was held to be eminently fitted for corrupting the young. One opponent of fiction wrote to the *Christian Observer* in 1817 expounding 'the duty of Christian parents to deny their dearest inmates those intellectual gratifications which cannot be separated from what has polluted many, and possesses at least the power of injuring all'.[18] In *An*

'Turning the Screw of Interpretation', *Yale French Studies*, 55–6 (1977), 94–207; Christine Brooke-Rose, *A Rhetoric of the Unreal: Studies in Narrative and Structure, Especially of the Fantastic* (Cambridge: Cambridge University Press, 1981), 128–229. Some of the more recent historicist analyses of the tale have criticized tendencies to make indeterminacy the end-point of interpretation, but have also (like my own reading) taken the tale's ambiguity as the basis of their critical projects; see Rowe, *Theoretical Dimensions*, 119–46, and Bruce Robbins, 'Shooting Off James's Blanks: Theory, Politics, and *The Turn of the Screw*', *Henry James Review*, 5 (1984), 192–8. However, the current trend towards historicist criticism of the tale has also produced renewed attempts to establish a definitive reading of the text, authorized by and as history; see e.g. Peter Beidler's historicized, pro-governess reading in *Ghosts, Demons, and Henry James: The Turn of the Screw at the Turn of the Century* (Columbia: University of Missouri Press, 1989).

[18] 'Excubitor', 'On the Expediency of Novel-Reading', (letter), *Christian Observer*, 16 (1817), 298, 301.

Essay on Light Reading (1808), the Revd Edward Mangin issued
the following warning on the subject:

The tender parent and conscientious guardian will feel surprise, not
unmixed with self-reproach, at the reflection of having, through criminal
inattention, connived at the perusal of some of those works which I shall
specify: or who, through indolence not less criminal, have neglected to
inquire how *all* the hours of their offspring or their pupils were passed;
and, by an indifference wholly unpardonable, have allowed the work of
moral and useful instruction, to which the day may have been dedicated,
to be demolished, like the web of Penelope, by the mischievous occupation of the night![19]

He went on to declare

that the parents, guardians, or preceptors, who authorise, or permit, or
connive at, or do not strictly prohibit the perusal of . . . [certain works of
fiction] to the youth whose morals they superintend, have to answer for
a crime more heinous than can well be named; for which no subsequent
care or caution can make reparation, either to the individual or the state,
and for which hardly any penitence can ever atone.[20]

In his essay 'Novel-Reading' (1879), Trollope warned of the same
need for vigilance in allowing the novelist to enter a household as
a 'tutor' for the young: 'What can be of more importance to us
than to know whether we who all of us encourage such tutors in
our houses, are subjecting those we love to good teaching or to
ill?'[21] And in his essay on 'The Future of the Novel', published
the year after *The Turn of the Screw*, James referred to the
Victorian obsession with young people's reading in terms which
strikingly resemble the tale's concern with absent parents and
guardians, domestic negligence, and potentially dangerous displacements of responsibility and authority with regard to the
education of the young: ' "You have kindly taken," they [the
young] seem to say to the fiction-mongers, "our education off
the hands of our parents and pastors, and that, doubtless, has been
very convenient for *them*, and left them free to amuse themselves" ' (*LC* i. 108). The role James assigns here to the 'fiction-
mongers' of the nineteenth century duplicates the role adopted by

[19] Edward Mangin, *An Essay on Light Reading, as It May be Supposed to
Influence Moral Conduct and Literary Taste* (London, 1808), 27–8.
[20] Ibid. 56.
[21] Trollope, 'Novel-Reading', 28.

Quint and Jessel, and then the governess, in *The Turn of the Screw*, as they take over the education of the children, leaving their uncle (conveniently for him) free to amuse himself. This duplication of offices suggests links between the educative or corruptive role of fiction in nineteenth-century culture, and the tale's concern with the education or corruption of the children at the hands of their caretakers.

The children were left with a governess who had fallen to the status of a servant through her liaison with one 'so dreadfully below' (62), and a servant who had assumed the role of a tutor in supervising Miles's education (68). Thus the question of their education becomes involved with the question of the influences of servants on children. The pernicious influence of servants was a common topic in treatises on the care of children, and the tale may be read, literally, as an exposition on this subject.[22] It may also be read, figuratively, as an allegory of the theme of the corruption of the young by fiction. Exposure to fiction and exposure to servants could both lead to the corruption of the manners and morals of children: in the issue of the need to protect children, these two topics in nineteenth-century culture, the servant problem and the fiction question, have much in common. A metaphorical association between the dangers of servants and the dangers of fiction makes sense given the similar effects each could have on innocent children. In the Edgeworths' *Essays on Practical Education*, the theme of the evil influence of servants, given a chapter in itself, is revived in the chapter on 'Books', where it is argued that nothing but harm can come from presenting even caricatured images of vice to the perfect inno- cence of children 'who have never lived with servants, who have never associated with ill-educated companions of their own age, and who in their own family have heard nothing but good con- versation, and seen none but good examples'; such children 'should be sedulously kept from contagion', from exposure to things outside the safe haven of family life.[23] Books of fiction, like

[22] The Edgeworths state that it is 'a common maxim' that 'it is the worst thing in the world to leave children with servants': see Maria and R. L. Edgeworth, *Essays on Practical Education*, new edn., 2 vols. (London, 1815), i. 156. For a reading of the tale in this light, see Elliot M. Schrero, 'Exposure in *The Turn of the Screw*', *Modern Philology*, 78 (1981), 261–74.

[23] Edgeworth, *Essays on Practical Education*, i. 413–14.

servants, can intrude on that life with bad language and a love of fashionable folly instead of virtue—and, although the Edgeworths do not mention this, with a knowledge of 'secret disorders, vices' (*TS* 53), giving children a precocious sexual awareness.

There was another way in which the concerns about servants and fiction were even more directly entwined: in the fear that servants could harm children by telling them stories, specifically ghost stories. An extreme example of this was the case of Bentham, who attributed much of his antipathy to institutional and legal fictions (and even the fictional element in all language) to his sense of the injurious effect of the ghost stories to which he was exposed in childhood by domestic servants.[24] The fear of ghosts that still plagued him in later life, despite his better judgement, fuelled the intensity with which he attacked what he saw as the no less fabulous and no less injurious fictions inherent in all power relations and processes of communication in social life. This hostility to fiction in Bentham's utilitarian philosophy was, of course, a major force encouraging hostility to the novel in Victorian culture. The subjection of children to fictional horrors at the hands of servants is the subject of a double censure by the Edgeworths: children should not associate with servants who tell them stories of goblins or play at being spectres, and children who have not been exposed to such behaviour should not see it described in books which represent it, even for the purposes of censure or ridicule.[25] The ambiguity of the governess's social position makes her role regarding such corruption of the children also ambiguous. She may be seen as either a servant-figure or a parent-figure, a harmful intruder upon the household or a trusted inmate working for its protection.[26] To a reader who believes that the ghosts are figments of the governess's imagination, invented by her, the tale may be seen as dramatizing the process of the

[24] Ogden, *Bentham's Theory of Fictions*, p. xv.
[25] Edgeworth, *Essays on Practical Education*, i. 417–19.
[26] On the socially and morally ambiguous position of the governess in English domestic arrangements, see M. Jeanne Peterson, 'The Victorian Governess: Status Incongruence in Family and Society', in *Suffer and Be Still: Women in the Victorian Age*, ed. Martha Vicinus (Bloomington: Indiana University Press, 1972), 3–19; and Mary Poovey, 'The Anathematized Race: The Governess and *Jane Eyre*', *Uneven Developments: The Ideological Work of Gender in Mid-Victorian England* (London: Virago, 1989), 126–63.

exposure of the children to the injurious fictions of a servant or tutor. The governess—tentatively at first, for she must 'defer to the old tradition of the criminality of those caretakers of the young who minister to superstitions and fears' (*TS* 88), and then explicitly—tells the children a ghost story, which she tries to force them to believe, and which is psychologically and physically damaging to them.[27] On the other hand, to a reader who believes that the governess, *in loco parentis*, is trying to protect the children from the corrupting influence of depraved servants, the tale may function as an allegory of the puritan battle to protect the young from the effects of fiction, especially in introducing them to the 'horrors' of unregulated sexuality. Indeed, one early reviewer of the tale suggested such an interpretation when, praising James as a 'moralist', he likened him to Jeremy Collier who, in the tradition of puritan hostility to works of imagination, wrote *A Short View of the Immorality and Profaneness of the English Stage* (1698).[28] Thus the governess's relation to this particular strand of puritan hostility to fiction is (of course) ambiguous; she may be either perpetrating or combatting the crime of fiction. Either way, the tale may be seen as dramatizing versions of the 'old superstition about fiction being "wicked" ' (*LC* i. 45).

On the other hand, *The Turn of the Screw* mocks this superstition by deliberately setting out to make the reader imagine the nature of the horrors that assault the children. James solves the problem of how to make his depiction of evil seem infernal enough by shifting responsibility for inventing the details of the horrors to the reader:

Only make the reader's general vision of evil intense enough . . . and his own experience, his own imagination, his own sympathy (with the children) and horror (of their false friends) will supply him quite sufficiently with all the particulars. Make him *think* the evil, make him think it for himself, and you are released from weak specifications. (*LC* ii. 1188)

[27] Without making a judgement on the reality of the ghosts, Joann Peck Krieg's reading of *The Turn of the Screw* as 'a cautionary tale . . . on the subject of tutelage' makes a similar point about the possible dangers of 'bring[ing] romance into the nursery-room'; see 'A Question of Values: Culture and Cognition in *The Turn of the Screw*', in *The Magic Circle of Henry James: Essays in Honour of Darshan Singh Maini*, ed. Amritjit Singh and K. Ayyappa Paniker (New Delhi: Sterling, 1989), 137.
[28] *New York Times Saturday Review of Books and Art* (15 Oct. 1898), 681–2; reprinted in Kimbrough, The Turn of the Screw: *An Authoritative Text*, 170.

Some early reviewers resented this. The reviewer for the *Independent* complained that the 'feeling after perusal of the horrible story is that one has been assisting in an outrage upon the holiest and sweetest fountain of human innocence, and helping to debauch—at least by helplessly standing by—the pure and trusting nature of children'.[29] Complaints about the disgusting nature of the evil suggested demonstrated the success of James's plan to force the reader to supply his own 'appreciation, speculation, imagination' (*LC* ii. 1188) of evil:

How can I feel my calculation to have failed, my wrought suggestion not to have worked, that is, on my being assailed, as has befallen me, with the charge of a monstrous emphasis, the charge of all indecently expatiating? There is not only from beginning to end of the matter not an inch of expatiation, but my values are positively all blanks ... Of high interest to the author meanwhile—and by the same stroke a theme for the moralist—the artless resentful reaction of the entertained person who has abounded in the sense of the situation. He visits his abundance, morally, on the artist—who has but clung to an ideal of faultlessness. (*LC* ii. 1188–9)

This ideal of faultlessness which corrupts the reader, this reticence which expresses more evil than expatiation, places *The Turn of the Screw* in an interesting relation to the late nineteenth-century debate on 'reticence' and 'candour' in English fiction. There were many complaints in the 1880s and 1890s that English fiction had been infantilized by censorship, as traditional fears about the evil influence of fiction on children forced novelists to write down to the level of 'the Young Person'.[30] *The Turn of the Screw* challenges this convention, not with 'candour', but with a sly reticence which allows the author to stay within the rules of acceptable representation while still indecently stimulating the reader's imagination; this tactic illustrates by practical experiment the idea that the reader, not the author, must be responsible for any evil effects of fiction on his or her imagination. The tale mocks the idea that the reader really needs protection from fiction, or that censorship really offers such protection; this mockery is made explicit in 'The Future of the Novel', in which James imagines young English readers complaining to the

[29] *Independent* 51 (5 Jan. 1899), 73; reprinted in ibid. 175.
[30] Linton, 'Candour in English Fiction', 11, 14. James made the same complaint in 'The Art of Fiction' (*LC* i. 63).

'fiction-mongers' about the blanks in their education which they
have been forced to fill in for themselves (*LC* i. 108), and remarks
that novelists 'need not, after all, be . . . more childish than the
children' (i. 109). The dangerous reticence of *The Turn of the
Screw* may also represent on James's part an act of revenge for the
way in which, in Victorian literary criticism, formal debates were
constantly displaced into moral ones; here, he lays epistemological and formal traps for the reader which become moral ones.

As Shoshana Felman declares, 'there is no such thing as an
innocent reader of this text'.[31] Where the tale's early readers
worried about the way in which they were morally implicated in
the evils they sought to condemn, more recent critics have found
that, no matter what perspective they take on the text, they
become formally implicated in the processes of interpretation
they aim to judge. Those who do not take the tale at face
value—and instead, like the governess, exercise the kind of attentive, daring readership demanded in 'The Art of Fiction'—are
forced to replicate the governess's suspiciousness and to participate in the 'crime' of 'detection'[32] for which they seek to condemn
her. Their readings, like the governess's, may be susceptible to the
fallacies induced by self-sustaining momentum: many readers
share the governess's discovery that 'The more I go over it, the
more I see in it' (60). Meanwhile, those who accept the governess's
report replicate the obtuseness of Mrs Grose, in contravention
both of the plea made in 'The Art of Fiction' that novels should
not simply be consumed as if they were puddings, and of the
warning in the tale's prologue that 'The story *won't* tell, . . . not in
any literal, vulgar way' (7). As well as forcing its readers to
imagine horrors and to engage in modes of reading which it calls
into question, the tale also draws many readers into a process of
fiction-making which has fallen under suspicion. Readers have
seized on the narrative gaps in *The Turn of the Screw* and have
filled them with their own explanatory fictions, such as John
Clair's argument that Miss Jessel is the children's mother, or Louis
D. Rubin's claim that Douglas is really the grown-up Miles.[33] Such

---

[31] Felman, 'Turning the Screw of Interpretation', 97.
[32] Ibid. 176.
[33] John A. Clair, *The Ironic Dimension in the Fiction of Henry James* (Pittsburgh: Duquesne University Press, 1965), 37–58; Louis D. Rubin, Jr., 'One More
Turn of the Screw', *Modern Fiction Studies*, 9 (1963–4), 314–28.

a mode of 'critical romance' may be, as Bruce Robbins argues, interpretatively productive,[34] but it also makes the reader complicit with a mode of imaginative excess which, in the governess's case, has had at best questionable, and at worst catastrophic, results.

If readers of this text cannot preserve their interpretative innocence from the imaginative 'horrors' of the tale, what of the author? In the preface written ten years after the tale's publication, James seems to disclaim involvement in or even awareness of the disturbing questions *The Turn of the Screw* raises about his own art, and evades the kind of serious judgements about the relation between fiction and life that the governess's narrative so problematically invites. Presenting the tale as merely a narrative 'Christmas-tide toy' (*LC* ii. 1183), he delights in the idea that it is of 'the very kind . . . least apt to be baited by earnest criticism' (ii. 1181–2), for it 'rejoices . . . in a conscious provision of prompt retort to the sharpest question that may be addressed to it'—the retort being that it is a 'perfectly independent and irresponsible little fiction' (ii. 1181). This deflection of earnest criticism is hardly a satisfactory answer to the interpretative problem raised by the text, and the enormous discrepancy between the questions the tale raises about how we should respond to fictions, and James's answer as given in the preface, seems in itself to require some interpretation.

One possibility is that James is distancing himself from a dubious enterprise of interpretation and representation. The governess has drawn the arts of reading and making fictions into disrepute—fulfilling puritan and philistine fears that fiction is 'wicked'—and the preface, in its evasive jocularity, now fulfils the puritan and philistine expectation that fiction must 'make itself humble in order to be forgiven' (*LC* i. 46). But the evasive strategies of the preface to *The Turn of the Screw*, like the self-inculpatory language of the preface to *In the Cage*, while appearing to comply with the expectations of anti-fiction rhetoric, also disrupt them. Declaring that the tale's best defence against earnest criticism lies in its character as an 'irresponsible little fiction', James reverses the terms of 'The Art of Fiction' which defended the novel against hostile criticism on the grounds of historical

[34] Robbins, 'Shooting Off James's Blanks', 198.

responsibility. In appearing thus to deflect serious attention from his work, James is in fact inviting a new kind of attention, for part of the tale's 'irresponsible' character is that it creates 'an annexed but independent world in which nothing is right save as we rightly imagine it' (ii. 1184). James thus reads back into *The Turn of the Screw*, through the notion of irresponsibility, the anti-historical, romance epistemology explored in the later novels, *The Ambassadors* and *The Golden Bowl*. *The Turn of the Screw* helped to clear the way for these explorations because it disrupts the historical epistemology which had governed James's earlier works. For the governess's tale is an 'excursion into chaos' (*LC* ii. 1184), with her—as reader and narrator—'strangely at the helm' (*TS* 19), and one aspect of this excursion is that it takes the reader into a chaotic region in which true and false cannot properly be distinguished. This means that it is impossible to dispose of the troublesome energies of the governess's fiction by handing them over to the disciplinary authority of history: the tale forces a deep questioning of the value of fiction in the world, without recourse to any such easy solutions. In the tale this is deeply problematic, but as the preface recognizes, it is also potentially liberating.

THE SACRED FOUNT

As another first-person narrative—James's only full-length novel written in this mode—*The Sacred Fount* also raises intense problems of narrative reliability. The narrator believes that in an intense passionate relationship, one partner always makes sacrifices to the benefit of the other, and that it is therefore possible to discover when two people are involved in an intimate relationship by the fact that one has become depleted in a quality with which the other has been enriched. His suggestive model is the case of the Brissendens, a married couple of his acquaintance who, when he encounters them at a weekend house party, seem to have undergone extraordinary changes since he last saw them. Mrs Brissenden, whom the narrator knows to be many years older than her husband, appears remarkably young, while her husband has preternaturally aged. Observing that another guest at the house party, Gilbert Long, has become cleverer than he remembered him to be, the narrator sets to work to discover a woman who is 'an intellectual ruin' (*SF* 38), and who must, therefore, be the source of her lover's improvement. The narrator's reading or plotting of the situation of his fellow guests is at first encouraged by some members of the party, who are inspired by his theory and make rival plots of their own which the narrator discounts; others resist the narrator's plot and undermine his confidence in both his findings and his method.

As in *The Turn of the Screw*, the absence of an authorial framework means that a confirmation of the narrator's version of the situation would involve finding corroborative views and objective evidence. In fact we can find evidence both to support and to undermine his case, and, as in *The Turn of the Screw*, systematic narrative ambiguity leaves the reader hesitating between opposed readings of the novel as uncanny tale or ironically presented example of unreliable narration.[35] A powerfully ironic perspective on the narrator's work is offered by Mrs Brissenden at the end of the novel when she offers her literal, vulgar reading of circumstances in refutation of his supersubtle one. The proliferation of competing interpretations in the novel resolves itself into this basic confrontation, familiar from *In the Cage* in the conflict between the girl's interpretation and Captain Everard's, and from *The Turn of the Screw* in the governess's and Mrs Grose's conflicting modes of perception. However, the fact that Mrs Brissenden's literal reading manages to silence the narrator does not mean that the novel reverts to the pattern of *In the Cage*, for Mrs Brissenden's victory does not signify that she has a monopoly on reality, or that she holds the authorized, historical

[35] Arguments for the unreliability of the narrator include Jean Frantz Blackall, *Jamesian Ambiguity and* The Sacred Fount (Ithaca, NY: Cornell University Press, 1965) and Bernard Richards, 'The Ambassadors and The Sacred Fount: The Artist Manqué', in *The Air of Reality: New Essays on Henry James*, ed. John Goode (London: Methuen, 1972), 219–43. The narrator's sanity and morality are defended in James W. Gargano, 'James's *The Sacred Fount*: The Phantasmagorical Made Evidential', *Henry James Review*, 2 (1980), 49–60; and Heath Moon, 'Saving James from Modernism: How to Read *The Sacred Fount*', *Modern Language Quarterly*, 49 (1988), 120–41. Charles Thomas Samuels and Shlomith Rimmon both find that the narrator's account can neither be confirmed nor denied; to Samuels, this is evidence of a 'confused' text (see *The Ambiguity of Henry James* (Urbana: University of Illinois Press, 1971), 25–39), while to Rimmon it is a technically masterful example of radical ambiguity (see *The Concept of Ambiguity*, 167–226).

perspective. In fact, in a letter to Mrs Humphry Ward, James spoke of 'Mrs. B.'s last interview with the narrator being all an ironic *exposure* of her own false plausibility, of course' (*Letters* iv. 186)—although this need not entail an endorsement of the narrator's theory either. She defeats the narrator with her authoritative tone, but her denial of the operation of miracles does not bring any hard 'facts' into the case; after all, she herself was one of several witnesses who independently attested to changes the narrator had perceived. Nevertheless, although the narrator's confrontation with Mrs Brissenden does not prove that he is wrong, it does extend the discussion of the doubts about the morality and value of his 'work' which his inner conflict on the subject has already raised. This is useful, because it opens up ideas of why, independently of the question of the narrator's reliability, fiction may be 'wicked'.

The narrator of *The Sacred Fount* is exceptionally self-conscious about his 'art', which is, in essence, the art of the novelist. Like the telegraphist and the governess, he employs interpretative and constructive skills similar to those set out for the 'young aspirant' (*LC* i. 59) of 'The Art of Fiction': the ability 'to guess the unseen from the seen, to trace the implication of things, to judge the whole piece by the pattern' (*LC* i. 53). Like the heroines of *In the Cage* and *The Turn of the Screw*, he is carried away by the momentum which the exercise of these skills generates, and is especially liable to the trap of assuming significance in everything, even—and indeed, most especially—in silence and absence. The narrator's exhaustive reflections on the process of creating his 'theory' provide abundant examples of the traits that he shares with the governess, the telegraphist, and the 'young aspirant' writer whom James imagined. Out of 'the terrible *fluidity* of self-revelation' (*LC* ii. 1316) which accounts for the density of these examples, I wish to concentrate on those aspects of the narrator's self-consciousness which show some of the disturbing qualities of the art of fiction.

Very early in his attempt to solve the riddle posed by his theory, the narrator doubts the moral acceptability of his activity. When Mrs Brissenden, who is at this stage still in his confidence, puts forward the idea that May Server must be the woman for whom they are looking, the intellectually ravaged partner of the so 'improved' Gilbert Long, and gleefully cries 'we have her; it's *she*!', the narrator reflects that 'the curiosity to which I had so freely surrendered myself began to strike me as wanting in taste' (44). The 'taste' that is 'wanting' in his enterprise soon resolves itself in his mind into a conception of moral responsibility which precludes the exposure of others to prying conjecture. In order to satisfy both taste and curiosity, the narrator tries to construct a network of imaginary rules governing his activity, which, by the discipline and sacrifice they demand, give his actions the sense of adherence to high standards. The basis of these rules is suggested by Ford Obert, who, at the beginning of the novel at least, has entered into the narrator's theory with great interest. 'To nose about for a relation that a lady has her reasons for keeping secret' (as the narrator puts it) is, Obert claims, 'made not only quite inoffensive, . . . but positively honourable, by being confined to psychologic evidence' (64). He insists: 'Resting on the *kind* of signs that the game takes account of when fairly played—resting on psychologic signs alone, it's a high application of intelligence. What's ignoble is the detective and the keyhole' (64). The narrator therefore sets about dignifying his enterprise by scorning direct inquiry. Yet this simply leaves speculation to rage unchecked, turning his whole field of observation into a mirror of his own vulgar curiosity, in which everything has a 'telling' (95) value, indeed a 'guilty significance' (37). The narrator's interest, despite his protestations of theoretical purity, is voyeuristic, as he wishes to uncover not only the existence, but the nature, of a relation which is '*Intimissima*' (32). At times he realizes that his art is simply gossip with a theory behind it; his obsession exposes Mrs Server to the scrutiny of others; he has 'dreadfully talked about her' (137). Yet his vision of her, hunted and searching for security, becomes simply another piece in the puzzle. 'Once my imagination had seen her in this light the touches it could add to the picture might be trusted to be telling' (95). The narrator has confined himself to psychological evidence, and yet, as he himself had earlier said, the 'psychologic glow' does not make the affair any more of his business (68). In 'The Art of Fiction' James had written that a 'psychological reason is, to my imagination, an object adorably pictorial; to catch the tint of its complexion . . . might inspire one to Titianesque efforts' (*LC* i. 61). Here, the 'telling' psychological reason is no longer 'an object adorably pictorial' but the victim of invidious exposure, and representation becomes a process exploitative rather than appreciative of its objects.

Confining himself to psychological evidence does not take away the taste of 'the detective and the keyhole' (64) from the narrator's activity. He makes another attempt to justify himself by claiming that his immersion in the affairs of others is 'but a more roundabout expression of interest and sympathy' (141), but in his case the plea of imaginative sympathy—one of the keystones of Victorian defences of the novel, and important in James's later rehabilitation of the value of fiction—is not convincing. Not only is there, as with the telegraphist's 'heroism of sympathy' (*ITC* 64), a fine line between imaginative sympathy and voyeurism, but this 'expression of interest and sympathy' becomes for the narrator, as for the governess, a matter of accusations and judgements. 'Are we accusing each other?' asks Grace Brissenden, to which the narrator replies, 'Dear no, . . . not each other; only with each other's help, a few of our good friends' (265–6). This conversation with Mrs Brissenden marks the collapse of his last attempt to make his enterprise respectable—his 'desire to "protect" Mrs. Server' (247). She now appears 'past all protection', for Mrs Brissenden, inspired by and competing with the narrator, has pursued her and 'there was now no rag of the queer truth that Mrs. Briss hadn't secretly—by which I meant morally—handled' (247). The narrator is caught between his desire to save Mrs Server from Mrs Brissenden's penetrating gaze, and his desire to save his theory from her competitive interpretations; the two motives are incompatible, and this accounts for much of the narrator's weakness in his conflict with Mrs Brissenden, in which he fails in both attempts. He had earlier tried to reconcile theory and practice with a formula equating intellectual and moral scruples: 'the process by which I had at last definitely inculpated Mrs. Server was precisely such a process of providential supervision as made me morally responsible, so to speak, for her, and thereby intensified my scruples' (153). But neither the rules of a game played by gentlemen, nor the 'morally responsible' scruples which define him as a providence, can rescue the narrator from his sense of keeping imaginative company with detectives and reporters. He continues to pursue an 'underhand process' in the service of an 'indiscreet curiosity' (127), seeking to catch an 'incriminated pair together—really together' (247). It is an activity out of place at Newmarch, where the narrator feels he is 'discrediting by musty secrets and aggressive doubts our high privilege of harmony and taste' and that therefore his imagination is liable to be treated to 'the snub that affects—when it does affect—the uninvited reporter in whose face a door is closed', while 'any preposterous acuteness might easily suffer . . . such a loss of dignity as overtakes the newspaper-man kicked out' (156). With his opportunistic reporters Matthias Pardon in *The Bostonians* and George Flack in *The Reverberator*, and the many aggressive journalists in the tales of the literary life, James identified 'the newspaper-man' with invasions of privacy and betrayals of artistic integrity; likening himself to such figures, the narrator knows that, as he tells Ford Obert, 'Our hands are not clean' (211).

The narrator's obsession has a price for him too. 'It was absurd to have consented to such immersion, intellectually speaking, in the affairs of other people. One had always affairs of one's own, and I was positively neglecting mine' (88). This was one of the commonplace warnings about the effect of reading too many novels, here applied to a character addicted to 'reading' the lives of others rather than proceeding with his own. The laws of sanity, as well as of civilized behaviour, warn him of his danger: 'I remember feeling seriously warned, while dinner lasted, not to yield further to my idle habit of reading into mere human things an interest so much deeper than mere human things were in general prepared to supply' (155). The moral is exactly that pointed out for both heroine and author in the preface to *In the Cage*. Yet the narrator does not heed his own warnings, and continues to find in the laws of composition a 'sovereign warrant for an interest in the private affairs of everyone else' (165). This exacts a further toll by increasing the self-consciousness of others. Surveying the results of his aggressive activity, the narrator reaches a point of 'alarm' which signifies the 'complete reversal' of his general 'estimate of the value of perception' (182). He comes to admire the state of being 'magnificently without it' (182), the almost paradisal state of Long and Mrs Brissenden before their fall (tempted by the narrator) into his world of obsessive observation and self-conscious analysis. The narrator realizes that this is yet another way in which he has made others pay the price of his folly: 'Wasn't it enough for *me* to pay, vicariously, the tax on being absurd? Were we all to be landed, without an issue or a remedy, in a condition on which that tax would be generally levied?' (183).

The 'tax' levied is the price of consciousness, which the narrator sees as a burden for others. The 'horror' expressed about the narrator's work at various times in the novel goes beyond a specific moral distaste for his processes of detection and exposure, to a horror of perception and representation themselves. Mrs Brissenden, trying to explain to the narrator why people are wary of talking to him, asks, 'Don't you sometimes see horrors?' (296), to which the 'critical' narrator asks in turn, 'is criticism the vision of horrors?' (297). He even wonders if she is about to suggest that he not only sees horrors, but perpetrates them (297); he has, after all, experienced 'that joy of determining, almost of creating results' (213). From this charge his opponent backs down, and settles for scoring the moral point that he seems to like discovering horrors without feeling any need to 'come down on them strong' (297). This allows the narrator to defend himself by countering that he simply likes to look things in the face, but to this Mrs Brissenden retorts: 'When they *have* no face, then, you can't do it!' (297). Is the narrator, then, simply bringing to light the horrors which already exist in the world, and which, more specifically, underlie the outward appearance of privilege and harmony at Newmarch? Or is he inventing horrors which do not really exist and therefore pursuing an occupation which is a horror in itself? Either way, Grace Brissenden wants nothing to do with his activity and faces him with 'an innocence, in particular, in respect to the relation of anyone, in all the vast impropriety of things, to anyone' (256). Innocence is knowing nothing, saying nothing; finding that really, relations start nowhere; being a person on whom everything is lost. In the end *The Sacred Fount* does not answer the question of whether it is 'things' or perceptions and narratives about them which are improper; in the narrator's world 'significance' is 'guilty' (37), but the ambiguity of the text obscures whether the guilt belongs to the interpreter or to the object of interpretation. Nevertheless, it casts grave doubts on the morality and usefulness of pursuing a 'vision of horrors' (297), which is what such fiction-making entails.

The Sacred Fount displays the art of fiction, as practised by the narrator, undergoing a crisis of conscience which is not simply tied to a crisis of realism. 'The state of my conscience was that I knew too much—that no one had really any business to know what I knew' (160). When Obert admits, with a 'sudden lowering of his voice in this confession—as if it had represented a sort of darkening of his consciousness' (218), that he has been watching his fellow guests, the narrator is amused. Yet he too accepts that observation and interpretation become the tools of enlightenment only at the price of 'a sort of darkening of his consciousness'. He may achieve 'the condition of light' (that is, 'the satisfaction of curiosity') only by paying with 'the sacrifice of feeling' (293): 'I was there to save my priceless pearl of an inquiry and to harden, to that end, my heart' (294).

This hardening of his heart involves a willingness to 'polish . . . off' (28) people for the benefit of his theory: 'The obsession pays, if one will; but to pay it has to borrow' (22). It borrows partly from his own life, diverting his attention from his own affairs, but it also borrows from the lives of others. Many variations on the theme of 'the sacred fount' are played in this novel, and one is that the subjects of the narrator's inquiry are depleted to the benefit of his curiosity: intellectually, he gorges on them. At one point Guy Brissenden accuses the narrator of being happy at his expense, and the narrator's response that his knowledge does not 'cost' Guy anything (122) is untrue; his sacrifice of other people's reputations and privacy is as damaging as the sacrifices of youth and intellect which he believes he has witnessed. When the narrator calls himself the 'most harmless man in the house' (113) he is, presumably, signalling the fact that he is not sexually predatory, but he practises imaginative and intellectual depredations which render him perhaps the most dangerous man in the house, of whom the other guests become increasingly wary.

The vampire theme may be taken even further, from the personal morality of the narrator to a general theory of fiction. Perhaps the real sacred fount is the world, which is consumed by art; such an idea is expressed by Miriam Rooth in *The Tragic Muse*, when she contends that the world exists only 'to pay for art' and urges Nick to 'make it pay, without mercy—squeeze it dry' (*TM* ii. 146). The world may pay for art, not only by buying its productions, but by giving itself up to representation. *The Sacred Fount* reverses the process of consumption explored in the tales of artists and writers, in which the writer is generally cast as the victim of his audience, exposed to and consumed by the insatiable curiosity of the public. In 'The Death of the Lion', where the crisis of the action is also set in a country house among the socially and economically privileged, the writer's public feeds parasitically upon him, finally destroying him as well as losing the manuscript of his new work; but in *The Sacred Fount* it is the maker of fictions who feeds upon those who constitute his material, not the victim but the perpetrator of acts of aggression and exposure. In nineteenth-century fiction debates, readers addicted to the consumption of novels were, Richard Altick writes, 'somewhat uncharitably termed "fiction vampires" ';[36] but *The Sacred Fount* raises the idea of vampire fictions, sustained by preying on the world for plots and subjects. The novel extends the point James had made in an essay on Daudet in 1883, that being entertained by fiction means 'that we have been living at the expense of some one else' (*LC* ii. 242), that is, of the characters whose sufferings are necessary for our interest and entertainment. Regardless of whether Mrs Brissenden and Long are, as the narrator suspects, feeding on their partners, it is the narrator himself who is the true vampire.

The Sacred Fount is an important document in the history of the problematic relations between authors and readers in late nineteenth-century England. Like James's earlier tales about the artistic life, *The Sacred Fount* illustrates a fundamental opposition of interests between producers and consumers of fiction; the difference is that, as we have seen, it shifts much of the blame for this on to the producer, whose activity is seen to be morally as well as epistemologically questionable. The novel both examines and enacts a process of communication so occluded that speaker and listener become radically disconnected; readers' difficulties with the novel mirror the problems which arise for characters within the novel in trying to understand the narrator. Mrs Brissenden's refusal to understand the narrator at the end of the novel is a rejection not only of his findings but of the whole mode of communication which he wishes to set up. The narrator himself, meanwhile, is really committed not to communication but to blocking communication. He admits that he found himself 'thinking with a kind of horror of any accident by which I might

---

[36] Altick, *English Common Reader*, 239.

have to expose to the world, to defend against the world, to share with the world, that now so complex tangle of hypotheses that I have had for convenience to speak of as my theory' (172). With this statement, 'horror' attaches itself to a third part of the fictional process: the material of a narrative may consist of horrors, the process of interpretation and representation may entail horrors, and now the idea of communicating the product of this to an audience evokes 'a kind of horror'. This attitude makes any kind of contract between author and reader—whether that involved in James's idea of historical narrative, or the kind of fictional contract suggested by Miriam Rooth in *The Tragic Muse*—impossible.

The idea of fiction as history rested as much on the contract between author and reader as on the referential nature of the narrative. As we saw in comparing the Countess Gemini's success in persuading Isabel to believe her story about Osmond and Madame Merle with Christopher Newman's failure to find an audience for his story about the Bellegarde family, much of the power to define a story as 'true' rests with its audience rather than its speaker. The narrator of *The Sacred Fount* realizes this as, faced with Mrs Brissenden's calculated obtuseness, he admits that 'she need, obviously, only decline to take one of my counters to deprive it of all value as coin' (311). Independently of the truth or falsity of his narrative, it is his failure to find an audience for it that deprives it of all value as a means of describing or directing experience. Yet this failure to communicate is partly self-determined—the narrator has a 'horror' of sharing his theory with others. Regardless of whether it corresponds to a prior reality, his story fails to achieve any imaginative connection with the world and remains intransitive, a purely self-directed and self-serving construction.

James's decision not to include *The Sacred Fount* in the *New York Edition* not only reflects the low esteem in which he held this novel (*Letters* iv. 185–6, 198), but suggests a more deeply rooted desire to disown the work, for the narrator of *The Sacred Fount* practises the arts of interpretation and representation in ways which threaten fundamentally to discredit James's whole fictional enterprise. Like *In the Cage* and *The Turn of the Screw*, *The Sacred Fount* examines a process of fiction-making on the part of its narrator which is in many ways 'wicked' (*LC* i. 45) and, when not actually destructive, is at best irrelevant to the world around it. The novel is 'some obscure, some ambiguous work of art' (*SF* 54) which puts forward no claims for the value of the art of fiction, but rather suggests a sense of exhaustion with the subjects and methods of the Jamesian novel. The same sense of exhaustion with the whole project of nineteenth-century realism is found in James's essay of 1899, 'The Future of the Novel', where traditional hostility to the novel is linked with a new alienation from the form. James speaks of a class of people

for whom the very form itself has, equally at its best and at its worst, been ever a vanity and a mockery. This class . . . is beginning to be visibly augmented by a different circle altogether, the group of the formerly subject, but now estranged, the deceived and bored, those for whom the whole movement too decidedly fails to live up to its possibilities. There are people who have loved the novel, but who actually find themselves drowned in its verbiage, and for whom, even in some of its approved manifestations, it has become a terror they exert every ingenuity, every hypocrisy, to evade. (*LC* i. 102)

As the tone and observations of the essay reveal, James is himself in many ways one of the 'estranged', and his description of the novel as a 'terror' links his questioning in this essay of the value of modern fiction to the deep doubts about the novelistic enterprise raised by his exploration of fictional horrors in *The Turn of the Screw* and *The Sacred Fount*. In 'The Future of the Novel' James returns to the concern that had sparked his defence of the novel in 'The Art of Fiction': the charge that the novel is

mere unsupported and unguaranteed history, the *inexpensive* thing, written in the air, the record of what, in any particular case, has *not* been, the account that remains responsible, at best, to 'documents' with which we are practically unable to collate it. (*LC* i. 101–2)

Yet he does not attempt to meet this charge, as he did in 1884, by attempting to claim for the novel the status of history. In fact, his earlier response is implicitly rejected when he says that the novel has 'never philosophically met the challenge' (*LC* i. 102)—it has practically met it, by producing masterpieces, but it has never produced a theoretical defence of its epistemology. That such defences of the novel had, of course, been produced, could easily be shown, but what is important to note is that James here implicitly discounts his own theoretical defence of the novel as history.

The essay leaves the novel philosophically undefended: James expresses a guarded confidence in the future of the genre, but does not yet propose a theory of fiction such as is to be found in his later critical works. In the same way, the fictional texts discussed in this chapter present the idea of fiction in a precarious, but potentially liberating, position. The contract between authors and readers capable of producing historical narrative has collapsed, but has not yet been replaced by a fictional contract. All three works reflect a historical situation in which the mistrust between producers and consumers of fiction led to relationships of sacrifice and depredation. Although the characters' desire to create plots is allowed to flourish, the radical disconnection between the producers and consumers of these plots leads to an equally radical disconnection between fiction and the world. The plots have only the status of fantasies, unable either to represent or to affect experience. The plot of the telegraphist is condemned in the tradition of hostility to the novel; yet, because her activity so closely follows the rules of fiction-making set out in 'The Art of Fiction', this condemnation casts doubt on the author's activity as well, a doubt only fully expressed in the preface. In *The Turn of the Screw*, the activities of the governess again stand in an ambiguous relation to the arguments of the nineteenth-century detractors and defenders of fiction. However, in this tale, not only is there no third-person historical perspective to mark off the heroine's plot from the author's for judgement, but the tale is constructed in such a way that it baffles any attempts to construct or retrieve such a perspective from evidence in the text. Like *The Sacred Fount*, the tale frustrates the desire to separate true from false narratives that is essential to both puritan attacks on, and James's defence of, the novel. This shifts the basis of the interest and value of the narrative away from the question of its conformity to an ideal of historical narrative, and towards other issues such as its moral function, and whether it intervenes constructively or destructively in the experience with which it is concerned. Although *The Sacred Fount* itself gives a negative picture of the value of fiction in these terms, like *The Turn of the Screw* it removes the standard of historical accuracy as the only criterion of the worth of narrative. The contract between author and reader set up in 'The Art of Fiction' has collapsed, but the way is opened for James, in later novels, to renegotiate the fictional contract on terms other than a fixed opposition between history and the imagination.

4

The Ambassadors and the Fictional Contract

THE 'DEEP taste of change' (*Amb.* 4) pervades the opening chapters of *The Ambassadors*, as Lambert Strether begins his encounter with Europe. The first stage of this encounter is described in terms which markedly draw attention to the idea that the novel is leaving behind the imaginative world of James's experimental phase, to enter new territory in its exploration of the relations between fiction and history. In this novel about questioning, 'Strether's first question' (3) is addressed to 'the young woman in the glass cage' (4), who gives him the answer in the form of a telegram from an old American friend; turning away, he meets Maria Gostrey, who becomes his first guide to 'Europe', and who helps him to find new ways of approaching the multifarious questions posed by his European experience. Walking away with his new friend, 'Strether had a rueful glance for the lady in the glass cage. It was as if this personage had seen herself instantly superseded' (6). In placing Strether so clearly outside the cage, James signals that the terms on which the earlier works had conducted their exploration of imaginative narrative have also been 'superseded'. Unlike the telegraphist, the governess, and the narrator of *The Sacred Fount*, whose plots are fundamentally unable to engage with reality or with the perceptions of others, Strether's imagination is set at liberty in the world, defined from the beginning as a mode of encounter rather than of retreat.

Through Strether's imaginative adventures, *The Ambassadors* explores fiction as a category of thought for addressing problems in social and moral life. The diplomatic encounters between the various ambassadors in the novel are largely conducted by means of a dialogue between historical and fictional propositions. Reviving James's 'international theme', the novel places great emphasis on questions of location and jurisdiction, and this leads to a highly developed concept of fictional space and its relation to the world outside it. Many of the characters' negotiations with each other involve a testing of the uses of jokes and lies, which explores the value of definitions of fictional discourse that were rejected in 'The Art of Fiction'. When the American hero comes to terms with European ideas and experience, it is by means of fictional contracts which, displacing the idea of the historical contract expounded in James's early novel theory, reflexively define the relation between author and reader in the novel as a whole.

Europe—even as represented by Liverpool, Chester, and London—offers Strether a sense of 'personal freedom', of being given over to 'the immediate and the sensible' (4). The quotation marks which so often enclose the word 'Europe' mimic its nature as a preconceived territory of the mind, set apart from the responsibilities of real life at home. As James had written in his 'Paris Revisited' (1875): 'We most of us transact our moral and spiritual affairs in our own country, and it is not cynical to say that for most of us the transaction is rather rapidly conducted. We wander about Europe on a sensuous and esthetic basis' (*PS* 5). The distinction James makes here was much more crudely enshrined in Anglo-American literary convention as 'the dreadful little old tradition . . . that people's moral scheme *does* break down in Paris' (*LC* ii. 1312). This view of Europe recalls, and shares a common puritanical origin with, the mapping of fictional space as definitively separate from the morally serious region of historical narrative; Strether's response to Anglo-American assumptions about 'Europe' will also involve a response to his culture's assumptions about the relative value of fiction and history.

At the beginning of the novel, Strether shares the popular American view of Europe. He does not doubt that Chad, the prodigal son he has been commissioned to reclaim for his mother, Mrs Newsome, has fallen victim to immoral influences in Paris. For himself, although he has come to Europe with work to do, it is someone else's work, which he intends to carry out using a set of imported cultural assumptions, and which he does not anticipate will involve his own 'moral and spiritual affairs'. Moreover, he hopes it will be rapidly completed, allowing him simply to enjoy Europe as a place where he can escape from his own work and personal problems. Yet he finds that his two aims— to settle Mrs Newsome's business for her, and to enjoy Europe for himself—are almost immediately in conflict. His success as an ambassador depends on his moral authority, and he senses that 'almost any acceptance of Paris might give one's authority away' (67). Strether does not share the ability of Mrs Newsome's second ambassador, her daughter Sarah, to have 'a good time' (263) while maintaining an unshakable faith in her own preconceived convictions and demands. Rather, he finds that any attempt to 'wander about Europe on a sensuous and esthetic basis' (*PS* 5), even so mild an attempt as a walk on the walls of Chester with his new friend, Miss Gostrey, involves 'what he would have called collapses' (*Amb.* 28), all of which, taken together, may amount in the end to the failure of his mission, and the collapse of the moral scheme which dictated the terms of that mission.

The task Strether has been given involves a combination of historical reconstruction and didactic intervention: he is to find out what Chad has been doing in Paris, and then, denouncing this way of life, he is to persuade Chad to return to Woollett in order to take up the moral responsibilities (and business opportunities) that await him there. As Chad's family sees it, the process of reconstruction is a question of details only, as they have already decided that, in broad outline, Chad's story will be found to be a version of the 'dreadful little old tradition': they believe he has fallen victim to a 'Particular Person' (67) who has dragged him, morally, into the gutter. Both the retrospective and the prospective arms of the scenario with which Mrs Newsome has equipped Strether reflect the epistemological and moral monism of her environment: the people of Woollett (Strether initially included) pride themselves on 'the faculty of seeing things as they were' (88), and believe that in every situation there is one 'real right thing' (113) that must be pursued. The principal representative of the voice of Woollett is Mrs Newsome, personally absent from Paris, but powerfully present to Strether through memory and through her letters; in Paris his friend Waymarsh, a native not of Woollett, Massachusetts, but of Milrose, Connecticut, sounds, if anything, an even purer note of the New England conscience. This note has a certain grandeur, as Strether never ceases to acknowledge—'the very voice of Milrose' is 'a plea for the purest veracity' (21)—but it is increasingly revealed to be inadequate to the kinds of attitudes and experiences with which Strether finds he has to negotiate.

The terms of Strether's mission as dictated by Mrs Newsome are first challenged by Maria Gostrey. An American who lives in Paris, Miss Gostrey is a sort of honorary European, who describes herself as 'a general guide—to "Europe," don't you know?' (14). 'Europe', in Miss Gostrey's hands, becomes a playground for an endless game of analysis and interpretation, in which 'the elements of Appearance' (7) are extremely important. Strether initially sees his interpretative mission as a matter of stripping away appearances to reveal the truth, but on his visit with Miss Gostrey to the theatre in London he learns how appearances may 'carry and complicate' one's vision, as the red velvet band around her neck becomes 'a starting-point for fresh backward, fresh forward, fresh lateral flights' (38), initiating an impressionistic play which disrupts received ideas and widens the range of possible responses. Maria Gostrey combines an openness to the effects of appearance with a knowledge of 'types' (39): as the narrator puns, 'she pigeon-holed her fellow-mortals with a hand as free as that of a compositor scattering type' (8) and when it is time to compose the histories of these people, the type is all in its proper cases in her mind. For her, historical reconstruction involves a great deal of composition, and she is vague about sources and the exactness of report: 'she admitted when a little pressed that she was never quite sure of what she heard as distinguished from things . . . she only extravagantly guessed' (41). Whatever possibilities of error this may involve, Strether very soon comes to rely on her 'free handling of the subject to which his own imagination of it already owed so much' (51). The 'fun' of going over things with her, of seeing his own situation as 'a *case*' ('he was now so interested, quite so privately agog, about it' (102)), gives him an amused detachment from his affairs— without diminishing their importance—which topples the distinction between business and pleasure on which his visit to Europe has been predicated.

In his attempt to reconstruct the narrative of Chad's life in Paris, Strether has two audiences who are also competing muses. Mrs Newsome demands and receives a serial report in the form of Strether's letters to her; these make up a whole epistolary narrative referred to in, but absent from, the novel. This lost narrative, the source of increasing problems for Strether as he finds himself unable to make his report conform to the version of events worked out in advance by Mrs Newsome, is later discredited when he identifies it with the meaningless rhetoric of journalism: 'Wouldn't the pages he still so frequently despatched by the American post have been worthy of a showy journalist, some master of the great new science of beating the sense out of words?' (247). Strether uses this image to express the insincerities that his narrative has come to acquire under the pressure of new realities which it cannot incorporate, but a much earlier use of related imagery reveals the inherent meanness in the range of interpretations of which Woollett is capable:

This echo—as distinct over there, in the dry, thin air, as some shrill 'heading' above a column of print—seemed to reach him even as he wrote. 'He says there's no woman,' he could hear Mrs. Newsome report, in capitals almost of newspaper size, to Mrs. Pocock; and he could focus in Mrs. Pocock the response of the reader of the journal. (123)[1]

The fact that none of his communications to or from Mrs Newsome is quoted in the novel is important, because it places this whole reconstructive narrative at a disadvantage in relation to its competitor, the dialogic narrative formed by Strether's confabulations with Maria Gostrey. Many events are presented to us as reports from Strether to Miss Gostrey, and much information is filtered through the medium of their conversations; the communications inspired by Miss Gostrey are privileged above those inspired by Mrs Newsome, as they define the narrative mode of significant portions of the novel.

Playful, sometimes tentative, and sometimes extravagant, this talk is dominated by Maria's injunction to 'Guess!' (125), foreshadowing the 'find out for yourself' theme of *The Golden Bowl*. It also owes much to the typical Jamesian conversational game of

---

[1] James vehemently objected to the use of headings in the pieces he sent to the *New York Tribune* in 1875–6, as Edel and Lind recount in their introduction to *Parisian Sketches* (pp. xxiv–xxv). Thirty years later he recorded the same dislike in his response to American newspapers and 'the idea of expression' embodied in 'vociferous "headings," with letterings, with black eruptions of print, that we seem to measure by feet rather than by inches, and that affect us positively as the roar of some myriad-faced monster' (QS 43).

suspended references and missing referents, a device which combines an uneasy epistemological uncertainty with an exploratory
freedom and the creative potential to make—through error—new
relations and interpretative leaps.[2] Nevertheless, beneath the
playful surface may lie a surprising accuracy. Miss Gostrey's
ability to reconstruct Mrs Newsome from the information
Strether gives her, down to the details of how she wears her hair,
displays an accuracy for which the Woollett mind, despite its
standards of veracity, is unprepared: 'He blushed for her realism,
but he gaped at her truth' (50). Such successes give a certain force
to Miss Gostrey's proposal of alternative scenarios for Chad's
experience to the single melodramatic plot conceived of in Woollett. She offers possible accounts of Chad's behaviour which
subvert Woollett's values as well as its version of events. She
suggests that Chad may have felt tainted by the immoral sources
of his family's wealth, or by the vulgarity of business, and have
sought the life of a gentleman in Paris (46); he may have been
'refined' rather than 'brutalised' in Paris (52); the woman with
whom he is involved may be 'charming' rather than, as Strether
believes, 'base, venal—out of the streets' (41). There is never any
evidence to support the first of these hypotheses, and Chad's
interest in advertising at the end of the novel rather seems to
disprove it. However, when Strether meets Chad for the first time
in Paris and finds him utterly transformed, 'refined', as Maria
had suggested, rather than 'brutalised', her second proposition is
vindicated, and this makes the truth of the third one undeniably
possible. Strether's task of reconstruction now becomes detective
work, for Miss Gostrey maintains that the miracle of Chad's
transformation can only be explained as the work of a woman,
and that in finding the woman Strether will find the key to Chad's
situation (125).

Strether's attempts to find this woman are frustrated by
the evasive answers he is repeatedly given when he asks for

---

[2] Referential ambiguity of pronouns as a technique placing demands on the
attention of James's readers is discussed by Vernon Lee in *The Handling of Words
and Other Studies in Literary Psychology* (London: John Lane, Bodley Head,
1923), 244; and by Seymour Chatman in *The Later Style of Henry James* (Oxford:
Blackwell, 1972), 57–8. See Ralf Norrman, *The Insecure World of Henry James's
Fiction: Intensity and Ambiguity* (London: Macmillan, 1982), 6–65 for an extended analysis of the technique as a means of dramatizing the relations between
characters in *The Golden Bowl*.

her identity. Chad assures him that he is not being kept in Paris by a woman, but asks Strether to meet his 'particular friends' (133), a mother and daughter with whom he has become close. Chad's friend, little Bilham, gives Strether the image of Chad as a revised edition of an old book, but when Strether asks straight out 'who's the editor?' (132), he does not answer; instead he offers the information that Chad, although technically 'free', is kept in Paris by 'a virtuous attachment' (133). To Strether, this answer seems to have 'settled the question' (133) of Chad's transformation.

> Nothing, certainly, on all the indications, could have been a greater change for him than a virtuous attachment, and since they had been in search of the 'word,' as the French called it, of that change, little Bilham's announcement—though so long and so oddly delayed—would serve as well as another. (134)

Tact (or pride) prevents Strether from asking the identity of the object of the attachment, and so his quest seems to have turned into an extended version of the common Jamesian hunt for a missing referent, the attempt to put a name to an unspecified 'she'. However, when he realizes that the object of the attachment is not the most obvious candidate, little Jeanne, but her mother, Madame de Vionnet, the nature of his quest changes. Little Bilham has characterized the attachment as 'virtuous'; this supports Miss Gostrey's intuition that the woman behind Chad's transformation must be 'good', indeed 'excellent' (125), and is itself corroborated by Chad who, in response to Strether's question, 'Is she bad?', assures him that her life is 'without reproach. A beautiful life. *Allez donc voir!*' (176).

Strether accepts the invitation to see for himself. As he turns his attention to discovering ways in which Madame de Vionnet, against all the prejudices of Woollett, may be 'good' and her attachment to Chad 'virtuous', Strether's experience anticipates William James's pragmatic critique of 'solving names' (such as 'God' or 'the Absolute') as answers to philosophical questions. William James wrote:

> But if you follow the pragmatic method, you cannot look on any such word as closing your quest. You must bring out of each word its practical cash-value, set it at work within the stream of your experience. It appears less as a solution, then, than as a program for more work, and more

particularly as an indication of the ways in which existing realities may be *changed*.[3]

As Strether discovers, the 'word' of little Bilham's formula is not a solution to his problem, but a programme for more work. He must not accept these terms 'good' and 'virtuous' as 'solving names', but set them at work in experience and find what 'cash-value' (in happiness or moral worth) they yield. The term 'virtuous attachment' implies a certain version of past events which Strether, in his process of reconstruction, agrees to accept as a kind of working hypothesis, which must be tested in experience.

The hypothesis is tested against several opposing perspectives and disconcerting pieces of information. Waymarsh's disapprobation is a constant challenge to Strether's point of view, and the discovery that Jeanne is to be subjected to an arranged marriage taxes his belief in Madame de Vionnet's nobility of character. However, Strether's faith surmounts these tests, as well as the attack on his position from Mrs Newsome's second ambassadorial delegation, the Pococks. Strether hopes that a recognition on their part of how Chad has changed for the better might provide a basis on which 'they might, as it were, have embraced and begun to work together' (270); however, the Pococks do not notice any change in Chad—or at least any change that is not 'hideous' (365)—and this blindness offers the same kind of challenge to his theory as Mrs Grose's blindness offers to the governess's theory of the ghosts in *The Turn of the Screw*, and as Mrs Brissenden's obtuseness offers to the narrator's vampire theory in *The Sacred Fount*. In wondering if he were 'utterly deluded and extravagant', Strether's doubts recall similar self-questioning by those earlier supersubtle readers of experience:

[3] William James, *Pragmatism: A New Name for Some Old Ways of Thinking*, and id., *The Meaning of Truth: A Sequel to* Pragmatism, first pub. 1907, 1909 (Cambridge, Mass.: Harvard University Press, 1978), 31–2. After reading *Pragmatism* when it appeared in 1907, Henry James gave complete assent to his brother's theory (*Letters* iv. 466). The most thorough examination of the relation between the works of the two brothers is made by Richard A. Hocks in *Henry James and Pragmatistic Thought: A Study in the Relationship between the Philosophy of William James and the Literary Art of Henry James* (Chapel Hill: University of North Carolina Press, 1974). Hocks maintains that William James 'names' processes which Henry James dramatizes in his fiction and embodies in his prose style (6), and that *The Ambassadors* is a 'textbook illustration' of this embodiment of pragmatist thought (152). See also J. N. Sharma, 'Humanism as Vision and Technique in *The Ambassadors*', in *The Magic Circle of Henry James*, ed. Singh and Paniker, 146–59.

Was he, on this question of Chad's improvement, fantastic and away from the truth? Did he live in a false world, a rank world that he had grown simply to suit him, and was his present slight irritation . . . but the alarm of the vain thing menaced by the touch of the real? Was this contribution of the real possibly the mission of the Pococks? Had they come to make the work of observation as *he* had practised observation crack and crumble, and to reduce Chad to the plain terms in which honest minds could deal with him? Had they come, in short, to be sane where Strether was destined to feel that he himself had only been silly? (271)

Reflection that his point of view has been corroborated by little Bilham, Madame de Vionnet, Jeanne, and Chad himself soon reassures him that his position is tenable: 'Wouldn't it be found to have made more for reality to be silly with these persons than sane with Sarah and Jim?' (271). Nevertheless, Sarah's continued resistance to both his methods and his conclusions helps to define for Strether the course he has chosen. Sarah avoids any challenge to her preconceived ideas by accepting 'no version of her movements or plans from any other lips' (282). Strether has accepted from Chad and Madame de Vionnet another version of his own plans (their idea that he is in Paris to 'let [himself] go' (282)) as well as another version of their history, and the combined frivolity and immorality of this involve him, for Sarah, in 'the performance of "Europe" ' (289), in which she has no intention of participating. Sarah wishes to return to Woollett with only 'so much producible history . . . in her pocket' (284), and no new perspectives on matters as to which she has already made up her mind. From her point of view, Strether's idea that Madame de Vionnet could be a 'revelation' to her is insulting (363), and his own attitude preposterous. Nevertheless, Strether articulates it, in pragmatist terms: Madame de Vionnet's 'life' is his business, 'only so far as Chad's own life is affected by it; and what has happened—don't you see?—is that Chad's has been affected so beautifully. The proof of the pudding's in the eating' (364).

   For support of his position Strether turns, increasingly, not to the evidence of Chad's transformation, but to its origin in Madame de Vionnet herself. It is his vision of her charm and variety which first, at Chad's party, allows him to articulate his moral view of her—a view which tallies with the character references he has been given by her Parisian friends. 'I couldn't, without my own impression, realise. . . . I understand what a relation with such a woman—what such a high, fine friendship—may be. It can't be vulgar or coarse, anyway—and that's the point' (207). This statement shows how Madame de Vionnet has 'taken all his categories by surprise' (201), including the categorization that separates moral and spiritual affairs from sensuous and aesthetic ones; here he suggests what he later explicitly admits, that his faith in the idea of the 'virtuous attachment' has an aesthetic motive.

This confusion of categories provides a complementary aspect to his early fears of being placed in a false position by allowing pleasure to erode his moral authority; in his European experience, work dissolves into idleness, but now play becomes serious. As well as testing the hypothesis of the 'virtuous attachment', Strether's experience also tests this broader idea, that one's moral and spiritual affairs may be conducted not in opposition to, but upon, a sensuous and aesthetic basis. In two important scenes, in Notre Dame and on Strether's visit to the country, exploration of this idea leads to the development of new relations between fiction and life. On each occasion, Strether seeks to escape from the problems of reconstruction and interpretation by finding sanctuary in a framed locus where the irresponsible pleasures of art are separated from the world of risk and judgement. However, both times authorial contrivance introduces a coincidence which turns the episode into a recognition scene forcing Strether to re-encounter the world and re-evaluate his activity in it.

Strether's impulse to visit Notre Dame is a passive, escapist one, 'the impulse to let things be, to give them time to justify themselves, or at least to pass' (216). He has found there before 'a refuge from the obsession of his problem' (215), and is conscious of the nature of its appeal for him. 'He was aware of having no errand in such a place but the desire not to be, for the hour, in certain other places; a sense of safety, of simplification, which, each time he yielded to it, he amused himself by thinking of as a private concession to cowardice' (216). It is a place where he is able 'to drop his problem at the door very much as if it had been the copper piece that he deposited, on the threshold, in the receptacle of the inveterate blind beggar' (216). Interpretative responsibility gives way to imaginative freedom as he feels how 'within the precinct, for the real refugee, the things of the world could fall into abeyance. ... Justice was outside, in the hard light, and injustice too; but one was as absent as the other from the air of the long aisles and the brightness of the many altars' (216–17).

This sense of Notre Dame as a sanctuary owes much to Victor Hugo's use of the cathedral as a place of asylum in *Notre-Dame of Paris*. Indeed, the debt is made explicit when Strether later reveals that his imaginative response to the cathedral was greatly influenced by 'the great romancer and the great romance' (220). In Hugo's novel, the hunchback Quasimodo, himself an outcast who has found sanctuary and an alternative world within the portals of Notre Dame, rescues the gypsy Esmeralda from the authorities executing judgment upon her, and claims asylum for her within the cathedral: 'Within the precincts of Notre-Dame, the condemned girl was indeed inviolable. The cathedral was a place of refuge. All human justice expired on its threshold.'[4] For Strether, too, the claims of human justice expire on the threshold of Notre Dame: he leaves behind him the competing claims of Mrs Newsome's a-priori principles and his own developing sense of the need to do justice to unfolding experience; he also leaves behind the demands of truth and conscience, always potentially in conflict and each continually being redefined. Immunity from the need to judge and be judged according to these shifting, conflicting standards is purchased with a coin given to the beggar at the door. Thus, the precincts of the cathedral define an imaginative zone which can be contrasted with the city around it, much as Europe and Woollett offer contrasting imaginative worlds. Europe is first seen as a region in which holidays may be taken from the strict laws of the New England conscience, although its very invitation to flout the rule of literal facts and preconceived beliefs makes it a more problematic region, epistemologically and morally, to inhabit. Seeking refuge from these problems in Notre Dame, Strether feels that here at last he can take 'the holiday he had earned' (216) in a region where neither the claims of history nor the risks of plotting can interfere with the freedom of pure imaginative play.

Notre Dame, as Strether responds to it, is a perfect instance of the 'playground' defined in Huizinga's theory of play—a space marked off from the rules and responsibilities of ordinary life, in

[4] Victor Hugo, *Notre-Dame of Paris*, first pub. 1831, trans. John Sturrock (Harmondsworth: Penguin, 1978), 351.

which 'a certain "imagination" of reality' can take place as a superfluous and disinterested activity.[5] Inside the cathedral Strether feels free to indulge in observation as a 'pastime' (217), without the responsibility that has attended his role as Mrs Newsome's deputed observer in Paris, or the risk that is involved in the interpretative observation taught him by Miss Gostrey. He plays a private game of supplying histories for people he observes in the cathedral; it is a game which he considers frivolous, but innocent—they are safe in their anonymity, as he is in his, and his imaginings are therefore without issue or effect in the world outside. His musings are 'vague and fanciful', and cast a romantic glow about their objects, whom he sees as 'figures of mystery and anxiety', 'those who were fleeing from justice' (217). His own temporary flight from justice he also treats indulgently, as harmless frivolity, believing that 'his own oblivions were too brief, too vain, to hurt anyone but himself' (217).

However, an implied authorial perspective and direct authorial commentary suggest a possible harsher judgement of Strether's activity, both for its frivolity and for its possible issue in error. Strether's attempt 'to reconstitute a past' for the cathedral is, we are told, carried out 'in the museum mood' and is an attempt to reduce that past to 'the convenient terms of Victor Hugo' (218), whose works he has just purchased in a magnificent edition of seventy volumes. Will his task of reconstruction regarding Chad and Madame de Vionnet be carried out in a similar way, seduced by the conveniently simplifying terms of romance? Would such a solution to his problem turn out to be 'a miracle of cheapness' (218), like his purchase of the Hugo romances which inspired it? In describing these volumes, great emphasis is placed on their binding, suggesting superficiality and lack of penetration, but also drawing attention to the idea of enclosure, the setting of boundaries which define the arena for narrative games but are impossible to set in the real world. The implied criticisms of ludic and romantic narrative-making come together with a rhetorical question: 'Were seventy volumes in red-and-gold to be perhaps what he should most substantially have to show at Woollett as the fruit of his mission?' (218). Suggesting that the Hugo

---

[5] J. Huizinga, *Homo Ludens: A Study of the Play-Element in Culture*, trans. R. F. C. Hull (London: Routledge & Kegan Paul, 1949), 4, 8–9.

romances may either replace or represent the achievement of his mission, this question implies two common charges made by opponents of fiction—that in choosing books over life one misses out on real experience, or that in trying to live through romantic fictions one's judgement is hopelessly led astray. The possibility is raised that Strether will either surrender to the charms of Victor Hugo and, failing to complete his mission at all, retire from the active world to a precinct of complete narrative immunity where irresponsible fictions are consumed and produced; or, that he will try to solve his problem by reducing it to the 'convenient' terms of a romantic plot and, judging it from a deluded perspective, produce an erroneous solution.

It is exactly as this question is asked—by Strether as well as by the narrator—that Madame de Vionnet approaches. Her appearance not only signifies the breaking of Strether's charmed circle of imaginative immunity and his relocation in the world of his 'problem', but raises the question of the relation between the two regions. For Strether realizes that Madame de Vionnet is one of the 'figures of mystery and anxiety' for whom he has been trying to invent a story. As an anonymous figure, she had 'reminded our friend . . . of some fine, firm, concentrated heroine of an old story, something he had heard, read, something that, had he had a hand for drama, he might himself have written, renewing her courage, renewing her clearness, in splendidly protected meditation' (217–18). The fact that Strether's activity is more compositional than reconstructive (something 'he might himself have written') is harmless enough while his subject is anonymous, but it has repercussions once he realizes who she is, especially as, we are told directly, Strether lacks the experience of her cultural milieu to understand what her presence in the cathedral may mean—his 'reading of such matters was, it must be owned, confused' (218).

Strether's discovery that the object of his interest is in fact Madame de Vionnet confirms his romantic sense of the identity between the real and the imagined woman, although an alternative ironic sense of the gap between the two is suggested by the context of implied authorial criticism of Strether's susceptibility to romance. 'She was romantic for him far beyond what she could have guessed' (219), and this sense of romance, together with Strether's 'confused' reading of the significance of her presence in the church, will have important effects on the way in which he readdresses the problems he left outside the precinct. His Protestant background gives him a naïve logic to argue his case for taking his romantic vision of Madame de Vionnet as evidence for her virtue. 'Unassailably innocent was a relation that could make one of the parties to it so carry herself. If it wasn't innocent, why did she haunt the churches?—into which, given the woman he could believe he made out, she would never have come to flaunt an insolence of guilt' (220). The Woollett mind's use of exclusive categories—innocent or guilty, true or false—will later be exposed as inadequate to experience, but in the mean time Strether's romantic vision sustains his argument. His response to the anonymous woman confirms the opinion he has already formed about Madame de Vionnet's relation to Chad. The attitude of the heroine before the altar

fitted admirably into the stand he had privately taken about her connection with Chad on the last occasion of his seeing them together. It helped him to stick fast at the point he had then reached; it was there, he had resolved, that he *would* stick, and at no moment since had it seemed as easy to do so. (220)

As Strether's view of the virtue of his friends' attachment still includes the mistaken belief that theirs is not a sexual relationship, his idle narrative play in the cathedral seems to have confirmed him in a deluded reading of the situation he is required once more to face. When the scene is read in these terms, the coincidence of Strether's meeting with Madame de Vionnet seems designed to show the dangers of allowing romance to flourish outside the jurisdiction of the real, and especially of attempting to read the real in terms of romance. The scene seems to be just another case of the author, as historian, inviting the reader to share his ironic perspective on the character's plot. Yet a very different reading is possible, which breaks away from this familiar model.

In the cathedral Strether is 'called upon to play his part in an encounter that deeply stirred his imagination' (217). This suggests both the idea of the calls of responsible involvement, and the idea that the author requires Strether to 'play' a 'part' which Strether might not have envisaged: in fact, it combines the two, equating the demands of the real world with those of the author.

However, it expresses both these demands in the language of artifice, and the requirement that Strether should play a certain part reminds us of the author's role, not as historian, but as a dramatist or fabulist, able to direct rather than just record his characters' actions. The model of fiction as history relied on the author having a more privileged access to the facts than his characters, but remaining passively faithful to those facts; however, the author's contrivance of coincidence at this point reveals not only privileged access to, but control over, the facts. This highlights the similarity between the author's activity and Strether's desire to recast experience imaginatively. Moreover, the engineering of a coincidence at this point forcing Strether to yield 'pastime' to 'encounter' (217) is a development with which Strether wholly concurs. Having had his vision of Madame de Vionnet inside the cathedral, he is extremely eager to leave the precinct and carry on their relationship in the world outside, using this vision as a basis. 'He had made up his mind and was impatient to get into the air; for his purpose was a purpose to be uttered outside' (220). This purpose is the decision to 'stick' to the idea of supporting her that his imaginative vision has encouraged; that vision was a product of the imaginative sanctuary, sheltered from the hard outer light of actual experience, but it is only in the outer air that it can have any value in experience. His decision to act upon it is presented not as a romantic delusion, but as a considered response to circumstances:

What had come over him as he recognised her in the nave of the church was that holding off could be but a losing game from the instant she was worked for not only by her subtlety, but by the hand of fate itself. If all the accidents were to fight on her side—and by the actual showing they loomed large—he could only give himself up. (223)

In earlier James novels, individual 'subtlety' and impersonal 'fate' had tended to be opposed. Here, 'fate' and 'accidents' (the author's control of events) fight on the side of Madame de Vionnet's plans and encourage Strether's imaginative tendencies. Strether takes the meeting as an invitation to intervene (author-like) in events. In asking Madame de Vionnet to breakfast and pledging his support for her, Strether has moved from reconstruction to intervention, capable of producing rather than merely responding to facts.

For his position now is less one of delusion than a self-conscious use of the elasticity provided by the absence of full knowledge. His relation to Madame de Vionnet is now defined by a contract which is strongly fictional in nature, the complex conditions of which are expressed obliquely through the reference point of 'the convenient terms of Victor Hugo' (218):

> While she rose, as he would have called it, to the question of Victor Hugo, her voice itself, the light, low quaver of her deference to the solemnity about them, seemed to make her words mean something that they didn't mean openly. Help, strength, peace, a sublime support—she had not found so much of these things as that the amount wouldn't be sensibly greater for any scrap his appearance of faith in her might enable her to feel in her hand. (221)

Strether signals his willingness to meet this need:

> The sign would be that—though it was her own affair—he understood; the sign would be that—though it was her own affair—she was free to clutch. Since she took him for a firm object—much as he might to his own sense appear at times to rock—he would do his best to *be* one. (221)

He is able to muster this appearance of faith in her, to be the firm object she takes him for, because he has had, under the influence of 'the great romancer and the great romance' (220), a vision of her as a 'fine, firm, concentrated heroine' (217). Strether and Madame de Vionnet are not swapping delusions, but extending imaginative credit to each other, setting up a circular system of fictions which can intervene creatively in reality: if he believes she is a fine heroine, he can stand firm for her; with his support, she can be the heroine he sees in her. (It is exactly this kind of credit that Robert Acton was unwilling to extend to Eugenia in *The Europeans*, unable to believe that 'a finer degree of confidence in this charming woman would be its own reward' (*TE* ii. 108).) The imperfect grasp of fact in this contract—for example, Strether's equation of church-going with innocence—gives it a certain instability, which may simply result in error, but which also gives it a provisional, exploratory character. Strether has already had the experience of making a statement—that he would 'save' Madame de Vionnet—and then having to wait to find out what he meant by it (225). His renewal of his pledge still has something of this prospective quality, although he is yet to realize how much; the meaning of his decision to support Madame de

Vionnet will only unfold through experience, together with the unfolding meanings of the terms 'innocent' and 'virtuous attachment'.

Inside Notre Dame, Strether, struggling to understand an alien form of religion, remembers the concept of indulgence. 'He knew but dimly what indulgence, in such a place, might mean; yet he had, as with a soft sweep, a vision of how it might indeed add to the zest of active rites' (218). His indulgence in idle imaginings about anonymous figures has a potential value in the world of 'active rites', as his 'vague and fanciful kindness' (217) for these figures could be channelled into an active imaginative sympathy for similar figures in the world outside. More particularly, when pastime yields to encounter and he puts his vision of Madame de Vionnet to work in experience, a direct link is made between his idle game of making up stories, and what, in pragmatist terms, is the discovery of truth. Dropping his problem at the threshold of the church, he sees it as an act of cowardice to 'dodge' the things of the world in this way, 'to beg the question, not to deal with it in the hard outer light' (217); when he picks up his problem again on leaving, he has emerged with a means of facing it. In the 'indulgence' of the precinct, he has discovered how to use fiction as a mode of problem-solving. Such uses of fiction are serious play, a concept foreign to Strether, with his New England dichotomies, but familiar to Madame de Vionnet, who, once again, has taken all his categories by surprise:

The thing that most moved him was really that she was so deeply serious. She had none of the portentous forms of it, but he had never come in contact, it struck him, with a spirit whose lightest throbs were so full. Mrs. Newsome, goodness knew, was serious; but it was nothing to this. (229)

Strether now bases his relationship to Madame de Vionnet, and his exploration of the meanings of the 'virtuous attachment', on a form of fictional play more serious than the 'portentous forms' of historical reconstruction he was originally commissioned to undertake.

Strether's experience in Notre Dame suggests how the reading of fiction could also be transformed from an apparently escapist activity into a serious confrontation of life. A reader may pick up a novel, as Strether enters the cathedral, under 'the impulse to let things be, to give them time to justify themselves, or at least to pass' (216); in an article of 1897 James recorded such a motive for plunging into a series of novels:

It was a supreme opportunity to test the spell of the magician, for one felt one was saved if a fictive world would open. I knocked in this way at a dozen doors, I read a succession of novels; with the effect perhaps of feeling more than ever before my individual liability in our great general debt to the novelists. The great thing to say for them is surely that at any given moment they offer us another world, another consciousness, an experience that, as effective as the dentist's ether, muffles the ache of the actual and, by helping us to an interval, tides us over and makes us face, in the return to the inevitable, a combination that may at least have changed. (*LC* i. 1399–1400)

This tribute to 'the great anodyne of art' (*LC* i. 1399) draws on a tradition of 'opiate' imagery used in both attacks on and defences of the novel, which emphasized the escapist value of fiction.[6] But Strether's attempt to escape his own problems by entering imaginatively into the lives of others—as novel-readers do—not only leads him to experience imaginative sympathy, the benefit of novel-reading most frequently cited in Victorian defences of fiction,[7] but radically affects his conduct of his own moral and social concerns. The use Strether makes of his 'reading' (218) of Madame de Vionnet as a romantic heroine suggests that fiction may not simply keep one occupied while waiting for reality to change, but may itself be the bridge to that changed reality: the game of fiction may have serious, practical results. Vernon Lee raised this idea in 'A Dialogue on Novels' in 1885:

Emotional and scientific art, or rather emotional and scientific play . . . trains us to feel and comprehend—that is to say, to live. It trains us well or ill; and, the thing done as mere play becoming thus connected with

---

[6] Stang, *The Theory of the Novel*, comments on Scott's use of opiate imagery for the novel (8). Stevenson wrote: 'The slightest novels are a blessing to those in distress, not chloroform itself a greater': see 'The Morality of the Profession of Letters', *Fortnightly Review* (Apr. 1881); reprinted in *Essays in the Art of Writing* (London: Chatto & Windus, 1905), 69. In contrast, in his essay 'On the Choice of Books', Frederic Harrison warned against the narcotic uses of literature (*Fortnightly Review*, NS 25 (1879), 510).

[7] See Stang, *The Theory of the Novel*, 65–7. The most eloquent exponent of the novel's duty to encourage imaginative sympathy was George Eliot: see e.g. *Adam Bede*, 3 vols. (Edinburgh: Blackwood, 1859), ii. 3–9; and 'The Natural History of German Life', *Westminster Review* (July 1856); reprinted in *Essays of George Eliot*, ed. Thomas Pinney (London: Routledge & Kegan Paul, 1963), 270–1.

practical matters, it is evident that it must submit to the exigencies of practical matters. From this passive acquiescence in the interests of our lives to an active influence therein is but one step; for the mere play desires receive a strange additional strength from the half-conscious sense that the play has practical results: it is the difference, in point of excitement, between gambling with markers and gambling with money.[8]

In investing the anonymous woman in the cathedral with the qualities of a 'fine, firm, concentrated heroine' (217), Strether is gambling with markers; in making the same imaginative and moral investment in Madame de Vionnet, he is, so to speak, gambling with money. The process and results of his gamble have important implications for James's developing theory of fiction.

The motive for Strether's excursion to the country is slightly different from that which led him to visit Notre Dame—then he had been desperately seeking an escape from his problem, whereas now, already enjoying a much greater confidence in his handling of it, he is celebrating the feeling of freedom that Sarah's departure from Paris has given him. The trip to the country is an even more extravagant and less apologetic expression of indulgence in the holiday spirit and of retreat to a zone of imaginative play. In the cathedral Strether had played the game of inventing stories for anonymous people; in the country, his game is to find and explore a landscape which matches a Lambinet painting he had once wished to buy in Boston. Strether presents his exploration of the Lambinet landscape (which he easily finds) as a game of reconstruction, a question of finding an original, but what he seems to be doing rather is turning a natural landscape into a work of art—the game seems to be based, not on the idea of a 'restoration to nature', but on the conceit of actually entering a painting and, miraculously, 'freely walking about in it' (398). 'The oblong gilt frame disposed its enclosing lines', and within it, the elements of the scene 'fell into a composition, full of felicity'; Strether finds himself 'boring so deep into his impression and his idleness that he might fairly have got through them again and reached the maroon-coloured wall' on which he had first seen the picture hanging (398). His fanciful attitude to his day also involves a literary element; if the scene is a picture by Lambinet, the events (as he anticipates them) are a story by Maupassant (399).

    [8] Lee, 'Dialogue', 388.

The sense of idleness and freedom prevails, and yet, in contrast to his state of mind inside Notre Dame, Strether does not feel detached from his problem; rather, building on his experience in the cathedral which merged 'pastime' and 'encounter', he has reconciled it with, and involved it in, his indulgence in leisure. Besides being 'amused' (402) by his outing, 'he had never yet struck himself as so engaged with others, so in midstream of his drama. . . . He had but had to be at last well out of it to feel it, oddly enough, still going on' (402–3). An expression of this sense of involvement is the time he spends thinking over his relationship with Madame de Vionnet, and the new terms, since Notre Dame and especially since the departure of Sarah, on which it is based. Once again, Victor Hugo serves as a pretext or point of reference for renegotiations of this relationship. In Notre Dame Strether had felt that Madame de Vionnet's talk of 'the great romancer' really signified a plea for an appearance of faith from him, to which he had responded with his proposed fictional contract. This is now taken even further when, in recalled or imagined conversations, Strether uses a discussion of 'the difference between Victor Hugo and the English poets'[9] to communicate his own appeal:

Yet it had served all the purpose of his appearing to have said to her: 'Don't like me, if it's a question of liking me, for anything obvious and clumsy that I've, as they call it, "done" for you; like me—well, like me, hang it, for anything else you choose. So, by the same propriety, don't be for me simply the person I've come to know through my awkward connection with Chad . . . Be for me, please, with all your admirable tact and trust, just whatever I may show you it's a present pleasure to me to think you.' (401–2)

This imaginative 'propriety' seems to be the result of the idea learnt in Notre Dame, that indulgence may help the performance of active rites: Strether now plots his relationship to Madame de Vionnet through the same kind of narrative-making games in which he had indulged in the cathedral, and prefers that she treat him likewise. His experience now in the country, where his game of finding the Lambinet landscape seems to be turning out so successfully, encourages the premise of this 'propriety': that life can indeed yield the fruits of indulgence.

---

[9] In the *New York Edition*, the reference to Victor Hugo is replaced by 'Shakespeare and the musical glasses' (*NYE* xxii. 251).

Yet there is something ominous, too good to be true, in the way that everything 'really and truly' (399) falls into place for him. When he admits that, if he were to see the actual Lambinet painting again, he might suffer 'a drop or a shock' (397), we may wonder if likewise, any disappointment or crisis will attend this exercise of restoring it to nature. So far, all that he has found has fitted within the frame, which 'had drawn itself out for him as much as you please; but that was just his luck' (402). Strether's luck, however, is generally bad luck, or so he has always felt.[10] Is the elasticity of the frame just a means of luring him into a trap? Perhaps Strether is in danger of being trapped inside this frame, and will only escape with its destruction, thereby losing the terms of indulgence which it offers him. Most blatant of all, in suggesting an imminent crash, is the comment that his drama is nearly finished, 'its catastrophe all but reached' (403). There is a double perspective in this statement; Strether's confidence that he has all but resolved his problem is undermined by the implicit authorial suggestion that a catastrophe, moral as well as formal, still awaits him.

Fact—the fact of the sexual intimacy between Chad and Madame de Vionnet—intrudes on his world of fancy as 'exactly the right thing' that his picture requires (407). The conflict between morality and aesthetics expressed in the tension between different meanings of the word 'right' indicates the problem with the imaginative 'propriety' (again both a moral and an aesthetic term) through which Strether has been operating. Aesthetic matters have their own rules which are independent of moral concerns, but an attempt to conduct moral concerns on an aesthetic basis is always potentially liable to a conflict of interests. This conflict now brings into relief the changes in Strether's values over the course of the novel. Initially, he had regularly tried to precipitate a crisis in order to hasten the resolution of his business; however, the delaying tactics of the Parisians averted this, and his exposure to pleasure which these delays entailed brought about the collapse of his old moral scheme and the creation of a new one. According to this new one, Strether does not even want to mention his 'awkward connection with Chad' (401), much less bring about a crisis in it. However, the imposition of this crisis upon him recalls him to some of his old attitudes.

[10] See e.g. 263, 281, 351.

The river scene may be read as the most masterly of James's ironic reversals in the tradition of the author's history defeating the character's plot. Strether's 'theory . . . had bountifully been that the facts were, specifically, none of his business, and were, over and above, so far as one had to do with them, intrinsically beautiful' (410). The evidence of sexual intimacy seems not only to explode the substance of this 'theory', but to throw into disrepute the means by which he had reached this position. He had, 'bountifully', extended an imaginative credit to Chad and Madame de Vionnet, basing his opinion of them on the fruits of narrative play rather than on a reconstruction of facts. Now that the facts can no longer be ignored, the values of play, idleness, and make-believe, all celebrated in his ramble through the countryside, turn sharply sour. The 'idle play' of the boat's oars are 'the aid to the full impression' (404–5) it makes—that full impression being a blast of disillusionment. Madame de Vionnet's parasol which makes 'so fine a pink point in the shining scene' (407) is, aesthetically, exactly the right thing for focusing the elements of the composition, functioning as does Miss Gostrey's red ribbon at the dinner in London (38), or the *omelette aux tomates* at the breakfast by the Seine (223). But, instead of being the starting-point for fresh flights of sensuous and aesthetic play, the parasol acts as an agent of deception, 'shifting as if to hide [the lady's] face' (407). Such a pretence 'out there in the eye of nature' (408) is an affront to old standards of veracity, and the 'violence' of this particular deception is averted only by other insincerities. Strether forces the others to recognize him by giving 'large play' (407) to the signs of joyful recognition, to which they respond with an equally face-saving 'performance' (411) to perpetuate the pretence that they are not lovers. While 'the amount of explanation called into play' makes the situation again elastic (408), play is no longer innocent and disinterested; as a means of making an awkward situation workable again, it is no longer free from the intention to deceive. Strether's unease throughout the evening crystallizes with the benefit of retrospective analysis: 'He kept making of it that there had been simply a *lie* in the charming affair—a lie on which one could now, detached and deliberate, perfectly put one's finger' (411).

In this frame of mind the conventions of fiction, explored in Notre Dame, now come to seem rather shabby. Where Madame de Vionnet had been, in the cathedral, the 'fine, firm, concentrated heroine of an old story' (217), Chad is now 'the coatless hero of the idyl' (407), a figure from melodrama or cheap romance. The complex blend of ironic awareness with suspension of disbelief inherent in the fictional contract has been reduced to a gentlemen's agreement not to give away a lady's deceptions:

It was as if [Chad] had humoured her to the extent of letting her lie without correction—almost as if, really, he would be coming round in the morning to set the matter, as between Strether and himself, right. Of course he couldn't quite come; it was a case in which a man was obliged to accept the woman's version, even when fantastic. (412)

The word 'fiction' is drawn into disrepute and used as another term for lying: 'fiction and fable *were*, inevitably, in the air, and not as a simple term of comparison, but as a result of things said' (410). Strether's moral difficulty is in having to swallow, not just 'the central fact itself' (413), but the fictions used to try to cover it up. 'It was the quantity of make-believe involved, and so vividly exemplified, that most disagreed with his spiritual stomach' (413). The equation of fiction with lies, and the dishonourable associations of play and make-believe, recall the familiar language of hostility to fiction, and the attitudes to which 'The Art of Fiction' responded with its defence of fiction as history.

That theory of fiction had led to a particular narrative practice: the presentation of the narrator as historian, the insistence on a moral and epistemological difference between the narrative-making activities of the characters and those of the author, and the defeat of the characters' plots by facts to which the narrator is faithful but for which he is not responsible. But in this scene, in which the intrusion of fact brings Strether's imaginative world crashing down around him, stress on improbability and coincidence combines with a dense network of reflexive images to foreground the way in which the narrative has been manipulated to achieve this effect. Manipulation of the narrative contrives the collapse of Strether's framed artistic world, but the framing devices emphasize the artfulness of the author's intervention.

Hints about the author's intentions are scattered throughout the chapter. The aside that Strether's motive for going to the country is 'artless enough, no doubt' (397) is a not particularly artless clue to the artfulness of the author's intentions. The insist-

ence on the arbitrariness of Strether's decision to leave the train
where he does highlights the improbability of his meeting his
friends—even perhaps insists on its being more improbable than
it really is. The remark that Strether 'threw himself on the general
amiability of the day for the hint of where to alight' (398) raises
the question of the 'amiability' of the author's plans for him in
placing the lost Lambinet and the found lovers in the same
apparently randomly chosen spot in the French countryside: 'the
train pulled up at just the right spot, and he found himself getting
out as securely as if to keep an appointment' (398). His appointment is with fate or, to put it less melodramatically, with facts—
both of which, in novelistic terms, mean the author's intentions
for him. The narrator suggests—and in so doing sets up a con-
fidential relation with the reader which makes Strether the butt of
patronizing irony—that it 'will be felt of him that he could amuse
himself, at his age, with very small things if it be again noted that
his appointment was only with a faded Boston enthusiasm' (398);
it is also an appointment with 'Boston "reallys"' (153), absolute
facts, for which Strether's enthusiasm has indeed faded. His
meeting with the lovers is called a 'marvel' (407), 'too prodigious,
a chance in a million' (407), 'the mere miracle of the encounter'
(408). Not only general exclamations of surprise, but more specific literary terms, are called upon to describe the coincidence—
it is 'as queer as fiction, as farce' (407), an occasion marked by its
'*invraisemblance*' (408). The characters play up 'the prodigy of
their convergence' (410) as a way of covering up the awkwardness of their situation—they 'could so much better, at last, on
either side, treat it as a wild fable than as anything else' (408)—
and through them the narrator is also able to draw our attention
markedly to the coincidence, even perhaps to make more of it
than the circumstance really warrants. As the scene is focalized
through Strether's consciousness, and much of it is narrated in
free indirect discourse, it is sometimes difficult to attribute responsibility for the language used; some of the language of coincidence and romance may have been actually spoken by the
characters, some may be Strether's way of describing the situation
to himself or summarizing the substance of their conversation,
and some may be the narrator's way of rendering the conversation and Strether's thought about the situation. In any case, the
characters' need to emphasize the coincidence to pass off their

awkwardness allows the narrator to press his own point about the artificiality of the plotting to which they have been subjected. Previously, Strether had noticed that one wall of the inn is 'painted the most improbable shade. That was part of the amusement—as if to show that the fun was harmless' (403). The piece of plotting which brings him together with his friends at this inn is equally improbable, although the *invraisemblance* is used in this case to show that the fun—of attempting to conduct his moral affairs on a sensuous and aesthetic basis—is not harmless at all. Strether worries that the others might secretly suspect him of 'having plotted this coincidence' (408), but the language in which the whole scene is narrated emphasizes the author's responsibility for the plot: fiction and fable are in the air, not just as a 'term of comparison'—as in reflexive references—but literally, 'as a result of things said' (410), of the nature of the events narrated.

The author hands his characters a situation so awkward that, 'arrange it as they would' (408), they can make nothing of it; the only way they can make it at all workable is to 'treat it as a wild fable' (408) which is, we realize, exactly what it is. The author arranges events to show the power of undeniable, 'natural' facts, but at the same time reveals that the 'facts' of his own narrative are not 'natural' but contrived. With the one piece of blatantly artificial plotting the author gives both his characters and himself away. He has done what, in 'The Art of Fiction', James accused Trollope of doing—committed the unpardonable sin of revealing that he is not a historian, but a fabulist capable of giving events any turn he likes best. In exposing the flaws in Strether's plotting of his situation, the author has torn off his own 'historic mask' (*LC* i. 1343). The conventions of fiction as history required verisimilitude and plausibility of narrative; that the plot of *The Ambassadors* at this point displays neither of these qualities is positively forced upon our attention. This means that the river scene differs significantly from ironic reversals in James's earlier novels, where the author's role as a historian was insisted upon, and we may ask if it really has the function of a complete reversal, forcing the hero to give up the plot that it has plotted to expose.

The river scene disproves Strether's theory that a 'virtuous attachment' must be sexually innocent, and in having held this theory he is shown to have been deceived and self-deceived. However, over the course of the novel, Strether has gradually been discovering that there are other ways in which an attachment may be virtuous, discoveries which have been linked to romantic ideas such as his vision of Madame de Vionnet in Notre Dame. In testing these ideas against fact, the encounter at the river tests whether Strether's moral vision has developed far enough for him to leave behind his original equation of virtue with sexual propriety (a Woollett equation) while still sustaining the moral implications of the imaginative superstructure built on that foundation. Drawing on James's famous definitions of the real and the romantic in the preface to *The American*, we may read the river scene as the intrusion of 'the things we cannot possibly *not* know, sooner or later, in one way or another' into an imaginative world created 'through the beautiful circuit and subterfuge of our thought and our desire' (*LC* ii. 1063). The 'possibly scandalous case' of romance (*LC* ii. 1058) is subjected to awkward questions, but this interrogation of the romantic by the real does not necessarily signify the negation of Strether's imaginings.[11] In looking back over the events of the day, Strether turns his thoughts from the quantity of so distasteful 'make-believe' in the lovers' actions to 'the other feature of the show, the deep, deep truth of the intimacy revealed' (413). The 'show' put on by Chad and Madame de Vionnet teaches Strether a 'deep, deep truth', for the fact of their intimacy is revealed by the very expertness with which the lovers silently communicate to each other how best to sustain their 'make-believe'. At the same time, the 'show' of the author's artifice has been employed to force Strether, not to abandon his theory, but to make it take account of facts. The intrusion of historical truth (through the vehicle of

[11] My reading is opposed to the view put forward by Robert E. Garis in 'The Two Lambert Strethers: A New Reading of *The Ambassadors*', *Modern Fiction Studies*, 7 (1961–2), 305–16. Garis argues that the river scene simply exposes Strether's delusions, demolishes his imaginative constructions, and demonstrates that he has learnt nothing in Paris—a view extended by David McWhirter in *Desire and Love in Henry James: A Study of the Late Novels* (Cambridge: Cambridge University Press, 1989), 67–81, as part of an argument that Strether's imagination is incapable of engaging with reality. Rather, I agree with Paul B. Armstrong that the river scene shows Strether achieving a 'postcritical faith' through a 'dialectic of faith and suspicion': see *The Challenge of Bewilderment: Understanding and Representation in James, Conrad, and Ford* (Ithaca, NY: Cornell University Press, 1987), 90.

deception and artifice) into his imaginative world does not lead to a merely passive consumption of literal, vulgar fact. Rather, it suggests William James's 'view of "reality," as something resisting, yet malleable, which controls our thinking as an energy that must be taken "account" of incessantly (tho [*sic*] not necessarily merely copied)'.[12] Strether's way of dealing with the outbreak of fact is to begin 'supposing' its various meanings: for it may mean (in the first edition) 'everything' (413), or (in the *New York Edition*) 'innumerable and wonderful things' (*NYE* xxii. 266), which temper, but do not disqualify, his attitude towards Chad and Madame de Vionnet and the virtue of their attachment.

The novel does not end with the ironic reversal of the eleventh book; a whole further book is devoted to the question of what Strether will make of the information he has been forced to take in. This is an important departure from the pattern of earlier works such as *In the Cage* where, in the face of new information, the heroine speedily capitulates to the superior force of the facts of the real world, and the story ends as soon as she has made an irrevocable commitment to these; even in *The Portrait of a Lady*, where Isabel's reverses of fortune occur in the middle of the novel, there is no respite from their effects in the second half, and true enlightenment does not come until near the end of the novel. In *The Ambassadors*, the initiative for defining the meaning of his own experience, and possibly intervening in the experience of others, passes back to Strether as he at last finds out what he meant by pledging to support Madame de Vionnet. As he indulges in some final pieces of retrospective and prospective plotting, two opposed perspectives on his activity are intertwined.

Although he decides to stand by both the substance and form of the resolutions he had arrived at before the encounter by the river, Strether does suffer something of 'a revulsion in favour of the principles of Woollett' (436). This interaction of the values of the old and the new morality places terms such as 'play', 'joke', 'lie', and 'appearance' in an ambivalent light, as the language of hostility to fiction is often used to narrate Strether's renewed commitment to the uses of fiction in understanding and directing experience. Most of this rhetoric is attributable to Strether rather than to the narrator, and his resolution of his problem is not

---

[12] William James, *Pragmatism*, 124.

made the object of any detached authorial evaluation. This means that the mixture of irony towards, and belief in, the powers of fiction is part of a single complex of attitudes, and is not separable into opposed authorial and heroic perspectives as in James's earlier works. The events of *The Ambassadors*, combined with its mode of narration, have led to a new set of attitudes towards fiction being formed.

Strether is recalled to his 'awkward connection with Chad' (401) by a telegram from Madame de Vionnet, requesting a meeting at which it is inevitable that she will ask him what stand he has taken on the affair, given the events of the day before. The possibility of not seeing her, but giving up the whole affair, holds a 'sharp' appeal for him (418), which is overcome not so much by a conviction of responsibility as by the atmosphere of the Postes et Télégraphes in which he writes his reply. The description of this place recalls not only the physical setting of *In the Cage*, but its world of false reports and misinterpretation, its view of the collective conduct of a huge, frivolous, pernicious narrative, and its use of the rhetoric of the argument that fiction is 'wicked'. Here we find again

the something in the air of these establishments . . . the influence of the types, the performers, concocting their messages; the little prompt Paris women arranging, pretexting goodness knew what, driving the dreadful needle-pointed public pen at the dreadful sand-strewn public table: implements that symbolised for Strether's too interpretative innocence something more acute in manner, more sinister in morals, more fierce in the national life. (418)

Here, Strether seems to have re-entered the world of *In the Cage*, so pointedly left behind in the first chapter of the novel when 'the lady in the glass cage' is 'superseded' by Maria Gostrey (6). Writing his telegram now, he identifies himself with 'the fierce, the sinister, the acute' and becomes 'mixed up with the typical tale of Paris' (418)—that dreadful little drama chronicling the breakdown of one's moral scheme. Yet Strether accepts this compromise of his innocence with a new humility and a new compassion for his countless anonymous partners in crime. 'They were no worse than he, in short, and he no worse than they—if, queerly enough, no better' (418). However, this more cynical version of the 'vague and fanciful kindness' (217) he had felt for his fellow fugitives in Notre Dame is followed by an immediate revulsion from the idea of indulgence in imaginative pleasures. It would be a pleasure to see Madame de Vionnet again in her beautiful, old apartments, but (he asks himself) 'what, precisely, was he doing with shades of pleasure now, and why hadn't he, properly and logically, compelled her to commit herself to whatever of disadvantage and penalty the situation might throw up?' (419). Strether now wants to reverse the 'propriety' (401) by which he had formerly wished to define his relationship with Madame de Vionnet: he feels he should meet her, not in a privileged zone of imaginative irresponsibility, but in a place bound by the ordinary discipline of the real and the right; rather than avoiding awkwardness, an ache for old spiritual standards makes him positively seek it, for only in 'awkwardness', 'danger', 'inconvenience', and 'sternness' can he avoid those 'shades of pleasure' connected with an indulgence and immunity which is now 'sinister' (419). He needs to feel 'that somebody was paying something somewhere and somehow, that they were at least not all floating together on the silver stream of impunity' (419).

This return to puritan morality is, however, more rhetorical than actual; filling in the day 'idling, lounging' (420), Strether finds that 'if he lived on thus with the sinister from hour to hour, it proved an easier thing than one might have supposed in advance' (419). He reflects that if the Pococks had unexpectedly returned and seen him now, they would have cause for scandal, but 'fate failed to administer even *that* sternness' (420). The author contrives no more coincidental recognition scenes to arrest the course of Strether's development, but leaves him to float on 'the silver stream of impunity', and see where it carries him.

It carries him to a decision to continue his support for Madame de Vionnet. In the terms that he attributes to her, his own impunity and his continuing support for her are entwined: 'Didn't she just wish to assure him that *she* now took it all [his ordeal] and so kept it; that he was absolutely not to worry any more, was only to rest on his laurels and continue generously to help her?' (420). The construction is logical in terms of her own morality, wherein the 'only safe thing is to give. It's what plays you least false' (427). It is questionable how innocent, how truly disinterested, is that use of the word 'play', but the game of giving she proposes falls in with the game (or contract) of the appearance of faith which Strether had felt she implicitly proposed in Notre Dame. Behind the appearance of faith lies the possibility of real faith, for the decision 'generously to help her' is underwritten by the reinstatement of the seemingly discredited theory which 'had bountifully been that the facts were, specifically, none of his business, and were, over and above, so far as one had to do with them, intrinsically beautiful' (410). As Strether later explains to Miss Gostrey, 'so much of it was none of my business—as I saw my business. It isn't even now' (440); while for the intrinsic beauty of the facts 'there was much to be said' (439). He is now able to explain and defend little Bilham's gentlemanly lie, under the influence of which he first rethought his attitude towards the relationship. He declares that

it was but a technical lie—he classed the attachment as virtuous. That was a view for which there was much to be said—and the virtue came out for me hugely. There was, of course, a great deal. I got it full in the face, and I haven't, you see, done with it yet. (439)

At the river Strether had received 'full in the face' facts which might have undermined his belief in the lovers, but here he makes clear that his overriding impression has been of the value of the relationship. In exploring the meaning of the term 'virtuous attachment', Strether has also explored new bases for knowledge and morality. The context in which little Bilham had spoken of the 'virtuous attachment' was one of humane scepticism and stoic acceptance: 'What more than a vain appearance does the wisest of us know? I commend you . . . the vain appearance' (150). Strether now defends the virtue of the attachment in the full ironic knowledge that he may be doing no more than clinging to a vain appearance. There are still elements of both the 'grandly vague' and the 'grandly cynical' (439) in his present stand: both attitudes have brought him out at the same point, a position in which irony and romance meet.

   In testing the value of a 'vain appearance' as the basis of committed action, the novel anticipates many aspects of the theory of truth William James called 'pragmatism', which may also be read as a theory of fiction. Like Mr Wentworth in *The Europeans*, Strether is subjected to the attempts of his foreign (or expatriate) friends to 'beguile him into assent to doubtful inductions' (*TE* ii. 223)—a dangerous power which was often ascribed to the novel as well. He gives provisional assent to Bilham's proposition, because it offers a means of orienting himself in the flux of experience, providing an intelligible point of reference in the midst of new things for which he has as yet neither names nor terms of judgement. Little Bilham seems to realize what William James later argued, that an '*outrée* explanation, violating all our preconceptions, would never pass for a true account of a novelty. . . . New truth is always a go-between, a smoother-over of transitions. It marries old opinion to new fact so as ever to show a minimum of jolt, a maximum of continuity.''[13] As Strether enters more deeply into the lives of his friends, the conservative term, 'virtuous attachment', is stretched by new experience until it yields a radically new meaning, a new truth: that virtue is more generously and variously defined than a strict puritanical morality would allow.[14] Little Bilham's words, which at first have the status of a 'vain appearance', come to satisfy William James's requirements for truth as 'any idea that will carry us prosperously from any one part of our experience to any other part', an opinion which 'gratifies the individual's desire to assimilate the novel in his experience to his beliefs in stock'.[15] Although the use of the term 'virtuous attachment' at first misleads Strether, with his increased experience his own use of the term shifts from error to fiction, as he is no longer duped by it but comes to understand its provisional, exploratory quality. Thus, when he is faced with information which would have contradicted his original understanding of the term, his new understanding of it is not disqualified. Rather, having gained 'the richest intimacy with facts',[16] his theory is able to survive as a means of understanding and possibly changing reality. The fictional nature of this is defined by a complex mixture of ironic detachment and willing suspension of disbelief.

[13] William James, *Pragmatism*, 35.
[14] The use of conservative terms to accommodate new intentions is also an important aspect of the working of legal fictions; see Lon L. Fuller, *Legal Fictions* (Stanford, Calif.: Stanford University Press, 1967), 15, 56–65. Fuller points out that scientific fictions also work on the same principle, whereby 'a new situation is made "thinkable" by converting it into familiar terms' (72). William James found in science a model for his own thinking about the employment of useful, although not necessarily true, formulations to bring old and new ideas together (*Pragmatism*, 33, 39).
[15] Ibid. 34, 36.
[16] Ibid. 23.

Strether has finally understood the language game played by his Parisian friends.[17] In calling the affair 'virtuous', little Bilham was, effectively, asking him 'what happens if we regard it as virtuous?' Maria Gostrey had played a similar game of 'what if?' when Strether first arrived in Paris—what if Chad is refined and not brutalized? what if the woman who has changed him is good? Strether's participation in this game suggests the possible results of imaginative participation in a work of fiction. Strether discovers two answers to the question behind little Bilham's statement. The first is that if he credits the relationship with value, he will gain a new perspective on an existing situation, bringing out aspects of it which he would otherwise not have been able to see. Long before he articulated his theory of pragmatism, William James had written that 'philosophic study means the habit of always seeing an alternative, of not taking the usual for granted, of making conventionalities fluid again, of imagining foreign states of mind'.[18] The reading (and writing) of fiction could mean the same thing; the habit of 'imagining foreign states of mind' is, of course, foregrounded in a literal sense by James's international theme, but any fiction requires the reader to enter imaginatively into some kind of alien experience. Strether's assent to little Bilham's description of the affair carries him from a conservative to a radical understanding of the term 'virtuous', and shows him how the apparently false description is really true. But there is another sense in which the proposition has an educative value, independently of its truth, and this is the second answer to little Bilham's implicit question. For Strether, imaginative sympathy leads to a whole new moral scheme, and there is a sense in which it becomes irrelevant whether Chad's and Madame de Vionnet's relationship really is virtuous or not: the point is that Strether believes that such a relationship could be virtuous, and this belief is part of a new approach to experience which he will continue to hold even if he doubts the degree to which the lovers—especially Chad—justify it. Like James's exercises in operative irony, little Bilham's formula 'implies and projects the possible other case,

[17] My interpretation of this expands on the view put forward by Ruth Bernard Yeazell of Parisian talk which, through its ambiguity, prevents Strether from drawing hasty conclusions: see *Language and Knowledge in the Late Novels of Henry James* (Chicago: University of Chicago Press, 1976), 71–6.
[18] William James, 'The Teaching of Philosophy in Our Colleges', *Nation*, 23 (1876), 178.

the case rich and edifying' which, regardless of whether he can give 'chapter and verse' for it, is justified by 'the sincerities, the lucidities, the utilities that stand behind it' (*LC* ii. 1229).[19] The power of the artist 'to *create* the record, in default of any other enjoyment of it' was defended by James as 'the high and helpful public and, as it were, civic use of the imagination' (ii. 1230), for 'where is the work of the intelligent painter of life if not precisely in some such aid given to true meanings to be born?' (ii. 1231). Fiction asks us to entertain new possibilities, and makes novel situations thinkable, simply by requiring the reader, at least for the duration of the reading process, to think them. Once the idea of a virtuous attachment outside the bounds of conventional morality becomes thinkable to Strether, he can set about helping to make it workable, by encouraging Madame de Vionnet to hold firm and trying to persuade Chad to keep faith with her. Arguing the virtue of the attachment becomes the basis of Strether's final diplomatic mission, the attempt to keep Chad in Paris. As he becomes an ambassador for Madame de Vionnet instead of Mrs Newsome, the changed terms of Strether's mission reflect the comments made by Sidney in his defence of poetry: 'And therefore, as in history, looking for truth, they may go away full fraught with falsehood, so in poesy, looking but for fiction, they shall use the narration but as an imaginative ground-plot of a profitable invention.'[20]

The theory of fiction that forms the basis of Strether's moral education in *The Ambassadors* is repeatedly tested against resistant facts and ironic perspectives, and this process continues to the end of the novel, becoming particularly intense in Strether's final meeting with Chad. Having made up his mind about Chad's situation in Paris, Strether now attempts to intervene directly in it. He tells Chad that he will be 'guilty of the last infamy' (445) if he leaves Madame de Vionnet, and he announces his intention of informing Sarah that he will not only be advising Chad not to leave Paris, but, if possible, 'absolutely preventing' him from even

---

[19] Hocks also notes the similarities between operative irony and William James's pragmatist, pluralistic thought (*Henry James and Pragmatistic Thought*, 98–102).

[20] Sir Philip Sidney, *A Defence of Poetry* (1595), reprinted in *Miscellaneous Prose of Sir Philip Sidney*, ed. Katherine Duncan-Jones and Jan Van Dorsten (Oxford: Clarendon Press, 1973), 103.

thinking of it (447). Chad meets this direct injunction with apparent insincerity and a jokey indirection. He throws in the topic of his new-found enthusiasm for advertising, which sits oddly with his protestations that he intends to stay in Paris and forgo the chance to run the advertising for his family's business. The way in which he describes his interest is a succinct but ghastly parody of Strether's whole experience in Paris: 'He appeared at all events to have been looking into the question and had encountered a revelation' (449–50). Chad continues to expound the seriousness of this new 'art', 'as if for the joke of it—almost as if his friend's face amused him' (450). When Strether uneasily asks why he speaks of a subject which is now irrelevant, Chad assures him that his 'interest's purely platonic' (450)—another ghastly parody, this time of the assurances Strether was given as to the virtue of his attachment to Madame de Vionnet. Is this assurance, too, a 'technical lie' (439) of which Strether is again to be the dupe? In Chad's hands, jokes and lies have become menacing quantities again, and his flippancy undermines the concept of serious play that has been developed through the novel. When he seems, to Strether, to dance 'an irrelevant hornpipe or jig' (451), Chad seems to have joined the ranks of those whom he had formerly accused of merely playing at life (260), his own family at Woollett. One feels sure that Chad is lying about his intention to stay in Paris, and the forms of his lies are both sinister and frivolous. This puts the whole story of his commitment to Madame de Vionnet in the light of a treacherous fiction, which finds its image in one of the many pleasing objects Chad had earlier put in Strether's way to seduce him into supporting his way of life. Once before when waiting for Chad at his apartment, Strether had found everything disposed for his convenience, including 'the novel half uncut, the novel lemon-coloured and tender, with the ivory knife athwart it like a dagger in a contadina's hair' (367). The fiction Chad makes available to Strether in Paris is just such an enticing mixture of beauty and excitement, offering both a chance to recover his lost youth (for it is like one of the 'lemon-coloured volumes' he kept as souvenirs of his youthful trip to Paris (64)), and a sense of potentiality (it is only 'half uncut'). But like a *contadina* with a dagger in her hair, Chad's fiction is also possibly dangerous and treacherous; having been seduced, Strether may yet be betrayed by it.

The open ending of the novel leaves unanswered the question of whether Strether will be betrayed by this particular fiction: we cannot conclusively say whether Strether has been right in defending the relationship as virtuous or successful in helping to preserve it. What is evident, however, is the deep change in Strether's thinking as he abandons a-priori principles for flexible encounters with experience on an imaginative basis. Strether's commitment to the moral and problem-solving value of the fictive imagination is challenged by Chad's association with the negative aspects of jokes, lies, and fictions, and by the revival of puritan attitudes in the description of the Postes et Télégraphes. Nevertheless, this challenge is not a disqualification, but simply emphasizes that motive and use define the value of fictions in the world. Strether is sceptical about his own narrative imagination and about the nature and uses of fiction in Chad's social circle, but he is not so sceptical as to believe that only arbitrary choices are to be made between available fictions. Rather, he discriminates on moral, practical, and aesthetic grounds, pragmatically limiting his scepticism to endorse fictions which may operate, at least, as a 'tribute to the ideal',[21] and at best may turn out to be practically workable revisions of experience.

The role of the author in guiding Strether's progress from delusion to fictional competence is highly emphasized. Authorial intervention in Notre Dame encourages Strether to encounter the world on the basis of his 'pastime' of imaginative play; in the river scene, coincidence forces him to take a closer account of facts. In engineering these encounters which teach Strether to balance freedom from and responsibility to facts, the author gives himself away as being implicated in the business of creatively shaping, rather than just passively recording, experience.[22] Ironic

---

[21] This phrase is used repeatedly in the novel, in many contexts: see e.g. 21, 49, 313–15.

[22] The debate over authorial intrusion in *The Ambassadors* is of only limited relevance to this. The survey of comments by the first-person narrator in John E. Tilford, Jr., 'James the Old Intruder', *Modern Fiction Studies*, 4 (1958), 157–64, usefully corrects the overstatement of the silencing of the narrating voice made by Percy Lubbock in *The Craft of Fiction* (London: Jonathan Cape, 1921), 147. However, both Tilford's argument and William B. Thomas's objections to it in 'The Author's Voice in *The Ambassadors*', *Journal of Narrative Technique*, 1 (1971), 108–21, are concerned with narrative method rather than with the fictional status of the text, with how events are narrated rather than with whether these events are shown to be fictitious.

perspectives on Strether's activity both rebound on the author and are shared by Strether himself, whose final view of his own narrative-making games reflects his propensity for 'sad ironic play' (287). The narrative model in which the author's 'history' is differentiated from the character's 'plot' has at last been abandoned, and the similarities between the projects of hero and author are revealed. This raises the idea of fiction not as a transcript of reality, but as a mode of encountering it, setting up a contract or game which calls for the reader's enlightened complicity, rather than attempting to delude the reader as to its historical status.[23] Lacking the intention to deceive, this activity cannot be classed with 'lies', for the fiction declares its fictionality. Like Strether, the reader is encouraged, not to measure the fiction against an a-priori standard of reality (as the model of historical narrative required), but to lend his or her provisional assent to the arrangement or interpretation of reality it offers. The novel provides an exploratory, imaginative space, into which we may enter in order to test new extensions of, new perspectives on, and new ways of orienting ourselves within, experience. Fiction, as a means of proposing new readings of experience, does not need to hide the fact that it is conducting its serious moral affairs on the basis of aesthetic play. The dichotomies of truth and fiction, seriousness and play, have been overcome, and with them the need for fiction to wear the mask of history.

[23] On fictional games and contracts, see Martin Price, *Forms of Life: Character and Moral Imagination in the Novel* (New Haven, Conn.: Yale University Press, 1983), 1–24, and Karlheinz Stierle, 'The Reading of Fictional Texts', trans. Inge Crosman and Thekla Zachrau, in *The Reader in the Text: Essays on Audience and Interpretation*, ed. Susan R. Suleiman and Inge Crosman (Princeton, NJ: Princeton University Press, 1980), 83–105.

5

History, Fiction, and Power in *The Golden Bowl*

THE GOLDEN BOWL is unique among James's novels in that its heroine, Maggie, has control over both history and plots: she is able to read the past correctly and to direct the future successfully. The novel thus seems to mark the furthest development in James's *œuvre* away from the early narrative model, where the author's control of history places him at an ironic distance from the characters' misreadings of the past and unsuccessful attempts to plot the future. The heroine's usurpation of authorial functions is not contested and defeated (as in earlier novels) but rewarded with one of James's few 'happy' endings; to judge by the success allowed to Maggie, *The Golden Bowl*—even more than *The Ambassadors*—endorses the radical power of fictions to intervene in reality.

The relations between past and future, history and plot, are regulated by the golden bowl itself. At once document and symbol, the golden bowl provides both the evidence which brings to Maggie's knowledge a passage of history and the inspiring form which indicates a response to that history. Both these functions can best be traced by beginning with the scene (chapters 33–4) in which Maggie presents the bowl to Fanny and Amerigo, forcing them to recognize its historical significance, and Fanny smashes the bowl, thereby suggesting to Maggie its possible prospective significance. The scene differs importantly from earlier Jamesian recognition scenes in that it appears to offer an uninterrupted flow between the discovery of history and the ability to plot the future; in *The Portrait of a Lady*, Isabel's recognition of the meaning of the past spells the end of her attempts to plot against it, while in *The Ambassadors* Strether's allegiance to his fictions continues in spite of, rather than because of, the impact of the recognition scene by the river. In *The Golden Bowl* the linked retrospective and prospective functions of the bowl at first appear to bring into unbroken relation the past truth it signifies, the fiction it inspires and the plot it licenses. However, this effect is in fact only achieved through the instability and perversity of the bowl's documentary and symbolic functions; once unravelled, the links between history, plot, and the bowl which connects them, may be seen to be obscure, perverse, even arbitrary. This has important consequences for the view of fictions explored in the novel.

'The golden bowl put on, under consideration, a sturdy, a conscious perversity; as a "document," somehow, it was ugly, though it might have a decorative grace' (*GB* 406). So considers Fanny Assingham in the scene in which Maggie asks for her response to the bowl and to the story of which it is 'evidence'— the story of a former intimacy and revived illicit relationship between Maggie's husband, Amerigo, and her stepmother, Charlotte. Maggie confronts her friend (whom she suspects of knowing more than she has admitted) and then her husband with the bowl, and their responses test the documentary function she has claimed for it.

Maggie sees the golden bowl as incontestable evidence of the secret relationship between her husband and her stepmother. By a strange coincidence, the bowl, which she had bought as a present for her father, is the same one that Charlotte, on a secret outing with Amerigo before his wedding, had considered buying, first for Maggie, and then for Amerigo himself. The shopkeeper who has sold the bowl to Maggie later comes to see her to confess that it is flawed and therefore not worth the price paid for it, nor worthy of the use for which it is intended. While at Maggie's house, he recognizes photographs of Charlotte and Amerigo and remembers their visit to his shop, which he describes to Maggie. He tells her of their wish to make presents to each other (429), and of his 'conviction' of their 'intimacy' which, despite their attempts at precautions and secrecy, they were not able to hide from him (446). From this testimony to their behaviour just before her marriage, Maggie infers that the pair were 'intimate' long before she met Amerigo, and that they have continued their affair since their respective marriages; this confirms her suspicions that they have been deceiving and making use of her, arranging their activities to enable them to conduct a relationship from which she is excluded. In Maggie's mind, there is no doubt

of the bowl's full character as evidence of this history: by means
of it, everything is 'fully, intensely, admirably explained' (407); it
makes her 'finally sure, knowing everything, having the fact, in
all its abomination, so utterly before her that there was nothing
else to add' (421).

The bowl's evidentiary status is reinforced by other documents—the photographs of Amerigo and Charlotte that prompt
the shopkeeper to tell his story, and the written evidence
that allows him to tell Maggie the exact date of their visit,
'by reason of a transaction of importance, recorded in his books,
that had occurred but a few hours later' (447). This network
of 'traces' confirms Colonel Assingham's view that Amerigo
and Charlotte could not have conducted an affair 'completely
without witnesses', that there must be 'evidence, up and down
London', that they will somehow have given themselves away
(383). Fanny Assingham believes that they will expertly have
'known *how*' to bury the evidence of their affair, but her belief
in their ability to cover their tracks is outweighed by the Colonel's plain (and patriotic) conviction: 'People are always traceable, in England, when tracings are required. . . . Murder will
out' (384).

However, although there is never any doubt about the accuracy
of Maggie's inferences, the connection between evidence and
significance seems rather strained. Amerigo, not surprisingly,
tries to argue this, and although his self-defence is of course
self-interested, he raises an objection which the reader may share:
'You're apparently drawing immense conclusions from very small
matters' (426), he warns Maggie. He offers an alternative explanation for his visit to the shop with Charlotte—the ostensible one,
of trying to find a present for Maggie—but Maggie will not be
moved from her interpretation of events. Later, he makes 'his
nearest approach to a cross-examination' (444) over the question
of the shopkeeper's motive for coming to see her and telling her
his story, and in going over it again, 'Maggie had felt her explanation weak; but there were the facts, and she could give no
other' (444–5). In the improbability of the man's motive for
confessing the flaw in the bowl Amerigo sees a possible loophole
in Maggie's argument, a chance to persuade her that she is
in error; were the reader not already in possession of the facts
(reported by the narrator in the first chapters of the novel), he

or she might also feel tempted to doubt the plausibility of her explanation. What is interesting is how little this worries Maggie—any *invraisemblance* simply cannot be helped; it does not, in her eyes, compromise her possession of the truth. The reader's position is a strange one: we know that Charlotte and Amerigo have been having an affair, but the golden bowl and the shopkeeper's story could only be evidence of this to a mind already (like Maggie's) predisposed to believe they are guilty.

The bowl's questionable status as evidence recalls the situation in *The Portrait of a Lady*, when the Countess Gemini confronts Isabel with the story of the deceptions practised on her by her husband and his former lover, Madame Merle. In fact, the resemblance between the 'something detected' (*PL* iii. 10) in each case is reinforced by the fact that the imagery used to describe the episode in the earlier novel is actualized in the later novel. Whereas 'Isabel sat staring at her companion's story as at a bale of fantastic wares that some strolling gipsy might have unpacked on the carpet at her feet' (*PL* iii. 187), Maggie is told her story by a set of circumstances attached to an actual object, extracted from the romantically heterogeneous collection of wares for sale in the Bloomsbury shop of an equally exotic (Jewish, polyglot) antiquarian. The use of the image in *The Portrait of a Lady* and of the object in *The Golden Bowl* both recall James's praise for Turgenev's realistic characterizations, part of his ability to construct a convincing illusion of his novels' referentiality: 'We feel as if the author could show us documents and relics; as if he had her portrait, a dozen letters, some of her old trinkets' (*LC* ii. 970). Yet, as I argued earlier, although the Countess's revelation is the means by which historical information is conveyed to Isabel, confirming various hints from the narrator to the reader, it is at the same time a point of stress where the distinction between truth and lies is confused, and the historical role of the narrator is both usurped and undermined by this notoriously untruthful character. There is a similar instability about the use of the golden bowl as a document. Of course, in neither case is there ultimately any doubt that the version of history revealed is true; in contrast to works such as *In the Cage*, *The Turn of the Screw*, and *The Sacred Fount*, where it is difficult or impossible to tell exactly what has happened, in the earlier and the later novels there are

definite facts, pieces of objective information. Yet there seems to
be a fortuitous accuracy about the stories told by both the Countess and the bowl; neither conforms to a forensic ideal. The
'conscious perversity' which Fanny attributes to the bowl recalls
the perversity behind the Countess's determination finally to tell
her story, suggesting not so much a plotted duplicity as her
notoriously irresponsible attitude to the truth and her love of
gossip and of trouble-making; yet Isabel, herself perverse, accepts
the information as something 'to which the very frailty of the
vessel in which it had been offered her only gave an intrinsic
price' (*PL* iii. 196). The image of the unreliable witness as frail
vessel most obviously evokes the bowl itself, structurally flawed
and materially weak, despite its sturdy appearance: although we
know that its witness is not in this case unreliable, we may
wonder if there is for Maggie, as for Isabel, a perversity in
accepting such testimony. *The Portrait of a Lady* also offers
another image associating a frail vessel with duplicity and treachery. The cracked porcelain cup of which Madame Merle, near the
end of the novel, warns Osmond to be careful, is a 'precious
object' (*PL* iii. 160) which may symbolize either her plot, which
is falling apart as the marriage between Isabel and Osmond
disintegrates, or indeed herself, whom she has earlier likened to a
vessel 'chipped and cracked' but (like the golden bowl) 'cleverly
mended' (*PL* i. 249); in either case, it suggests something not to
be trusted.[1]

Ironically, the episode betraying the intimacy of the lovers took
place at a time when they were not intimate and when, although
they may have been commemorating the past, they had every
intention of leaving it behind them and pursuing new courses.
There are therefore two things to be noticed about the bowl's
function as a document. First, it is a perverse document—it
signifies what is not; it signifies the affair by referring to a time
when there was no affair and no intention of one. Secondly, its
power to signify depends on what is brought to it, rather than

[1] The image of 'frail vessels' appears again in the preface to *The Portrait of a
Lady*, where James quotes George Eliot to support his investment of narrative
meaning in female centres of consciousness (*LC* ii. 1078–9); here, the emphasis is
on emotional appeal rather than epistemological uncertainty, although it should
be remembered that 'centres' such as Maisie, Fleda, and the telegraphist create
both.

what is extracted from it: Maggie brings her suspicions, and finds confirmation of them; Fanny brings her determination not to admit suspicion, and finds in the bowl a signification of innocence where Maggie had found one of guilt.

The bowl's unstable quality as a document is most fully brought out under Fanny's consideration. Although she is already sure that Amerigo and Charlotte are guilty, Fanny takes refuge from the burden of knowledge in her ignorance of the precise connection to be made between the bowl and Charlotte's and Amerigo's liaison: 'I don't know, you see, what you now consider that you've ascertained; nor anything of the connection with it of that object you declare so damning' (406). Yet she inwardly accepts Maggie's conviction as having an authority independent of the bowl's character as evidence. 'There was a force in the Princess's mere manner about it that made the detail of what she knew a matter of minor importance' (408–9), and this reinforces Fanny's earlier sense of the validity of intuitive knowledge, explained to her husband during one of their interminable discussions about Maggie: 'It isn't a question of belief or of proof, absent or present; it's inevitably, with her, a question of natural perception, of insurmountable feeling. She irresistibly *knows* that there's something between them' (382). Now Maggie has what she considers to be proof, and makes it the foundation of her allegations ('I think I may say that *I* depend on it' (408)). Yet Fanny continues to deny—and indeed to refuse to hear—the connection made between the bowl and what it is supposed to signify.

Before her discovery of the bowl, Maggie had felt:

Her grasp of appearances was thus out of proportion to her view of causes; but it came to her then and there that if she could only get the facts of appearance straight, only jam them down into their place, the reasons lurking behind them, kept uncertain, for the eyes, by their wavering and shifting, wouldn't perhaps be able to help showing. (324)

The bowl tells a story which brings appearances and causes into line, and it is thus, to Maggie, a simplifying object. To Fanny, however, it is 'that complicating object on the chimney as to which her condition, so oddly even to herself, was that both of recurrent wonder and recurrent protest' (415). The element of 'protest' in her response to it is the desire to detach appearances from causes, as Maggie has connected them. Fascinated by the cup, she approaches it,

> quite liking to feel that she did so, moreover, without going closer to her companion's vision. She looked at the precious thing—if precious it was—found herself in fact eyeing it as if, by her dim solicitation, to draw its secret from it, rather than suffer the imposition of Maggie's knowledge. (408)

In Fanny's mind, the bowl is an autonomous object, separable from the 'vision' it has inspired in Maggie, and she hopes to extract a reading of it different from the one Maggie has imposed upon it. Extraction of meaning, however, is not invited by the bowl itself, compellingly present but oddly impenetrable with its 'sturdy, . . . conscious perversity' (406); to Fanny, 'it was inscrutable in its rather stupid elegance, and yet, from the moment one had thus appraised it, vivid and definite in its domination of the scene' (406). As obvious as 'a lighted Christmas-tree' (406), it is both absorbent and repellent of meanings, which cluster about it without seeming to emanate from it. As Fanny had immediately realized on seeing it, 'the question was obviously not of its intrinsic value' (403). This observation may be glossed by James's contrast, in the novel's preface, between the idea of a 'value intrinsic' and a 'compositional resource' (*LC* ii. 1324). Perhaps then, it is as a compositional resource that the bowl's meaning will surface, that it will have, or appear to have, a referential value?

The problem of referentiality is raised in the earlier episode concerning the bowl, when Charlotte and Amerigo visit the Bloomsbury shop (the episode which Maggie takes as the reference for the bowl itself). As the pretext of finding Maggie a gift lapses, the question arises of Amerigo giving Charlotte a present, as a '*ricordo*' of their day together. Charlotte sees no logic in this: 'A *ricordo* from you—from you to me—is a *ricordo* of nothing. It has no reference' (77). Reference is dependent on will and desire: 'You don't refer', Charlotte tells Amerigo. '*I* refer' (77). She refers because she wishes to recall, not just this episode, but their whole past; Amerigo, who has privately resolved to make a complete break from the past, does not refer. Logically, then, Charlotte should give Amerigo a present, but this suggestion is disposed of as impossible—he cannot afford such references in his new life. If he had allowed it, she would have given him the golden bowl, not just as a *ricordo* of the one day, but as a reference to all their past intimacy. The discussion between Charlotte and Amerigo over the bowl's possible status as a *ricordo* puts forward the idea that referential value is not intrinsic, but contingent upon the compositional uses by which an object such as the bowl may be turned into a 'document' of one kind or another. This recalls the second, more aggressive half of William James's pragmatist programme, where, given that the relation between words and things ('truth') is always manufactured and arbitrary, in the forging of referential relations a creative compositional sense is advocated over the impossible attempt to discover intrinsic correspondences.[2]

In *The Golden Bowl*, *ricordi* and references are essentially disconnected. This rules out the historical model of narrative, which depends on the idea of a correspondence between word and thing, discourse and story. Yet *The Golden Bowl* is a novel in which the 'historical' is highly valued. Lacking stable historical referents, *ricordi* may nevertheless work to signify a pure historicity, as they confer historical significance on objects and scenes while having a value which is in fact purely self-referential. Like the documentary fragments obsessively pored over in modernist literature, the *ricordi* in *The Golden Bowl* are valued because they seem to indicate a process of historical signification which has in fact been broken; now the records refer only to their own lost documentary status, and have only obscure, unstable, and ambivalent connections with things outside themselves. At Fawns, Maggie and Adam go out into the garden through 'a door that had a slab with a date set above it, 1713, but in the old multiplied lettering' (111); the significance of this is never explained—the apparatus of historical documentation seems to be generating its own value (for it does, obscurely, function as a multiplier of 'historic' value for the conversation which ensues), but without the need to make reference to things other than itself. In a sense, the records of Amerigo's family at the British Museum function in this way—at best, their significance is free-floating

---

[2] William James distinguishes reality from truth, which is our belief about reality. Reality may be glimpsed, but all that can be grasped is some substitute for it, already prepared by human thinking for our consumption: 'If so vulgar an expression were allowed us, we might say that wherever we find it, it has been already *faked*' (*Pragmatism*, 119–20).

and reinterpretable. The ambiguous testimony about Amerigo's family given by these documents—Amerigo calls them 'abominable' (5), but Maggie finds in them 'beautiful associations' (400) —recalls the varying hypotheses which Hyacinth Robinson is able to form about his parentage on the basis of reports in *The Times*, which he also consults in the British Museum (*PC* iii. 86). A visit to the Museum may be linked to the discovery of truth (Maggie visits on the day she buys the golden bowl) or to the decision to plot and deceive (Charlotte visits before she comes to Amerigo with the proposition that they revive their affair). The records of Amerigo's family are a kind of touchstone for the Ververs' attitude towards him but they can testify fallaciously, as they do when Maggie, not yet having heard the shopkeeper's story, derives a sense of peace and satisfaction from them, a conviction that 'everything would come out right' (400). Even before this, the status of the records and their reference is ambivalent. When Colonel Assingham suggests that Amerigo may have invented his descent from the famous explorer in order to gain credit in the eyes of the Ververs, Fanny retorts: 'The connection's a true thing—the connection's perfectly historic', as he may check by consulting the roomful of family archives at the British Museum (56). However, she also calls the 'historic' Amerigo 'the make-believe discoverer' (55), thereby curiously destabilizing the chain of record and reference.

The function of the British Museum in *The Golden Bowl* also highlights the importance of power exercises in determining meaning. The Museum is part of the imperial theme of the novel,[3] established on the first page with descriptions of the precious objects in shop windows (like the bowl itself) that lie 'tumbled together as if, in the insolence of the Empire, they had been the loot of far-off victories' (1). The Museum, also full of such loot, is an expression of the power of the British Empire to appropriate historical records (even of countries over which it does not directly rule, such as Italy), control access to them, determine how they will be arranged and presented, and thus take charge of their meaning. Its authority as an institution can even confer meaning and authenticity by itself—in Fanny's mind, if something is in the

---

[3] Possible sources for the imperial theme of *The Golden Bowl* are discussed by Bernard Richards in 'Henry James's "Fawns" ', *Modern Language Studies*, 13 (1983), 154–68.

Museum, it must be true. Similarly, the Ververs have the economic power to appropriate Amerigo's family history for their own uses, securing associations of which they can be proud for Maggie's son (400), and thus purchasing for him a historical identity, summed up in his name, 'the Principino'. In the same way, Maggie uses her emotional and imaginative power to build up a museum of 'historic' moments which, finally, constitute her incontestable version of the truth.

Thus, in *The Golden Bowl* historical records are highly valued but their meaning often seems arbitrarily determined, negotiable according to power or desire. Amerigo finds it difficult in English culture to ascertain 'a discerned relation between a given appearance and a taken meaning' (252), and the same indirections that channel meaning in this highly masked society operate at levels even more fundamental. There is a discontinuity between given appearances and taken meanings which is focused in the attempt to underwrite the bowl's symbolic uses with a documentary status: the bowl may mean 'the whole of [Maggie's] situation' (407), mutually exclusive things, or nothing.[4]

Fanny's determination to extract from the bowl a meaning different from that imposed on it by Maggie shifts attention away from the question of the accuracy of Maggie's reading to the question of its usefulness in comparison with other possible readings. This marks the shift of interest in this novel, through *The Ambassadors*, away from the epistemological obsession of James's early and middle works. In Maggie's use of the bowl as evidence, intuitive knowledge masquerades as historical knowledge—a potentially dangerous situation resembling the Countess Gemini's willingness to make accusations 'without researches' (*NYE* iv. 364), and the governess's confounding of suspicion and knowledge in *The Turn of the Screw*. The kinds of questions such earlier works have trained us to ask—how can she know? is she deluded?—come to mind, but are irrelevant. We know that Maggie's surmises are correct and that we are not dealing with a case of deluded consciousness or unreliable narration. Rather, a different question needs to be asked: if Maggie has made the bowl mean one true thing, what other true things can it be made to

---

[4] On the bowl as 'a field of form, a formal nexus', and the source of a network of images, see Laurence Bedwell Holland, *The Expense of Vision: Essays on the Craft of Henry James* (Princeton, NJ: Princeton University Press, 1964), 348–9.

mean? This is what Fanny asks herself, and the bowl's referential instability helps her to cast around for new compositional meanings.

Although she knows it to be retrospectively correct, Fanny rejects Maggie's reading of the bowl as evidence, because it is prospectively destructive. 'I don't believe in this, you know' she says (415) and smashes the bowl, the evidence of Charlotte's and Amerigo's adultery: 'Whatever you meant by it—and I don't want to know *now*—has ceased to exist' (416). Of course, she does know what was meant by it, but her idea is that when the evidence is destroyed, its reference will also cease to exist. This is in accord with her belief that 'the forms . . . are two-thirds of conduct' (277); if forms generate conduct, a broken bowl will generate a broken relationship. While the bowl is the confirmation of the suspicion that 'everything has happened' (321), the smashed bowl underwrites the fiction that 'Nothing *has* happened' (284). Socially, Fanny makes her presence signify the same thing as the bowl's absence—for Maggie she becomes a value, but 'a value only for the clear negation of everything', signifying the 'unimpaired beatitude' of Maggie and Amerigo (435). In a way, then, Charlotte's statement in the Bloomsbury shop is prophetic: Fanny smashes the bowl and claims that whatever Maggie meant by it 'has ceased to exist' (416), and by the time Maggie has finished rearranging their lives the reference, as well as the sign, has truly been destroyed. The bowl (or the idea of it) has indeed become 'a *ricordo* of nothing. It has no reference' (77).

Or rather, it begins to have a new reference. The idea of the bowl, whole, 'as it *was* to have been' (440), becomes an image for the projected 'unimpaired beatitude' that Maggie intends to produce. There is thus an important shift of reference: as evidence, the bowl referred to the adultery of Charlotte and Amerigo; as an image for the future it refers to the saved marriage of Maggie and Amerigo. Once again, reference is the product of will, but there are further perversities: it is only when it has been broken that the bowl can refer to the whole relationship of Maggie and Amerigo, and the *ricordo* itself has to be destroyed in order to make this new reference possible. Moreover, the image employed is completely fictional: even when it was whole, the bowl was always flawed, yet Maggie wishes to take it as the image for a flawless happiness, without a crack.

The use of a fictitious bowl as the sign for the goals Maggie seeks to achieve is appropriate because these goals are themselves only to be achieved through the use of fictions. Waiting for Amerigo, who is late in returning from the house party he has attended with Charlotte at Matcham, Maggie 'knew herself again in presence of a problem, in need of a solution for which she must intensely work' (309). When she discovers that the problem is, indeed, Amerigo's infidelity with Charlotte, Maggie does not choose to respond in the manner expected of wronged wives—with accusations, demands, hysteria. Rather, she chooses to work, intensely but indirectly, to solve this problem, finding her solution in the form of a fiction.

The idea of fiction as a mode of problem-solving was explored in *The Ambassadors*, having been associated in less developed form with characters such as Eugenia in *The Europeans* and Miriam in *The Tragic Muse*. In each case, some form of lying was involved, as a means of proposing new ways of interpreting or arranging experience. The basis of the fiction employed by Maggie is first suggested by Fanny to Colonel Assingham as a way of dealing with the possibility that Amerigo and Charlotte may be deceiving their *sposi*. 'What was the basis, which Fanny absolutely exacted, but that Charlotte and the Prince must be saved—so far as consistently speaking of them as still safe might save them?' (269). The Assinghams develop this into a compact of ignorance:

'We know nothing on earth—!' It was an undertaking he must sign.
So he wrote, as it were, his name. 'We know nothing on earth.' It was like the soldiers' watchword at night. (284)

The epistemological dead-end which, in earlier works by James, was so often the last word on the characters' attempts to interpret their own experience, here becomes the starting-point for a new attempt to resist some kinds of experience and make possible other kinds. Fanny articulates this emphatic blankness: 'Nothing—in spite of everything—*will* happen. Nothing *has* happened. Nothing *is* happening' (284). There is surely a self-referential joke here—of the kind taken to extraordinary lengths in *The Sacred Fount*—as this sounds like the familiar complaint of readers that 'nothing happens' in a Jamesian novel; yet the parodic formula is also the essence of a radical fiction which aims to wipe out some events and leave room only for certain other, chosen, ones to take place: in other words, to control history.

It is in terms of this idea of saving ignorance that Fanny decides that she must lie for Maggie and

> lie *to* her, up and down, and in and out—it comes to the same thing. It will consist just as much of lying to the others too: to the Prince about one's belief in *him*; to Charlotte about one's belief in *her*; to Mr. Verver, dear sweet man, about one's belief in everyone. So, we've work cut out—with the biggest lie, on top of all, being that we *like* to be there for such a purpose. (376)

Thus, when Maggie, full of suspicions, but not yet in possession of the evidence of the golden bowl, implores Fanny to tell what she knows about Amerigo and Charlotte, she says, 'I see no "awfulness"—I suspect none' (370); in reply to Maggie's direct question whether Charlotte and Amerigo are 'in act and in fact' lovers (371), she swears by her 'positive word as an honest woman' that she has never entertained this idea (374). Although with 'the outbreak of the definite' accompanying the discovery of the golden bowl (409) Fanny later abandons the pretence of ignorance when talking privately with Maggie, her belief that denial may somehow be a saving value continues to give Maggie the basis for a public line of action—the idea, imaged by the smashed bowl, that 'nothing has happened'.

How does this fiction, which is the basis of Maggie's success, compare with the fiction of the 'virtuous attachment' in *The Ambassadors*? In that novel, little Bilham's lie becomes the basis of an exploratory, and to some extent redemptive, fiction: the idea, as Strether accepts and uses it, involves the notion that the relationship may be made virtuous by calling it virtuous (and that Madame de Vionnet may become a heroine if spoken of as such), but it also demonstrates that giving credit for virtue may reveal ways in which the relationship is already virtuous. Like William James's theory of pragmatism, it raises the possibility of changing the future by means of a creative discrepancy between language and reality, but it derives this possibility only from a practice, faithful to reality, of exploring the meanings of terms by finding their cash-value in experience. By contrast, the central fiction of *The Golden Bowl*, as propounded by Fanny, but even more as taken over by Maggie, is concerned only with prospective redefinitions of experience. The lovers will, under pressure of the idea, become innocent, but Maggie has little interest in using this proposition to discover ways in which they may be regarded as already 'innocent'. For her, the future is available for redefinition, but the meaning of the past is not negotiable. Or rather, the only retrospective function of her fiction is not to reinterpret the past, but to erase it. Her use of fictions resembles the potentially totalitarian uses of pragmatism for which William James was criticized.[5]

The precise differences between Maggie's and Strether's use of fictions can only be brought out by a more detailed comparison. I wish to look especially at three areas: lies, jokes and games, and the development of fictional contracts.

Leo Bersani describes *The Golden Bowl* as a drama 'involving the mutation of lies into redemptive fictions'.[6] As he points out, the action of the novel concerns the struggle for supremacy between competing arrangements of reality, rather than a straight-forward battle between a truth and a lie; Maggie opposes an arrangement of the couples which she had, unwittingly, abetted, and now 'the only status given to the truth she denies is that of a compositional invitation which she has merely to withdraw'.[7] Maggie's lie resists not so much the truth as a rival power of arrangement: 'I live in the midst of miracles of arrangement, half of which, I admit, are my own' (367). Thus, the power to control the truth resides with the best liar, and the contest between Maggie and Charlotte becomes most intense when, on the terrace at Fawns, Charlotte demands to know whether Maggie has any complaint against her. Charlotte's lie—that she has consciously committed no fault—is pitted against Maggie's lie—that she does not feel wronged and accuses Charlotte of nothing. At first the advantage seems to lie with Charlotte: pre-empting accusations, and forcing Maggie to agree to her innocence, she seems to have

[5] In a sustained attack on pragmatism, Vernon Lee suggested that the 'will-to-believe' raised the possibility of the violent imposition of the will of an arbitrary power on others; see *Vital Lies: Studies of Some Varieties of Recent Obscurantism*, 2 vols. (London: John Lane, Bodley Head, 1912), i. 90. Marius Bewley argues that the governess in *The Turn of the Screw* exemplifies the possible evil side of pragmatism: see *The Complex Fate: Hawthorne, Henry James and Some Other American Writers* (London: Chatto & Windus, 1952), 149.

[6] Leo Bersani, 'The Jamesian Lie', *Partisan Review*, 36 (1969), 58.

[7] Ibid. 73.

turned all the elements of Maggie's 'challenge', gradually built up to unsettle Charlotte's sense of success, into 'a mixture that ceased to signify' (462). However, Maggie, inspired by the example of Amerigo's lie to Charlotte (that Maggie knows nothing), which had 'given her the clue and set her the example' (464), sees how their shared lie places her with Amerigo in a complicity against Charlotte. It in fact sets a limit, not to further action on Maggie's part, but to further action on Charlotte's; it gives her no more challenges to make, nowhere else to go with her uncertainty and distress. In an image which recalls Roderick Hudson's attempt to prove himself worthy of Christina Light (*RH* ii. 137–41), Maggie finds in her lie both a way of accomplishing what she desires and a new, perverse morality:

she had kept in tune with the right, and something, certainly, something that might be like a rare flower snatched from an impossible ledge, would, and possibly soon, come of it for her. The right, the right—yes, it took this extraordinary form of her humbugging, as she had called it, to the end. It was only a question of not, by a hair's breadth, deflecting into the truth. (465)

How does this use of the lie differ from that explored in *The Ambassadors*? The primary difference is the question of the intention to deceive. Strether finally classifies little Bilham's lie as only 'a technical lie' (*Amb.* 439): its purpose is to offer Strether a perspective from which he may discover new meanings of the term 'virtuous', rather than to deceive him about literal actions and events. On the other hand, Maggie's lie to Charlotte creates a 'baffled consciousness' for which she finds the image of a caged bird. 'The cage was the deluded condition, and Maggie, as having known delusion—rather!—understood the nature of cages' (449). The glass pane against which Maggie had 'flattened her nose' in the attempt to find out about Amerigo's and Charlotte's affair becomes a wall of Charlotte's cage, 'the glass Mrs. Verver might, at this stage, have been frantically tapping, from within, by way of supreme, irrepressible entreaty' (520). The glass cage recalls the situation of the telegraphist in *In the Cage*, so pointedly left behind by Strether at the beginning of *The Ambassadors*. Between them, Amerigo and Maggie have put Charlotte in the caged, deluded condition of so many of James's earlier heroes and heroines while they stand outside the cage with authorial privilege. Maggie lacks the 'provision of irony' (489) necessary to enjoy this position and indeed has a large store of imaginative sympathy for Charlotte; nevertheless, her successful lying gives her the control of the future which functions as an ironic commentary on Charlotte's own attempts at power through falsification. Like *The Ambassadors*, *The Golden Bowl* differs from earlier James novels in that it allows its protagonist out of the cage of delusion with a power to create rather than merely accept experience; however, for Maggie this is achieved only at the price of putting Charlotte in the caged condition, and the imagery of imprisonment and bafflement associated with Charlotte for the rest of the novel—especially the image of her being led about by Adam on a 'silken noose' (521)—turns the whole issue of victory through fictions sour. In *The Ambassadors* the use of the 'technical lie' had led to the discovery of new knowledge; in *The Golden Bowl*, the lie intended to deceive is an expression of the power to baffle and enclose, rather than enrich, consciousness.

This can be seen in the ways in which deception is associated with the word 'right'. The various uses of this word to describe various compositional experiments conducted by different characters throughout the novel generate a formal and moral complex reminiscent of the shifting meanings of the words 'right', 'good', and 'virtuous' in *The Ambassadors*. However, in *The Golden Bowl* the discovery of the right form generating the right conduct is not exploratory and provisional, as in *The Ambassadors*, but a question of power, leading to a unitary ideal: different versions of the 'right' cannot coexist, since they must serially defeat and usurp each other. Thus, Charlotte's and Amerigo's affair expresses their interpretation of the 'right' way to make use of their situation, a situation created for them by Fanny's idea of the 'right' way to behave towards her friends—by marrying them off. The lovers' idea of the right puts Fanny's fatally in the wrong. When Charlotte points out that Fanny is condemned to silence by her inability to admit that she has been 'frivolously mistaken', Amerigo replies: 'All the more that she wasn't. Everything's right, . . . and everything will stay so' (242). As a deceptive point of view, this proposes new interpretations of the word 'right' which are utterly invalidated by Maggie's own deceptions. Against the fiction that everything is right she proposes her own, that nothing has happened, generating a new view of the right which places

Charlotte's and Amerigo's adventure into speculative philosophy, like Fanny's reliance on conventional morality before them, in the light of a frivolous mistake. Maggie's view of the right prevails because she is the most successful liar and her lies are definitive rather than exploratory.

Jokes and play are less important in *The Golden Bowl* than in *The Ambassadors*, although Maggie's whole plan of indirect action may be seen as confirming Amerigo's observation that 'it was the English, the American sign that duplicity, like "love," had to be joked about. It couldn't be "gone into" ' (9). In *The Golden Bowl* the use of fictive issues as indirect routes to serious questions often has a sad or desperate quality, as the characters find themselves 'avoiding the serious, standing off, anxiously, from the real' (469). The player who derives most 'fun' (62) from the game of indirection is Fanny Assingham, but even her activity is ominously likened to the game of 'forfeits' (198). The smile that covers Maggie's 'humbugging' is described as 'convulsive', a smile 'that didn't play, but that only, as might have been said, worked' (517). Maggie often refers to the process through which she must 'intensely work' (309) as a game, but the many game images in the novel are curiously unplayful. With her father 'she might yet, as at some hard game, over a table, for money, have been defying him to fasten upon her the least little complication of consciousness' (348). In another image she is her father's gambling partner, frustrated by her need to protect him from the truth; 'there was a card she could play, but there was only one, and to play it would be to end the game' (311):

That hideous card she might in mere logic play—being by this time, at her still swifter private pace, intimately familiar with all the fingered pasteboard in her pack. But she could play it only on the forbidden issue of sacrificing him; the issue so forbidden that it involved even a horror of finding out if he would really have consented to be sacrificed. (365)

Games that involve such horrors reveal the high stakes of the power-plays expressed in this novel through competing lies and fictions; like Maggie's smile, these are games which do not so much play as work.

In *The Ambassadors*, Strether's game in Notre Dame, in which he invented identities for various unknown people in the cathedral, led directly to the establishment of a fictional contract with

Madame de Vionnet which becomes the basis for his entire shift
of values and loyalties. Similar contracts operate in *The Golden
Bowl* and contribute to, although they do not entirely account
for, Maggie's success. In a fictional contract, something that is
not (yet) the truth is proposed as a way of solving a problem
where circumstance is in conflict with need or desire: the fiction
is a bridge between the actual and the desired state of affairs. The
partner in the contract agrees to suspend disbelief in order to try
out the possible rearrangement of reality which is being proposed. Both parties must be aware of the discrepancies involved:
the contract is invalidated by deceit, error, or delusion. A kind of
fictional contract is established between Amerigo and Maggie
after Maggie confronts him with the bowl as evidence that she
'knows' of his affair with Charlotte. Maggie states her knowledge, but feels a 'sudden split between conviction and action':

They had begun to cease, on the spot, surprisingly, to be connected;
conviction, that is, budged no inch, only planting its feet the more firmly
in the soil—but action began to hover like some lighter and larger, but
easier form, excited by its very power to keep above ground. It would be
free, it would be independent, it would go in—wouldn't it?—for some
prodigious and superior adventure of its own. What would condemn it,
so to speak, to the responsibility of freedom—this glimmered on Maggie
even now—was the possibility, richer with every lapsing moment, that her
husband would have, on the whole question, a new need of her, a need
which was in fact being born between them in these very seconds. (421)

Conviction is concerned with 'the things we cannot possibly *not*
know, sooner or later', but action pursues 'the things that can
reach us only through the beautiful circuit and subterfuge of our
thought and our desire' (*LC* ii. 1063). Reversing the pattern of
The Portrait of a Lady, in *The Golden Bowl* imagination displaces detection as the epistemological mode governing the characters' understanding of their experience.[8] Maggie phrases her
account of what the bowl signifies less as an accusation, requiring

---

[8] This shift of attention away from proving 'some fact in issue' (254) is central
to Alexander Welsh's reading of *The Golden Bowl* in *Strong Representations:
Narrative and Circumstantial Evidence in England* (Baltimore: Johns Hopkins
University Press, 1992), 236–56. I agree with Welsh that the novel preaches 'the
lesson that experience involves distortions of reality and only rarely shares the
same ideal aim as the finding of a fact' (254); however, unlike him I find Maggie's
fiction as punitive and conclusive as the modes of proof she rejects.

an admission, denial, or explanation, than as a statement of the fruits of her own intelligence, demanding some more imaginative tribute. Presenting the bowl primarily as evidence, not of Amerigo's guilt, but of the fact that she is not 'too stupid to have arrived at knowledge' (440), Maggie implicitly says to her husband: 'Look at the possibility that, since I *am* different, there may still be something in it for you—if you're capable of working with me to get that out' (422). For his part, Amerigo, while considering the value of this, does not waste time on conventional responses; 'for though he had, in so almost mystifying a manner, replied to nothing, denied nothing, explained nothing, apologised for nothing, he had somehow conveyed to her that this was not because of any determination to treat her case as not "worth" it' (443). Rather, after their second interview, Maggie 'had imagined him positively proposing to her a temporary accommodation', 'the tacitly offered sketch of a working arrangement': this is, that if she will leave him his 'reserve', he will give her in return 'something or other, grown under cover of it', even though he does not yet know what this will be (443).

Maggie's articulation of the contract she believes her husband is proposing to her (for, like her own offer, it is unexpressed) has a certain desperation in the face of the failure of expected responses—'she *had* to represent to herself that she had spiritually heard' some such offer (444)—but it gives her the provisional sense of a new distribution of confidence, which sees Amerigo working with her in a deep plan from which others, especially Charlotte, are excluded, and this 'sketch of a working arrangement' foreshadows the final arrangement of the couples for which she is aiming. And so it works out: Maggie offers Amerigo a view of herself as desirable which, provisionally accepting, he comes to believe in; Amerigo asks her to accept an idea of him as not having any crime for which to answer and indeed, finally, he does not. Through these undertakings, the fiction of 'unimpaired beatitude' (435) realizes itself. The process involves, on Maggie's part, a deliberate cultivation of the blindness that, earlier in the novel, Amerigo had found so irritating. At Matcham he had found her innocent faith in him, 'the extraordinary substitute for perception' in her consciousness, 'a state of mind that was positively like a vicarious good conscience, cultivated ingeniously on his behalf, a perversity of pressure innocently persisted in' (237).

After her discovery of the truth, Maggie persists in this 'perversity of pressure', not innocently or deludedly but in full knowledge of its discrepancy from the truth, and with Amerigo knowing that she knows this. Maggie's coercive, saving blindness is an artistic imitation of delusion which defines what must be excluded from her vision of the future. The result is successful—the vicarious good conscience cultivated on her husband's behalf is, with his acquiescence, able finally to grow independently and to correspond to some reality. Amerigo's complicity with the indirections of this method is such that, at the end of the novel, when Maggie finally asks whether he accepts and recognizes her knowledge, he makes no distinction between 'truth' and 'good faith' (535), his interest in his past with Charlotte effectively displaced by his fascination with the fictions Maggie has proposed.

The complicity between Amerigo and Maggie places Charlotte in a 'deluded condition' (449) precluding her from full participation in fictional contracts, which rely on an enlightened attitude by both partners towards what is involved. Maggie's relations with Charlotte are also characterized by an intention to deceive which again violates the spirit of a fictional contract. Indeed, the kiss of 'conscious perjury' (465) that seals the apparent understanding reached by Maggie and Charlotte after their conversation on the terrace at Fawns darkly parodies the kind of agreement reached by Maggie and Amerigo (or Strether and Madame de Vionnet). Each is 'conscious' of lying, but each intends to deceive the other, and it is only under the pressure of circumstances that Charlotte will, in reality rather than just in appearance, accept the version of herself—as Adam's loyal wife and Maggie's loyal friend—that Maggie offers her.

Moreover, while Maggie forces Charlotte to accept her fictions, it is only after she is sure of her success with Amerigo that she will participate in any fictions proposed by Charlotte. In their encounter in the garden at Fawns at the end of the novel, when Maggie's victory over Charlotte for Amerigo's attention is secure, Maggie gives her stepmother a space in which she can create her own fiction—the idea that Maggie has worked against her relationship with Adam, and that it is only by returning to America with him that Charlotte can save their marriage. Maggie works with Charlotte on this idea (which exactly suits her own plans) and lies to endorse it; however, it is not clear whether she has really deceived Charlotte. If she has not, the situation has elements of a fictional contract—Maggie and Charlotte agreeing to a fictional proposition under cover of which they can rearrange their situation more advantageously for all. However, if Charlotte is really deceived (and self-deceived) into thinking that her idea is true, or even that Maggie thinks she believes it, then the situation involves elements of delusion that make it an expression of competing plots rather than complicit fictions. Maggie feels that Charlotte, defending her interests, 'might truly have been believing in her passionate parade' (512); the amount of deceit and delusion involved is unclear, but there is little sense that Maggie and Charlotte are really working together. Indeed, Charlotte's proposed fiction is absolutely controlled by Maggie's intentions for her, and Maggie directs her friend's reading of their situation just as, in this scene, she literally directs her reading of fiction. As a 'pretext' (506) for approaching Charlotte in the garden, Maggie brings her the first volume of a novel of which Charlotte has, mistakenly, taken only the second. While Amerigo occupies himself in London, possibly with 'books to arrange' (502), Maggie pursues her plan for their marriage through her own arrangement of books. The 'pretext' of helping Charlotte both allows Maggie to carry out, and itself figures, one of her 'miracles of arrangement' (367) whereby she corrects arrangements made by other characters and substitutes her own definitive order: '*This* is the beginning; you've got the wrong volume, and I've brought you out the right' (508). Charlotte attempts to take control of her situation with a present tense assertion which is poised between being a false account of the past and a sincere intention for the future: 'I place my husband first' (511). But this statement of priority simply reflects the new beginning Maggie is offering her as a replacement for the false start constituted by her affair with Amerigo, which now has the status of the 'superfluous' volume that Maggie 'obligingly' takes up (510). Throughout this encounter, Maggie is at pains to play up her own weakness, to pretend that she is accepting terms dictated by Charlotte, but in fact the agreement they reach is a supreme expression of her sense of herself as an 'author' (454), absolutely controlling the lives of those around her.[9]

---

[9] I cannot agree with Yeazell that, in 'granting the others the power to invent

One of Maggie's coercive lies to Charlotte is an estimation of Charlotte's worth: 'You must take it from me that I've never thought of you but as beautiful, wonderful and good' (465). This fiction becomes the basis upon which Maggie closes her relations with her father. The whole issue of how much Adam 'knows' is never resolved, and so the question of whether Maggie and Adam have been working together in some kind of tacit complicity is never answered, for Maggie or for the reader. At her last meeting with her father, the topic of what she will lose with the loss of Charlotte begins as one of the fictive issues which relieve her from having to address the unspeakable topic of her loss of her father. However, in offering her opinion of Charlotte's worth Maggie finds in herself a 'felt sincerity' (544) which surprises her. The proposition that 'Charlotte's great' (545) becomes a basis to close upon—a means of closing the novel, but perhaps also of closing some tacit contract towards which Maggie and Adam have been working. Adam calls his marriage to Charlotte a risk that they believed in and that has worked, and in his tribute to Charlotte's beauty Maggie discerns a new tone which suggests a felt sincerity on his part also. 'They were parting, in the light of it, absolutely on Charlotte's *value*'; they allow this articulated value to fill the room, leaving it 'as if to give it play' (546). As a basis for closure of the novel, this 'value'—in some ways consciously fictive, yet arguing a 'felt sincerity'—offers the only real hint of the kind of exploratory open-endedness offered in *The Ambassadors*. The value of Charlotte, discovered through the tacit contract between Adam and Maggie always to speak of her as valuable, has possibly both a retrospective and prospective meaning, a meaning not imposed but discovered and given room to play.

Yet this is a potential development of the role of fictions which is carried out of the novel when Charlotte and Adam drive away. The peculiarly static quality of the final scene between the four characters fixes the values through which Maggie's plot has

their own saving fictions', Maggie 'does not always control the terms of the discourse' but rather 'conquers by affirming the imaginative autonomy of her victims' (*Language and Knowledge*, 107). Rather, I concur with Mark Seltzer's argument in *Henry James and the Art of Power* (Ithaca, NY: Cornell University Press, 1984), 61, that Maggie produces in others compulsions which require them to choose the regulative norms she invokes.

worked, and shows how it has come to resemble the bowl which inspired it; 'the whole scene having crystallised' as soon as Charlotte has taken her place in the room (541), Maggie's arrangement of her 'good things' (542) is complete. Visually, the effect is that of the completion of a human and cultural museum; in terms of narrative, the crystallization of the scene perfects a crystalline structure, a determination of the interaction of character and event so tightly knit that, like the idea of the flawless bowl, it cannot be split apart. Earlier, before she had any evidence for Amerigo's and Charlotte's infidelity, Maggie had felt that if Amerigo could only say the right thing to her, 'everything might crystallise for their recovered happiness at his touch' (330). She comes to realize that she must take upon herself the initiative for finding the idea around which their recovered happiness will crystallize and, in forcing others to acknowledge its truth, she finds a crystalline strength in her own coercive imagination: 'as hard . . . as a little pointed diamond, the Princess showed something of the glitter of consciously possessing the constructive, the creative hand' (392–3). The image of crystal is also linked with duplicity—Maggie's reassurance to Charlotte that she has never suspected her is extended under 'a twinkle of crystal and silver' (486)—but not with the kind of endless change and variety associated with the vision of Paris as a glittering jewel in *The Ambassadors* (*Amb.* 67). This is appropriate, because whereas Strether's use of fictions celebrates variety, Maggie's power comes from singleness of vision—the discovery of the one structure in which the elements of her situation crystallize.

In her ruthlessly unitary vision Maggie leaves behind many of the questions important in earlier works by James. The preface to *The Turn of the Screw* distinguishes between a 'crystalline' record of events and a crystalline explanation of them (*LC* ii. 1185)—a distinction essential to works which explore deluded perspectives or unreliable narration, and offer implied authorial positions distinct from these. But in *The Golden Bowl* the exploration of such a distinction never leads to any moment of real arrest, such as that when the governess in *The Turn of the Screw* asks herself 'if he *were* innocent, what then on earth was *I*?' (*TS* 166), or when Strether asks if he is 'deluded', 'fantastic and away from the truth' (*Amb.* 271), and the idea of possible discrepancies between information and interpretation is never underwritten by an ironic authorial perspective. At one point Maggie calls her suspicions of Amerigo 'the adventure of an imagination within her that possibly had lost its way' (341), and when she finds the bowl, which confirms these suspicions, she has indeed allowed herself to 'wander a little wild' (399) in the depths of Bloomsbury; yet her suspicions are vindicated, and the bowl testifies accurately. Adam offers some criticisms of the privileged social basis of their lives which, reverberating with terms reminiscent of *The Turn of the Screw*, also obscurely raise doubts about the epistemological basis of their experience. Adam speaks of the 'immorality' of their situation, of 'something haunting—as if it were a bit uncanny' in their wealth and comfort, which allows them to retreat from the world, as if 'sitting about on divans, with pigtails, smoking opium and seeing visions' (353–4). No less bizarre than this image is the suggested intrusion of a completely foreign set of literary and moral values into the novel: ' "Let us then be up and doing"—what is it Longfellow says? That seems something to ring out; like the police breaking in—into our opium den—to give us a shake' (354). Yet the authorities which in earlier James novels had policed the opium dens of the characters' imaginations—authorial irony, indifferent fate, immutable history—never do break into *The Golden Bowl*. Late in the novel Maggie raises the possibility that she has been building her plot on a mistaken perception: coming up against Charlotte's confidence in her relationship with Adam, she realizes that if there is still so much firm ground between them, perhaps 'it was only the golden bowl as Maggie herself knew it that had been broken. The breakage stood not for any wrought discomposure among the triumphant three—it stood merely for the dire deformity of her attitude toward them' (457). I disagree with Dorothea Krook's contention that this constitutes for Maggie a moment of self-doubt 'as radical and portentous' as that experienced by the governess in *The Turn of the Screw*,[10] for Maggie immediately proceeds to tackle the problem raised by the possibility of confidence between Charlotte and Adam, not as one of truth, but as one of power—she must outmanœuvre Charlotte in the bid to determine what the broken bowl stands for.

[10] Dorothea Krook, *The Ordeal of Consciousness in Henry James* (Cambridge: Cambridge University Press, 1963), 311.

Varieties of interpretation are, for Maggie, rivals to be defeated or, as Leo Bersani has pointed out, mere time-fillers which keep her imagination occupied during the essentially passive work of waiting for others to accept her primary interpretation.[11] Substantial portions of the text are given over to the narration of events and speeches which exist only in Maggie's imagination; often what appears to be real dialogue is given a phantasmal status by the admission that it is only 'what, in her mind's ear, Maggie heard' (350), that a speech apparently made by Amerigo is 'what, while she watched herself, she potentially heard him bring out' (390), that another is a speech that Charlotte 'might in fact have but just failed to make' (315). The quotation of imagined speeches testifies to Maggie's authorial propensities, as the world of *The Golden Bowl* is increasingly subsumed into Maggie's formulations of it.[12] However, the most revealing thing about these imagined speeches is their frequent redundancy; although some of them influence Maggie's action—as when she imagines the terms of the contract Amerigo may be offering her (443–4), most of them are 'foredoomed ingenuities of her pity' (520)—foredoomed, because they will be sacrificed, as having no place in her plan. The many repressed questions and potential speeches that are reproduced in the text are a kind of narrative excess, which gives the illusion of far greater variety of action, far more concrete interaction between the characters, and a much more generous entertainment of the views of others, than actually takes place. Over a family lunch with the priest, just before her final confrontation with Charlotte, Maggie goes over the possibilities of how each member of her circle may have become involved in the affair: of such possibilities 'there were always too many, and all of them things of evil when one's nerves had at last done for one all that nerves could do . . . She might, with such nerves, have supposed almost anything of anyone' (500)—even of

[11] Bersani, 'The Jamesian Lie', 76.

[12] As Norrman points out, this creates uncertainty and ambiguity in the text, although I think he underestimates the extent to which it reflects an effective, not just a desired, power of language over reality (*The Insecure World*, 118–29). Sharon Cameron argues that the unspoken utterance reflects a desire to legislate the thoughts of others, while revealing that shared reference is only a fiction; although the plot is resolved by Maggie thinking for others, the device creates a radically enigmatic 'problematic of referring'; see *Thinking in Henry James* (Chicago: University of Chicago Press, 1989), 83–121.

the Colonel or the priest. Her imagination working overtime, 'she was in the midst of a passage, before she knew it, between Father Mitchell and Charlotte' (501); yet such passages are fundamentally disconnected from the single narrative vision she is patiently waiting to crystallize. Like the extraordinarily varied narratives in which she, and the narrator, indulge at a metaphorical level, these alternative stories are expressions of the overflow of a feverish narrative imagination unable quite to confine itself to the austere discipline of the single story it has decided to endorse.[13]

Maggie's plot resembles the bowl not only in its unitary structure, but in its opacity: it is not a transparent window on a prospective reality any more than the bowl, as evidence, functions as a transparent window on a retrospective reality. What Maggie has aimed for is a perfect happiness, like the bowl as it ought to have been—'The bowl with all happiness in it. The bowl without the crack' (440). This image for her plotted future is called an 'obscured figure' (440), for, as we have seen, the idea of the unflawed bowl is purely fictitious, and the shift of references necessary to produce this image (the bowl initially refers to a wrong situation, which must be destroyed, and then to a right one, which must be achieved) makes the connection between image and idea obscure. Similarly, Maggie takes great pains to make the connection between her aims and her actions obscure to

[13] Carren Kaston notes in *Imagination and Desire in the Novels of Henry James* (New Brunswick, NJ: Rutgers University Press, 1984) that Fanny Assingham's imagined scenarios also 'introduce an irresponsible superfluity of plot, more than the novel could possibly use' (157), and argues that Maggie's superiority to Fanny as an authorial figure rests on the fact that 'she is willing to pay for the direction in which her design pushes the plot' (158), payment being made by forfeiting other possible plots (such as the plot of continued intimacy with her father). Similarly, David McWhirter argues that the need to limit the play of imagination (choosing one story at the expense of all others) is essential to both Maggie's ability to achieve her desire and the author's ability to pursue his plot and close his novel (*Desire and Love in Henry James*, 142–99). This accords with Martha Craven Nussbaum's argument that the novel shows how mature commitments are based on choices which necessitate failures of response in other quarters; see 'Flawed Crystals: James's *The Golden Bowl* and Literature as Moral Philosophy', *New Literary History*, 15 (1983), 25–50. However, my point is that Maggie carries this process too far, rendering her plot static and inflexible in its exclusion of all variant interpretations. For an alternative reading of the role of metaphor as a component, rather than an overflow, of Maggie's method, see Yeazell, *Language and Knowledge*, 41–9. Gabriel Pearson also emphasizes the coherence as well as excess of metaphor in the novel; see 'The Novel to End All Novels: *The Golden Bowl*', in *The Air of Reality*, ed. Goode, 354–60.

the others—indeed, if possible to sever any traceable connection between intention and effect. The success of her plot lies in its inscrutability and it becomes, finally, as inscrutable as the symbolic nature of the bowl itself. With regard to the tacitly complicit plot between Maggie and Adam to force Charlotte to return with him to America, it is explained that the father and daughter had, between them, 'so shuffled away every link between consequence and cause, that the intention remained, like some famous poetic line in a dead language, subject to varieties of interpretation' (531). The same could be said of Maggie's whole plot to recover and reinstate her happiness with Amerigo. Like the bowl which, functioning as evidence, had exhibited a similar discontinuity between causes and effects, Maggie's plot is a form which must be reckoned with by others, inscrutably and perversely confronting them, both inviting and defying interpretation. As perverse document and inscrutable symbol, the golden bowl coordinates evidence and plot in this novel in which a pervasive referential instability licenses the production of arbitrary fictions. This severance between intention and effect, which exploits the general problem in English culture of ascertaining 'a discerned relation between a given appearance and a taken meaning' (252), makes Maggie's plot an arbitrary imposition on reality, lacking the dynamic interaction with experience that characterized the use of fictions in *The Ambassadors*.

The idea that Maggie's fiction has an arbitrary relation to her world (as she finds it) brings us back to James's criticisms of Trollope which helped, negatively, to define his idea of fiction as history. James had criticized Trollope for declaring his authorial presence in such a way that he allows his fiction to 'give itself away' (*LC* i. 46), reminding us that he is not reporting a true story but 'telling us an arbitrary thing' (*LC* i. 1343). However, as we have seen, James's own fiction is dotted with such moments of reflexive irony—stress points, which threaten the model which absolutely distinguishes fiction from history—the most extreme example of which is the river scene in *The Ambassadors*. Maggie's account of her discovery of the significance of the bowl, which forms the central recognition scene in *The Golden Bowl*, has a similar quality. She uses the language of romance to stress the unlikeliness of the coincidence, the implausibility of her luck. The bowl is 'too strangely, almost, to believe', her proof (404); it

has 'turned witness—by the most wonderful of chances' (405); it
has brought her 'miraculously' to knowledge (408). The Prince,
arguing the arbitrariness of the conclusion she has drawn from it,
describes the coincidence in formally reflexive terms: 'I agree
with you that the coincidence is extraordinary—the sort of thing
that happens mainly in novels and plays' (428). This moment of
reflexive arrest, reminding us of the fictionality of the text, brings
James close to the kind of dropping of the historic mask for
which he criticized Trollope. Maggie is enabled to understand
and act upon the significance of the bowl because of 'the wonder
of [her] having found such a friend' (428) in the Bloomsbury
shopkeeper, whom several critics have identified with James's
authorial presence in the novel.[14] Through the shopkeeper, 'clearly the master' (74), whose fingers play over his merchandise 'as
those of a chess-player rest, a few seconds, over the board, on a
figure he thinks he may move and then may not' (76), who speaks
with such authority and possession of ' "My Golden Bowl" '
(80), James reveals his own responsibility for and power over the
novel, at the same time as he arranges for Maggie to be enabled
to assume control over her own situation. Simultaneously endorsing Maggie's authorial powers and confessing his own, at this
point James has moved as far as possible from his early practice—
designed to reinforce the idea of the narrative as history—of
disclaiming his work's fictionality while blocking his characters'
plots.

   In making a commitment to Maggie's plot, the author gives free
play to a particular idea of fiction, fundamentally different from
the model of historical narrative. Maggie's powers of authorship
are identified with a certain kind of novel, as is seen in her
manipulation of Charlotte's actions when she confronts her in the
garden at Fawns. The book over which she conducts her 'parley'
with Charlotte (508) is 'an old novel . . . in the charming original
form of its three volumes' (506)—a form which was obsolete
when *The Golden Bowl* was written. In 1894, the two most
powerful circulating libraries, Mudie's and Smith's, had joined
forces in presenting publishers with an ultimatum which rendered
the three-volume novel uneconomic to produce, and led to its

---

[14] See Holland, *The Expense of Vision*, 345–6; Kaston, *Imagination and Desire*,
154–5; and McWhirter, *Desire and Love in Henry James*, 158–60.

virtual disappearance within three years.[15] Arbitrarily determined by the success of Scott's *Waverley* in 1814, the 'three-
decker' had been the standard format of the Victorian novel, the
staple fare of the circulating libraries, and had become part of the
rhetoric of literary debate and novelistic metacommentary. Reference to the three-decker provided a way of talking about the
Victorian novel as if in quotation marks, evoking a whole cluster
of formal, thematic, and institutional associations. Typically, it
was identified with a romantic (sensational or sentimental) content, and so could be referred to in the rhetoric of realism as a
(rejected) standard of unreality.[16] It was associated with an audi-
ence-centred aesthetic, and 'the third volume' denoted a conventional happy ending, such as James had objected to in 'The Art of
Fiction' (*LC* i. 48).[17] Most notoriously, it meant an arbitrarily
imposed length, the effort to conform to which led to the use of
devices such as authorial intrusion in order to lengthen the novel
artificially.[18] In short, the qualities typically attributed to the
three-volume novel are the antithesis of the ideal of historical
narrative described by James in his early criticism. The effect of
the format in distorting narratives was so well known that Trollope joked about it in *Barchester Towers*, thereby engaging in just
the kind of authorial intrusion to which James had objected as an
infringement of historical integrity:

And who can apportion out and dovetail his incidents, dialogues, characters, and descriptive morsels, so as to fit them all exactly into 930 pages,
without either compressing them unnaturally, or extending them artificially at the end of his labour? Do I not myself know that I am at this

[15] The collapse is recounted by Griest, *Mudie's Circulating Library*, 171–5;
Keating, *Haunted Study*, 25–7; and Charles E. Lauterbach and Edward S. Lauterbach, 'The Nineteenth Century Three-Volume Novel', *PBSA*, 51 (1957), 281–4.
[16] See William Makepeace Thackeray, *Vanity Fair: A Novel without a Hero*
(London: Bradbury & Evans, 1848), 43, 621. Further examples are found in
Griest, *Mudie's Circulating Library*, 92. See also James's parody of the three-
volume novel in his letter to Thomas Sergeant Perry, 5 Aug. 1860 (*SL* 40–1).
[17] In *Barchester Towers* Trollope joked about the violation of this rule: 'A late
writer, wishing to sustain his interest to the last page, hung his hero at the end of
the third volume. The consequence was, that no one would read his novel'; see
Barchester Towers, 3 vols. (London: Longman, 1857), iii. 289.
[18] Griest (*Mudie's Circulating Library*, 92–119) discusses the effects of length
requirements on the form and content of the novel; these, and more mechanical
forms of 'padding' such as chapter chopping and increasing the leading and
margins, are discussed in Lauterbach, 'The Nineteenth Century Three-Volume
Novel', 272–81.

moment in want of a dozen pages, and that I am sick with cudgelling my brains to find them?[19]

In his review of *Far from the Madding Crowd* in 1874, James had criticized the use of 'conversational and descriptive padding' which gave the reader the sense of 'a simple "tale," pulled and stretched to make the conventional three volumes', and took the opportunity to remind Hardy of his responsibility to respect the autonomy of his data. James complained that 'the tyranny of the three volumes' (*LC* i. 1045) (which reflected the power of institutions—the circulating libraries—over literature) subjected the narrative to an external constraint violating the independence of its material. It is 'the tyranny of the three volumes' that Maggie exercises over her world, creating a factitious, inflexible form, arbitrarily imposed on experience, which reflects an irresponsible but despotic power. As such an author, Maggie's status is highly ambiguous. In conferring upon Maggie the powers of the three-volume novelist, James was not only endorsing an affront to the ideal of the historical narrative, but in one sense supporting the irresponsible powers of fiction, thereby making a pointed challenge to the old hostility to the novel. As Guinevere Griest notes, by the end of the century, 'the three-decker seemed to have inherited the obloquy formerly directed against fiction'.[20] In 1894 an article in the *Spectator* claimed that the Society of Authors, which supported the abolition of the format, had 'put the three-volumed novel on the index'.[21] Maggie is invested with the power of forbidden books, and in a way her success, which vindicates the value of fictions that escape from or rearrange reality, defies the whole nineteenth-century tradition of hostility to fiction. But attacks on the three-decker, although sometimes the vehicle for general attacks on fiction, more often stemmed from a belief that the format was itself detrimental to fiction, inhibiting its freedom and condemning it to reflect the demands of an external, institutional power, rather than engage in a flexible interaction with life.[22] These criticisms may also be made of

[19] Trollope, *Barchester Towers*, iii. 289; see also ibid. iii. 163.
[20] Griest, *Mudie's Circulating Library*, 183.
[21] 'Novels as Sedatives', *Spectator*, 73 (1894), 108.
[22] In George Gissing's *New Grub Street: A Novel*, 3 vols. (London: Smith, Elder, 1891), ii. 70, the three-volume novel is described as a 'triple-headed monster, sucking the blood of English novelists'.

Maggie's fiction, contributing to our sense of unease with her victory.

Maggie's success reinstates several values discredited in 'The Art of Fiction' and James's early works: the value of lies, of jokes (although less so than in *The Ambassadors*), and of arbitrary things. But it does so at the expense of another, paramount, Jamesian value. At the end of the novel Charlotte maintains her dignity within the only role allotted to her in Maggie's plot, just as Maggie herself has, inscrutably, worked to put her there, by clearing her actions 'of any betrayal, any slightest value, of consciousness' (541). Although the novel records, in depth, the feverish workings of an isolated consciousness (Maggie's), the power of her imagination to change reality is achieved only by blocking interaction between the consciousnesses of the various characters, and it is upon the draining away of the value of consciousness as anything to be expressed or communicated to others that the novel closes. Indeed, Maggie not only acknowledges that she does not know what her father feels, but confesses that she does not even know what she herself feels; if she did, she says, 'I should die' (504). Maggie may have left behind cages of delusion, but she has created cages of consciousness, impenetrable to others. In the end, no one really knows what anyone else has known or felt or believed, and as John Carlos Rowe points out, the resolution of the novel is achieved at the expense of all 'intersubjectivity'.[23] Maggie's extravagant propensity for imagining the thoughts and emotions of others (which takes up more and more narrative space in the novel) does not fill this lack. Her imaginings represent only a specious intersubjectivity; they reflect an impulse to dictate, not to consult, the consciousnesses of others and, as I argued earlier, the material they introduce to the narrative is fundamentally irrelevant to the plot she single-mindedly and successfully pursues. The trouble for Maggie is that she will, finally, need to consult the consciousness of another if she is to find out what her success has meant. In the last paragraphs of the novel she realizes that only Amerigo can assign a value to her achievement in saving their marriage: 'She had thrown the dice, but his hand was over her cast' (547). The value of her

---

[23] John Carlos Rowe, *Henry Adams and Henry James: The Emergence of a Modern Consciousness* (Ithaca, NY: Cornell University Press, 1976), 223.

success lies not in Amerigo's actions, which have conformed perfectly to her plot, but in his consciousness, which still remains essentially hidden from her. As, at the end of the novel, Maggie closes her eyes with 'pity and dread' (548), it is uncertain whether she has indeed begun to gain access to her husband's consciousness and, if so, whether she will find there what she is looking for.

Uncertainty of meaning does not, however, mean openness of plot, and it would be hard to imagine a plot more effectively closed than Maggie's. This is largely because of the perpetual displacement of flexible values, such as 'consciousness', into forms fixed as 'historic'. In spite of—or rather because of—its lack of respect for the data of experience, Maggie's plot acquires, through its sheer persuasive force, the status of history; it must be accepted by the others—there is nothing speculative or provisional in her rearrangement of reality. But the process of her success has nothing to do with the bases of historical narrative expounded by James in his early writings on the novel: faithfulness to received experience and deference to natural causality. Rather, her success reflects a ruthless power to erase, not only the meanings of past events but the shared consciousness of the events themselves, and to impose on others, not just a version of history, but the very events of which it consists. The value of the 'historic' now reflects not an organic connection between narrative, language, and reality, but the personal power to rewrite these connections. The final meeting between the two couples is the last in a series of 'historic' scenes where character and event crystallize into this final form of the human museum. The artifacts in Maggie's museum, like the *ricordi* in the British Museum, finally matter less as a system of reference to external realities (certainly not to past realities), than as an enclosed system testifying to the power that brought them together in this way.

The glass cages of consciousness in which the characters are imprisoned become the glass cases of Maggie's museum, which is the product of a fiction so powerful that it ceases to be fiction and attains the status of history. Maggie's success testifies to the power of a subjective vision in changing reality, but only by sacrificing the subjectivity of others. Amerigo's telegram to Charlotte, endorsing her decision to marry Adam and thus making way for her to plot the revival of their affair, asserts the principle that '*We must lead our lives as we see them*' (205). Like Isabel

Archer's similarly worded rejection of Lord Warburton's marriage proposal (*PL* i. 151), this expresses a supreme belief in the individual's liberty to plot his or her own experience. But in *The Golden Bowl*, the characters must all lead their lives as Maggie sees them, and her fundamentally corrective role places her in the position of history with regard to other people's plots. Like Isabel, Amerigo and Charlotte are punished for their wish to see life from their own point of view (*PL* iii. 230), and it is in this punitive role that Maggie's imaginative power is expressed. Maggie's crystalline vision brings the Jamesian narrative full circle: by not, for an instant, deviating by a hair's breadth into the truth (465), she creates a plot which does not conform to, but replaces, history. In doing this, in creating 'a single rightness' (330), her totalitarian radical fiction sheds the provisional and pluralistic quality of fictions explored in *The Ambassadors*. ' "Oh, I'm not afraid of history!" She had been sure of that' (5); but in 'consummately, diabolically' (281) gaining control over history, Maggie's fiction gives up the dynamic interaction with reality, and with the subjective views of others, intrinsic to Strether's fictions.

6

Counter-Realities: James's Last Phase

In 'The Future of the Novel' (1899), James abandoned the attempt to mount a philosophical defence of fiction against traditional charges of false epistemology, leaving the novel to be justified by the appearance 'from time to time' of 'some purely practical masterpiece'. His own late novels may be seen as offering such an *ad-hoc* defence of the genre as that essay proposed: ' "Why am I not so unprofitable as to be preposterous? Because I can do *that*. There!" ' (*LC* i. 102). But *The Ambassadors* and *The Golden Bowl* do not merely stand as 'practical' defences of the novel form; they also dramatize and explore theories of fiction which powerfully address philosophical and social objections to the fictive imagination while defying the authority of a historical epistemology. The theoretical defences of fiction found in these novels became the basis of James's late critical practice, which interrogates and largely abandons his earlier concern with a historiographical model for the novel. Three essays in particular from his last published critical collection, *Notes on Novelists* (1914), embody the radical theoretical shift between James's early and late thinking about the novel: 'Honoré de Balzac, 1902', a revised reading of the novelist who had most fully realized the younger James's ideal of fiction as history; 'The New Novel' (1914), in which James's assessment of modern English novelists decisively rejects many of the techniques associated with both naturalism and 'scientific' historiography; and 'The Novel in "The Ring and the Book" ' (1912), in which the novelistic imagination is liberated from the authority of historical facts and texts. These essays embody in a particularly concentrated form the anti-historical aesthetic and epistemology operating more diffusely throughout the prefaces to the *New York Edition*. However, *Notes on Novelists* was only published after the outbreak of war in 1914, and its intellectual defiance of a historically defined conception of experience was thus immediately thrown into question by this revelation of the seemingly irresistible force of history. James inscribed a copy of the book to Edmund Gosse 'Over the Abyss':[1] the war had, he felt, pulled the ground from beneath their civilization, and in particular from beneath the whole business of reading and writing fiction. The experience of war presented a formidable challenge to James's late theory of fiction, as the novelist's imagination attempted both to fathom and to span the abyss of history which opened in 1914.

Taking Liberties with History

For the late as for the early James, Balzac was 'the greatest master' of the art of fiction (*LC* ii. 119), 'the first and foremost member of his craft' (*LC* ii. 90). In his early reviews and essays James had repeatedly invoked Balzac as the very model of the novelist as historian. In 1913 he still characterized Balzac as 'an historian unprecedented, an historian documented as none had not only ever been, but had ever dreamed of being' (*LC* ii. 143), but his three late essays on Balzac register important reservations about the methods he employed to achieve this effect. While still marvelling at his powers of 'observation and certification' (ii. 146) and at the 'rank tropical forest of detail and specification' (ii. 123) in his novels, James now finds that this concentration on material detail limits the depth and range of Balzac's characterizations (ii. 149–50), while design and meaning in his work are sometimes overwhelmed by a 'flood of general reference' (ii. 124). Similar reservations had always tempered James's enthusiasm for Balzac's achievement, but when clearly focused and analysed, as they are in 'Honoré de Balzac, 1902', they call into question the whole idea of the historiographical model for fiction that James had made Balzac represent.

James's argument now was that 'the artist of the Comédie Humaine is half smothered by the historian' (*LC* ii. 94). In 1867, in his review of Anne Manning, James had praised Balzac for

---

[1] Edel, *The Life of Henry James*, v. 564.

having eschewed the 'unobstructed sky' of the story-teller in order to restrain his imagination, like the historian's, beneath a 'vast fabric of impenetrable fact [that] is stretched over his head' (*LC* i. 1154). In 1902, praise has turned to pity and regret: Balzac could not 'work in the open' because he 'had no "open" ' (*LC* ii. 103); he was trapped in a 'cage' formed by 'the complicated but dreadfully definite French world that built itself so solidly in and roofed itself so impenetrably over him' (ii. 101); and in the end his 'catastrophe' was that 'the sky . . . came down on him' (ii. 103). The image of 'hard labour' (ii. 101) associated with an imagination so constrained picks up James's earlier image of the historian as one who works 'on his hands and knees, as men work in coal-mines' (i. 1154), but intensifies its disciplinary aspect: Balzac's imagination is now seen to work 'much in the manner of a criminal condemned to hard labour for life' (ii. 101). Such excessive disciplining of the imagination by the real is now deprecated, and the application to Balzac of the cage image usually associated in James with delusion suggests that cages of fact could be as damaging as cages of fantasy to the free commerce between fiction and the world on which the transitive value of imaginative narrative depended. Endorsing such commerce, James revised his earlier attitude towards 'those smashes of the window-pane of the real' (ii. 113) which allow romance to enter Balzac's novelistic cage of facts. In his essay of 1875 on Balzac, James had dismissed as wildly improbable the episode in *Les Illusions Perdues* in which Madame d'Espard and Madame de Bargeton reject Lucien de Rubempré, and had commented that Balzac's aristocrats 'really seem at times to be the creatures of the dreams of an ambitious hairdresser who should have been plying his curling-irons all day and reading fashionable novels all the evening' (*LC* ii. 65). Here, Balzac's failure of realism is presented in terms of a readerly miseducation by fiction; James's image is drawn directly from anti-fiction rhetoric, particularly in the element of snobbery in its presentation of an 'ambitious' working-class reader led socially astray by inaccurate novels. However, in 1902 James defended the same episode on the grounds that it is '*done*' and 'all we can do is to say that the true itself can't be more than done and that if the false in this way equals it we must give up looking for the difference' (ii. 113). As Peter Brooks notes, this response 'appears to signal a greater willingness to trust the reading experience and the "pleasure of the text," rather than any preconceived notion of representation',[2] and it thus resembles Strether's decision to trust unfolding experience rather than judge by a-priori standards. James continues: 'If the great ladies in question *didn't* behave, wouldn't, couldn't have behaved, like a pair of nervous snobs, why so much the worse, we say to ourselves, for the great ladies in question' (ii. 113). He now defends Balzac in the same terms he would employ in the prefaces to justify the presentation of his own 'supersubtle fry': 'If the life about us for the last thirty years refuses warrant for these examples, then so much the worse for that life' (ii. 1229; see also ii. 1180–1). The verbal repetition links James's new reading of Balzac to his own exposition of operative irony as the 1902 essay takes up implications of Balzac's fictional programme that had been passed over in 1875. Then, James had read Balzac's claim 'to start an opposition . . . to the civil registers' (ii. 40) as a commitment to reproducing social data, but in the later essay he saw and defended the way in which Balzac's programme of 'competition' involved significant departures from this data.[3] It is in this sense that the plots of James's characters compete with the given circumstances of their lives, a tendency which was consistently blocked in James's early fiction, but was given more room to play and greater power over reality in the later works. James's redefinition of Balzac's romantic episode from the fantasy of a novel-reading hairdresser to an imposing vision of novelistic authority occurred at around the time that the hero of *The Ambassadors* and the heroine of *The Golden Bowl* were being given freedom to pursue fictions which were not crushed by the judgements of the old antipathy to the novel, but allowed to flourish as analogues for the author's own avowedly fictional enterprise.

In linking romantic affronts to the real with the exercise of the oppositional imagination that he called operative irony, James suggests a new insight into the relation between realism and censorship. The image of the smashed window-pane in 'Honoré de Balzac, 1902' repeats an image used in 'The Future of the Novel' (1899) for resistance—specifically, female resistance—to

[2] Banta (ed.), *New Essays*, 54.
[3] This is discussed by Vivien Jones in *James the Critic* (London: Macmillan, 1985), 68.

the long reign of the censors over the English novel. In that essay James noted with approval that 'we may very well yet see the female elbow itself, kept in increasing activity by the play of the pen, smash with final resonance the window all this time most superstitiously closed' (*LC* i. 109). In James's early thinking about the novel, the alignment of novelist and historian had been seen as a way of combatting censorship and claiming a new freedom for fiction; now, the shared image for the release of imaginative energy that will come from smashing both the window-pane of the real and the window-pane of superstition suggests a complicity between realism and censorship in Victorian culture, and a new awareness that a truly oppositional imagination may work most effectively by affronting rather than respecting historical models of narrative.

In 1867 James had praised Balzac for being 'as averse from taking liberties with [his material] as we are bound to conceive Mr. Motley, for instance, to be from taking liberties with the history of Holland' (*LC* i. 1155). In 1902, such an importation of historiographical standards for the novel is decisively rejected, for the 'laws' governing the activities of historian and story-teller now seem irreconcilable: 'the reporter, however philosophic, has one law, and the originator, however substantially fed, has another; so that the two laws can with no sort of harmony or congruity make, for the finer sense, a common household' (*LC* ii. 94). In 'this perpetual conflict and final impossibility' lies what James again refers to as 'Balzac's catastrophe' (ii. 94). His work is marked by a 'monstrous duality' (ii. 96) as the imaginative principle is 'perpetually dislocated by the quite opposite principle of the earnest seeker, the inquirer to a useful end', that is, the principle of research (ii. 95). James comments that Balzac is 'clearly quite unwitting that in handing over his *data* to his twin-brother the impassioned economist and surveyor, the insatiate general inquirer and reporter, he is in any sort betraying our confidence' (ii. 96). This charge that the dislocation of the law of the story-teller by the law of the historian constitutes a betrayal of the reader's confidence reverses James's famous indictment of Trollope for a 'betrayal of [his] sacred office' (i. 46) in not handing over his material to the methods of the historian. The charge against Balzac is significant in that it shows James dissociating readerly confidence in fiction from a historical epistemology, just as in *The Ambassadors* and *The Golden Bowl* questions of confidence are worked out by ignoring or defying historical modes of proof.

The language in which James describes the divergence of the responsibilities of novelist and historian is also revealing about his place in the changing configuration of theoretical positions that helped to create the modernist era in English fiction. James's assertion that history and fiction cannot make 'a common household' (*LC* ii. 94) recalls one of Burton's comments on the *Arabian Nights*, approvingly quoted by Hall Caine in his romance manifesto of 1890, 'The New Watchwords of Fiction': 'Fiction is not the mere handmaid of History; she has a household of her own'.[4] James, of course, never espoused the ideological programme which underwrote this and many other late nineteenth-century manifestos of romance, but he did come to share their questioning of the cultural and epistemological authority of currently dominant modes of realism, a questioning which helps to place *Notes on Novelists* as an early document in English modernism.[5]

Like the late nineteenth-century champions of romance, James now objected to the domination of modern fiction by a social realism which worked through naturalistic modes of close notation of the material world. The romantic reaction against this often had a moral basis, and while James was far from adopting the kind of idealist rhetoric used by Caine, Lang, or Saintsbury in their attacks on realism, he had his own long-standing quarrel with naturalism on the grounds of 'taste'. However, as Vivien Jones observes, 'In *Notes on Novelists* the conservative idealist and the modernist merge',[6] particularly in the essay on Zola in which the moral-aesthetic appeal to 'taste' is now part of a challenge to the epistemological grounds of Zola's 'scientific'

---

[4] Hall Caine, 'The New Watchwords of Fiction', *Contemporary Review*, 57 (1890), 484.

[5] The ground James shared with the supporters of romance was often obscured by the common perception of him as an ally of the naturalists; see, for example, Saintsbury, *Essays on French Novelists*, 16–17. However, Caine makes an implied reference to James as one of the first champions of American 'teacup Realism', who 'are themselves turning their backs on their own manifesto, and coming as near to Romanticism as their genius will let them' ('The New Watchwords of Fiction', 487–8). For surveys of the late nineteenth-century romance movement in England, see Graham, *English Criticism of the Novel*, 64–70 and Keating, *Haunted Study*, 344–51.

[6] Jones, *James the Critic*, 99.

realism through the opposed idea of a more technically self-conscious 'game of art' (*LC* ii. 891). This brings James closer to the more sophisticated theorists of romance such as Stevenson, who sought to expose the technical bases of, and thereby demystify, the truth-telling claims of naturalist 'detailism', and so contributed to the modernist dismantling of the cultural authority of nineteenth-century realism.[7]

James's sense of both the survival and the exhaustion of this authority in the twentieth century provides the irony behind the title of his essay 'The New Novel' (1914). The essay begins by suggesting that 'a change has come over our general receptive sensibility not less than over our productive tradition' (*LC* i. 129) as the novels of the early twentieth century raise 'the possibility of hugging the shore of the real as it had not, among us, been hugged' (i. 130). However, James also warns that to argue thus may be 'to enrich the case', for 'overstatement is easy and overemphasis tempting' (i. 129): in fact, as the rest of the essay makes apparent, the 'new' novel is dominated by the methods of the old, carrying to extremes and reducing to a merely mechanical exercise the reality-effects of the nineteenth-century novel. James's assessment of the works of social realism which, to his eyes, dominated the early twentieth-century literary scene, involves a marked reassessment of the values of the 'historical' novel he had formerly advocated. In the 1870s and 1880s James had borrowed from the concerns of historiography to place the question of evidence at the heart of his conception of serious fiction; now, the aesthetic of '*saturation*', of immersion in a 'body of reference' (i. 128), is called 'that simple state of possession of much evidence' (i. 154) and mocked as a grossly reductive expression of the novelist's function. Similarly, the role of the reader of this evidence is now regarded as hopelessly passive. James had once praised the fact that 'Balzac is always definite; you can say Yes or No to him as you go on; the story bristles with references that must be verified' (*LC* ii. 38). In 1914 he finds that the same quality in Arnold Bennett's novels contributes only 'a source for us of abject confidence, confidence truly *so* abject in the solidity of every appearance that it may be said to represent our whole relation to the work and completely to exhaust our

---

[7] See Stevenson's 'A Note on Realism', *Magazine of Art* (1883); reprinted in *Essays in the Art of Writing*, 93–107.

reaction upon it' (*LC* i. 136). Mere verification of '*constatations
pure and simple*' (i. 140) is a poor substitute for the collabora-
tive making of meaning through fiction explored in James's late
novels.

Although James's barely disguised contempt for the aesthetic of
'saturation' in 'The New Novel' radically revises his earlier estimate of 'solidity of specification' as the 'supreme virtue of a novel'
(*LC* i. 53), his impatience with the construction of the reader
as passive consumer shows a continuity of concern with 'The
Art of Fiction'. This is suggested in his use of related imagery
in the two essays. In 'The New Novel' he picks up the common image of the naturalist novel as a 'slice of life' and elab-
orates it to create a picture of childish, unreflecting consumption:
the slice of life may attempt 'to butter itself thick', there may be
'jam super-added to the butter', but it is clear that this 'manna'
descends 'from quite another heaven than the heaven of method'
(i. 144). The use of nursery food as an image for bland and stolid
consumerism recalls the protest in 'The Art of Fiction' against the
comfortable belief 'that a novel is a novel, as a pudding is a
pudding, and that our only business with it could be to swallow
it' (*LC* i. 44). What the images suggest is that, ironically, in their
resistance to technique, distrust of 'art', and generally consumer-
ist, utilitarian conception of fiction, the exponents of a domestic-
ated naturalism were perpetuating the attitudes towards fiction
held by the philistine British public which had once been so
outraged by the challenge of naturalism. But the images also
suggest that techniques associated with historical narrative could
encourage the kind of passive consumption of novels that James
deplored. Vivien Jones rightly observes that James's quarrel with
the 'new' novel was that it embodied what Barthes calls ' "readerly"
rather than "writerly" modes' of narrative,[8] but James's late
critique of the effects of 'solidity of specification' also suggests a
recognition that his own earlier historical model of narrative had
also been an essentially 'readerly' mode.

The reader's 'imaginative collaboration' (*LC* i. 803) in the
fiction-making process is celebrated in James's essay of 1912,
'The Novel in "The Ring and the Book" ', and this appreciation
of a 'writerly' text involves an even more explicit defiance of the

---

[8] Jones, *James the Critic*, 158; see Barthes, *S/Z: An Essay*, trans. Richard Miller
(New York: Hill & Wang, 1974), 4.

authority of history than is found elsewhere in *Notes on Novelists*. The essay was a public performance of a private reading
practice which had become inveterate with James by this time. He
wrote to Howard Sturgis in 1903 that he could only read a novel
'critically, constructively, *re*constructively, writing the thing over
. . . *my* way' (*Letters* iv. 286).[9] Finding the potential novel in *The
Ring and the Book*, James indulges in a process of rewriting
which determinedly eschews the historian's responsibility to documents. The pressures of this responsibility are foregrounded in
Browning's poem, which constantly wrestles with the authority
of its documentary sources. However, James, taking Browning as
his source, allows no documented fact to stand in the way of the
processes of rearrangement and reconstruction to which he subjects Browning's volumes, in pursuit of 'the novel they might have
constituted' (*LC* i. 792). The reading process through which
James creates his imaginary novel focuses two principles central
to the theory of novelistic composition explored in the prefaces
to the *New York Edition*. The first is the idea that fiction grows
best from slight sources: James's early view of Browning's poem
as a composition 'tragically spoiled' and 'smothered in the producing' (*LC* i. 792) bears out the concern of the prefaces with 'the
fatal futility of Fact' (*LC* ii. 1140) when it is allowed to feature in
the process of composition as more than a mere 'germ' of suggestion.[10] James wishes to avoid the problems, encountered by
Browning, that are raised 'when we take over, as the phrase is,
established data, take them over from existing records and under
some involved obligation to take them as they stand' (*LC* i. 797).
Refusing to recognize any such obligation, James's method in
'The Novel in "The Ring and the Book" ' exemplifies a second
general principle of the prefaces, the principle that 'The historian,
essentially, wants more documents than he can really use; the
dramatist only wants more liberties than he can really take' (*LC*
ii. 1175). Under this dispensation, James exhibits a supreme
indifference to Browning's obsession in *The Ring and the Book*
with closing the gap between source and poem, fact and fiction.
Rather, he makes almost in passing the point that Browning is so
reluctant to accept—that the poet's 'offered' story is 'a very
different matter' from his 'borrowed' one (i. 794)—and himself

---

[9] See also *Letters* iv. 238, 576, 617, 686.
[10] See *LC* ii. 1138–40, 1307–9.

offers a story very different from the one he borrows. This is in effect an acceptance of the inevitable disjunction between story and discourse which the whole array of 'historical' techniques in his early theory had been designed to, disguise. Untouched by Browning's yearning for 'repristination' (book 1, line 23), James accepts and even celebrates the secondariness which is the source of such anxiety in Browning's poem.

James not only flaunts the fictionality of his imaginary novel, but in its subject-matter defies the nineteenth-century condescension towards fiction and its readers which had made the novel more susceptible to moral censorship than any other literary genre. In 'A Dialogue on Novels' (1885), Vernon Lee had discussed the impossibility of writing *The Ring and the Book* as a novel in order to illustrate the disadvantages under which the novelist, compared with the poet, was placed in Victorian culture. A character in the dialogue, Baldwin, asserts:

> Now the plot of 'The Ring and the Book' is one which no English novelist would dare to handle; Mudie would simply refuse to circulate a novel the immense bulk of which consisted in the question, discussed and rediscussed by half-a-dozen persons: Has there been adultery between Pompilia and Caponsacchi? Has Guido Franceschini tried to push his wife into dishonour, or has he been dishonoured by his wife?[11]

Uncompromisingly basing his 'novel', like Browning's poem, on 'the exhibition of the great constringent relation between man and woman at once at its maximum and as the relation most worth while in life for either party' (*LC* i. 809), James asserts that there is no part of the sexual nature of Browning's poem 'that doesn't positively plead for our perfect prose transcript' (i. 810). With this statement, James was defying the upsurge of action in the early twentieth century against the representation of sexuality in fiction, in which writers such as Wells, Joyce, and Lawrence were subjected to the same forces of censorship that had operated in the 1880s against an earlier generation of novelists.[12] He was also triumphantly defying the Victorian hierarchies of genre which had expressed hostility to fiction by subjecting it to a stricter moral surveillance than other forms of literature. James no longer meets the question of censorship by appealing to the

---

[11] Lee, 'Dialogue', 397–8.   [12] Keating, *Haunted Study*, 268–79.

freedoms offered to more highly esteemed literary genres such as history: 'The Novel in "The Ring and the Book" ' insists on both its freedom and its fictionality, thereby healing a split which was the primary cultural cause of James's early attempts to align the novel with history.

Such an alignment was now seen by James as both unnecessary and undesirable. Speaking in 'The Novel in "The Ring and the Book" ' of 'the so-called historic fiction' as 'so beautiful a case . . . of a muddlement of terms' (*LC* i. 797), he disowned the attempt made at the beginning of his career to use the term 'historical novel' to denote a narrative ideal, to force history and romance 'to look upon the other with the cold glance of the speculator', and 'to imagine a mind in which their distinctive elements and sympathies should be combined' (*LC* i. 1154). The 'mistake' of attempting to combine the functions of novelist and historian was brought home to James in a particularly personal way when he angered his relatives by rewriting portions of William James's letters for publication in *Notes of a Son and Brother* (1914). Speaking as a novelist, James defended his 'ethic' and 'aesthetic' of revision (*Letters* iv. 800), claiming that he had liberated the potential meanings of the text, and by falsifying documents had produced imaginative truth. But as a historian, he conceded that such tampering with the evidence was indefensible, and vowed: 'Never again shall I stray from my proper work—the one in which that danger is the reverse of one and becomes a rightness and a beauty' (*Letters* iv. 803). Here, as in his contrasting of historian and dramatist (*LC* ii. 1175), reporter and originator (*LC* ii. 94), James found that the work of the novelist was to be defined through deep violations of the historian's code of practice.

The late James's commitment to the authority of the imagination in shaping and revising experience found its most radical expression in his essay of 1910, 'Is There a Life After Death?'. Considering the power of the imagination to affect the very material conditions of existence, James approaches science as simply 'the most assured show' of 'appearances' (*LD* 218), and consciousness as a mode of 'reaction against so grossly finite a world—for it at least *contained* the world, and could handle and criticise it, could play with it and deride it' (*LD* 220). He justifies taking 'these inordinate intellectual and irresponsible liberties with the idea of things' (*LD* 223) by dissolving the difference between desire and belief: 'If one acts from desire quite as one would from belief, it signifies little what name one gives to one's motive' (*LD* 232). In literary terms, this pragmatic impulse translates into a collapse of the boundaries between romance and realism, fiction and history. James's exploration of the capacities of fiction as an imaginative and narrative mode opposed to the processes of history leads to the redefinition of history itself that we find in *The American Scene*. Having apologized for one of the subjective digressions which do not merely impinge upon, but more or less constitute, his record of his visit to America in 1904–5, James wrote: 'I draw courage from the remembrance that history is never, in any rich sense, the immediate crudity of what "happens," but the much finer complexity of what we read into it and think of in connection with it' (*AS* 182). This definition, which covers both historical matter and historical discourse, expresses the complete absorption of history into fiction; whereas, in his early criticism, James had offered definitions of the novel in terms of historical discourse, he now defines history in terms of fictional processes of reading and plotting. But with the outbreak of war in 1914, this understanding of history was put under severe pressure.

WAR AND COUNTER-REALITY

'We must for dear life make our own counter-realities', James wrote to Lucy Clifford in 1914.[13] The Great War threw the accepted values of James's culture into disarray and, he felt, seriously discredited his whole literary enterprise, but it also made urgent calls on the imagination to resist or assimilate new experience. Between the outbreak of war and his death in 1916, James produced writings, some intended for private and some for public audiences, which explored the uses and limits of an oppositional imagination in the face of the seemingly irresistible force of history.

To James the war meant the irrevocable loss of the life he had known and about which he had written. In a letter to Howard

---

[13] Edel, *The Life of Henry James*, v. 519.

Sturgis in 1915, he made the death of their friend Ned Boit the occasion to mourn the death of a whole way of life: 'I do indeed "understand how one's heart reaches back into the past"—that incredible past in which we once lived unimagining of these horrors and not knowing that we were fantastically happy' (*Letters* iv. 753). James uses the rhetorical figure of the fall from paradise, the plunge from innocence to experience, to describe the ironic gulf the war had opened between past and present. This use of the trope of irony soon became the most generally accepted way of imaginatively regulating the relation between the war and the pre-war world, as Paul Fussell has illustrated in *The Great War and Modern Memory*.[14] Fussell shows how experience extremely susceptible to literary organization, such as the contrast between the idyllic pastoral of the summer of 1914 and the hopelessness of the winter of that year, led to the creation of rhetorical patterns which have since passed into cultural mythology. It has become a historical commonplace to counterpoint the horror of the trenches with the material advances and ideological complacencies of the Victorian age, the latter both thrown into relief and undermined by the former. As Fussell argues, all wars reflect ironically on the ages that produced them, but the Great War offered a sharper irony than any before or since, because it was 'a hideous embarrassment to the prevailing Meliorist myth which had dominated the public consciousness for a century. It reversed the Idea of Progress.'[15] If, as Hayden White contends, a 'historical field' must be subjected to 'prefiguration' according to some rhetorical pattern before it can be written about,[16] the First World War in relation to the nineteenth century is always prefigured by the trope of irony.

James commented on the 'ironic beauty' of the weather in the first weeks of the war (*Letters* iv. 718), and wrote to Rhoda Broughton that 'the huge shining indifference of Nature strikes a chill to the heart and makes me wonder of what abysmal mystery, or villainy indeed, such a cruel smile is the expression' (*Letters* iv. 714). The fear is partly prospective—what kinds of suffering will

[14] Paul Fussell, *The Great War and Modern Memory* (London: Oxford University Press, 1975), 3–35.
[15] Ibid. 8.
[16] Hayden White, *Metahistory: The Historical Imagination in Nineteenth-Century Europe* (Baltimore: Johns Hopkins University Press, 1973), p. x.

this war produce?—but is also retrospective, as he wonders 'what abysmal mystery, or villainy indeed' has lain behind the war, or beneath the smile of civilized progress that masked its coming. Looking back and finding an ironic gap between the hopes and beliefs of his generation and the actualities to which they have led, one impulse is simply to discount the issue as false, impossible. In a letter to Grace Norton in October 1914 James admitted the temptation 'to say "Oh, *this* wasn't in the bargain; it's the claim of Fate only in the form of a ruffian or a swindler, and with such I'll have no dealing" ' (Lubbock ii. 428). The impulse is to leave past experience intact, not to reinterpret it in the light of new knowledge. However, the facts of present experience—the lists of the dead, the Belgian refugees in Chelsea and Rye, the long hospital wards full of injured soldiers—impinged on James's life in ways that could not be ignored, and demanded, moreover, the respect owed to the sufferings of others. The past and the present forced themselves on his attention as two mutually contradictory versions of the story of nineteenth-century civilization; if the account implied by the present were true, then that offered and accepted in the past must have been false. For James the war provided the sense of an ending, and like the end of a novel it created a position of retrospection from which sense could be made of what had gone before. Ruthlessly teleological, most of James's letters defer to the war as providing the last word that places all that preceded it, offering a privileged sense-making perspective, an authoritative interpretation.

Many years earlier, James had applied the same sort of teleological vision to the eighteenth century as seen through the French Revolution. In his essay 'Madame de Sabran' in 1875, James had written:

A part of our kindness for the eighteenth century rests on the fact that it paid so completely the price of both corruptions and enthusiasms. As we move to and fro in it we see something that our companions do not see—we see the sequel, the consummation, the last act of the drama. The French Revolution rounds off the spectacle and renders it a picturesque service which has also something besides picturesqueness. It casts backward a sort of supernatural light, in the midst of which, at times, we seem to see a stage full of actors performing fantastic antics for our entertainment. But retroactively, too, it seems to exonerate the generations that preceded it, to make them irresponsible and give them the right to say that, since the penalty was to be exorbitant, a little pleasure more or less would not signify. There is nothing in all history which, to borrow a term from the painters, 'composes' better than the opposition, from 1600 to 1800, of the audacity of the game and the certainty of the reckoning. We all know the idiom which speaks of such reckonings as 'paying the piper.' The piper here is the People. We see the great body of society executing its many-figured dance on its vast polished parquet; and in a dusky corner, behind the door, we see the lean, gaunt, ragged Orpheus filling his hollow reed with tunes in which every breath is an agony. (*LC* ii. 653)

In his letter to Howard Sturgis about the blissful ignorance of the pre-war years, James found that the war performed a similar 'picturesque service' for such naturally aristocratic figures as Ned and Iza Boit: 'They both seem to me to have been thrown back, as by the violence of our awful present, into the same sort of old-régime fabulous air into which the French Revolution must have thrown of a sudden the types of the previous age' (*Letters* iv. 754). In drawing this parallel between the way the French Revolution rounded off and 'composed' the eighteenth century and the effect the war was having on his perception of his own age, James anticipated the common twentieth-century habit of taking 1914 as the point at which the nineteenth century, imaginatively, ended. But whereas he had considered that the French Revolution retroactively exonerated the generations that preceded it, in James's eyes the war retroactively incriminated the society that produced it. The day after England entered the war he expressed this sense to Howard Sturgis:

The plunge of civilization into this abyss of blood and darkness . . . is a thing that so gives away the whole long age during which we have supposed the world to be, with whatever abatement, gradually bettering, that to have to take it all now for what the treacherous years were all the while really making for and *meaning* is too tragic for any words. (Lubbock ii. 398)

Later that month he again expressed, this time to Rhoda Broughton, his sense of betrayal: 'The tide that bore us along was then all the while moving to *this* as its grand Niagara—yet what a blessing we didn't know it. It seems to me to *undo* everything, everything that was ours, in the most horrible retroactive way' (*Letters* iv. 713). In September 1914 he reiterated, to William

Roughead, his belief that the war 'makes all the past, with this hideous card all the while up its sleeve, seem now a long treachery, an unthinkable humbug' (*SL* 254–5).

Except for the elevation to the 'fabulous' of Ned and Iza Boit, which is more an expression of nostalgia than an investment of value, James allowed the war to authorize a much more sinister teleology than the French Revolution. One reason for this is that although he linked 'the audacity of the game' of eighteenth-century civilization to 'the certainty of the reckoning' (*LC* ii. 653), he was able to separate the agents of destruction from its victims, and thus, whatever the 'certainty' of their doom, to throw in his lot imaginatively with the latter. A similar reasoning motivates the hero of his novel about civilization and revolution, *The Princess Casamassima*. Hyacinth Robinson's sense of the imminent destruction of privileged institutions at the hands of the people only intensifies his impulse to exonerate these institutions of blame for the doom they are preparing for themselves. In the case of the war, James cannot do this, because he cannot externalize the agent of destruction. He acknowledges of the war what he could not or did not choose to acknowledge of revolutionary movements—that this threat to civilization was a product of civilization itself, an oblique expression of its nature. Hence his repeated use of the word 'treacherous' in his war letters: civilization, tending all the time towards this end, had deceived those who had believed in it, and the war had exposed this.

James's war letters identify the whole of nineteenth-century civilization as he had known it and participated in it as an error, a delusion, a fantasy, a lie. The false account civilization had given of itself is seen as an unreliable narrative, now corrected and brought to an end by the incontrovertible historical fact of the war. War presents itself to James's mind as the final reality, making at best a joke and at worst a lie of what civilization had purported to be. The relation between war and civilization is a version, writ large, of the opposition of history to plot which I have traced throughout James's work. In fact, in a letter to the sculptor Hendrik Andersen in 1912, James had, with uncanny prescience, used war imagery to describe life's criticism of art. He warned Andersen against producing

brilliant castles in the air, brilliant as you will, cut off from all root-taking in this terribly crowded and smothered and overbuilt ground that stretches under the feet of the for the most part raging and would-be throat-cutting and mutually dynamiting nations. I don't, in fine, see where your vision, subject to such murderous obstruction and control and annihilating criticism, 'comes in' . . . (*Letters* iv. 641–2)

The war now provides such 'annihilating criticism', not just of Andersen's grandiose schemes, but of all the arts of civilization. James's retroactive vision of the significance of 1914 means that the relation between nineteenth-century civilization and the war is not simply that between events in a sequence (an ironic reversal) but that between discourse and story, false and true accounts of the same series of events. A whole authoritative narrative of the nineteenth century is embedded in the single event of the outbreak of war, and this narrative unmasks the true face of civilization as destruction and savagery. Thus for James, the irony offered by the sequence of events—that civilization at its height could be followed by its opposite, war—is overtaken by the even more sinister irony to be found in the discrimination of false from true narratives—that the relation between war and civilization is one not of opposition but of complicity.

This discovery placed James's fiction in a false position, as he noted in a letter to Hugh Walpole in February 1915:

The subject-matter of one's effort has become *itself* utterly treacherous and false—its relation to reality utterly given away and smashed. Reality is a world that was to be capable of *this*—and how represent that horrific capability, *historically* latent, historically ahead of it? How on the other hand *not* represent it either—without putting into play mere fiddlesticks? (Lubbock ii. 462)

The idea of the potential for the war being somehow encoded in all the experience he had witnessed is referred by James, with a distressed emphasis, to historical inevitability—the war has all along been '*historically* latent, historically ahead of' the reality about which he wrote. It is a personal irony of James's career that at the time when his fictional theory and practice had moved furthest from deferring to the authority of history, history asserted itself with seemingly irresistible force, its inevitability not only blocking future imaginative liberties, but rendering vain and pretentious the liberties taken with it in the past. In the preface to *The Spoils of Poynton* James had cavalierly dismissed 'the fatal futility of Fact' (*LC* ii. 1140) as irrelevant in defining or limiting the scope of his fictions. Now the fact of the war gave James a chastened sense of his own pretensions as a maker of fictions, and threatened to make the production of any fiction irrelevant.

In 1874, in an essay on Turgenev, James had observed: 'The personal optimism of most of us no romancer can confirm or dissipate, and our personal troubles, generally, place fictions of all kinds in an impertinent light' (*LC* ii. 999). The personal and collective troubles encompassed by the war placed his fictions 'in an impertinent light', in the sense, not only of being presumptuous in their counterplotting of reality, but of being irrelevant, arbitrary, their relation to potential as well as actual reality 'utterly given away and smashed' (Lubbock ii. 462). The charge of telling his readers 'an arbitrary thing' (*LC* i. 1343) was one which the earlier James had sought to avoid by deferring to an idea of historical inevitability. However, the image of the canopy of historical fact imprisoning the novelist's imagination (*LC* i. 1154), which had already been degraded into a 'cage' limiting Balzac's imaginative achievement (*LC* ii. 101), now took on even more sinister overtones. In a letter to his niece Peggy in October 1914, James explained that everything they might talk about 'can't but consist of our huge oppressive and obsessive matter here. *That* is the only thing that exists for us—it crowds our whole sky from pole to pole' (*Letters* iv. 725). James's fictions were composed without calculating on the presence of this imprisoning canopy of impenetrable fact, and with its sudden appearance were rendered arbitrary.

The entire context for James's novels was now gone; he wrote to Peggy James that 'all social life has gone to smash; nothing exists but *the* huge enormity' (*Letters* iv. 784). Congratulating Rhoda Broughton on having brought out her latest book before the outbreak of war, James wrote: 'I am utterly pulled up in the midst of a rival effort by finding that my job won't at all consent to be done in the face of it. The picture of little private adventures simply fades away before the great public' (*Letters* iv. 714). This recalls his comment on Hawthorne's predicament as a writer during the American Civil War: 'It was not a propitious time for cultivating the Muse; when history herself is so hard at work, fiction has little left to say' (*LC* i. 449). However, writing to congratulate Edmund Gosse on his article 'War and Literature', James registered his respect for those who continued with their work and 'created life and force by doing' (*Letters* iv. 720). About his own work he continued to feel ambivalent. The publication of his *Notes on Novelists* struck him with 'a kind of painful inevitability in its so grotesquely and false-notedly coming out now' (*Letters* iv. 721)—again he ascribed an inevitability to the historical irony that had placed his work in a false light. On the other hand, he also told himself that 'nothing serious and felt and sincere, nothing "good," is anything but essentially in order today' (*Letters* iv. 721). Although his 'poor old "values" [had] received such a shock', 'this is all the more reason why one should recover as many of them as possible and keep hold of them in the very interest of civilisation and of the honour of our race' (*Letters* iv. 720).

Yet it was not possible to continue to write as if the war had not happened, and James was faced with the problem of trying to work out what kind of fiction could escape the charge of impertinence and irrelevance. Should one try to work out a mode of utterance which confined itself beneath the canopy of impenetrable historical fact, or would it be possible (or proper) to attempt 'one of those smashes of the window-pane of the real' (*LC* ii. 113) and an escape in the balloon of romance? Should one's energies be directed towards assimilation of new knowledge and experience, or towards resistance of it? In *The Princess Casamassima* James had explored the role of the individual imagination (Hyacinth's) and the literary artifact (the novel) in addressing a social situation which is 'so bad that the imagination recoils, refuses' (*PC* ii. 76). In the 1880s, although he acknowledged the horrors of the social situation, James, like Hyacinth, did not regard them as invalidating the creative, consolatory, or escapist qualities of art; refusing political knowledge and commitment, the imagination can recoil back into the pleasures of art. However, because of the intimate connection he saw between war and civilization, such a choice did not seem possible for James in 1914. The imagination 'recoils, refuses', but has nowhere else to go, as James testified in several letters to friends. He agreed with Edith Wharton that 'the irrelevance of all remark, the utter extinction of everything, in face of these immensities, leaves me as "all silent and all damned" as you express that it leaves *you*'; the only possible response is silence and the only relief is inconscience, as he finds the war 'a nightmare from which there is no waking save by sleep' (*Letters* iv. 715). Expressing impatience with the facility of D'Annunzio's poetry, James wrote to Wharton: 'What's magnificent to me in the French themselves at this moment is their lapse of expression' (*Letters* iv. 716). His comment recalls the point in *The Sacred Fount* at which the narrator says of the victimized May Server, standing on the edge of abysses of civilized violence: 'She went through the form of expression, but what told me everything was the way the form of expression broke down' (*SF* 131–2). Later, novelists such as Ford Madox Ford in *Parade's End* would evolve a mode of narrative for depicting the experience of war (both for soldiers and civilians) through the general breakdown of accepted forms of expression. However for James, in the first shock of war, the only adequate response seemed at times to refrain from expression altogether.

This he did not do. However, he did abandon the novel he had been writing, *The Ivory Tower*, and resumed work on a fragment of a ghostly, romantic tale of time-travel which he had laid aside in 1900, *The Sense of the Past*. The standard explanation for this decision has been given by Percy Lubbock, who argues that James stopped work on *The Ivory Tower* in 1914 because 'it was impossible to believe any longer in a modern fiction, supposed to represent the life of the day, which the great catastrophe had so belied', whereas work on *The Sense of the Past* was possible because its 'unreality' was 'now remote enough to be beyond the reach of the war' (Lubbock ii. 394). This accords with James's explanation of his thinking to Edith Wharton:

It's impossible to 'locate anything in our time.' Our time has been *this* time for the last 50 years, & if it was ignorantly & fatuously so the only light in which to show it is now the light of that tragic delusion. And that's too awful a subject. It all makes Walter Scott, him only, readable again. (*HJ & EW* 316)

However, it could be argued that the task of representing the 'horrific capability, *historically* latent' in society—now rejected as 'too awful a subject'—had always been a major concern of James's fiction: James had always represented the false nature of civilization and the latent and potential horrors of social life. As early as 'A Passionate Pilgrim' (1871) his hero had called the civilized security of Oxford 'a delightful lie' (*CT* ii. 293). Civilized institutions and manners, the social expression of various collectively held fictions about human behaviour, provide fragile bridges over the abysses of unspeakable personal motive that haunt all his later fiction, but do not always redeem the futility and brutality that may inhere in a highly refined social existence. In the card-playing scene in *The Golden Bowl*, 'the amount of enjoyed, or at least achieved, security represented by so complete a conquest of appearances' acts on Maggie's nerves 'with a kind of provocative force', tempting her to smash the protective surface of achieved forms and show that if she should choose to break the fictional contract of civilized life, 'all this high decorum would hang by a hair' (*GB* 452). Even in its fragmentary form, the symbolism of *The Ivory Tower* promises James's most fully realized exploration of the relation between the surface pleasures and benefits of civilization and the abysmal price paid for them. Within the ivory tower, a rare and precious work of art, is kept a letter which, it is hinted, contains an account of the corruptions and dishonest business practices which have produced the wealth to purchase it. The idea of the protective shell of civilization carrying around within it, '*historically* latent', the story of its own dark side, matches James's retroactive sense of the nineteenth century carrying about, hidden from view, its other, latent, self-negating history. The novel's capacity to represent society's 'horrific capability' for its own destruction is especially powerful if one acknowledges the role of economic interests as a cause of war. An unwillingness to do so may have contributed to James's decision to abandon the novel. Far from being irrelevant to the war and to James's retroactive sense of his own age, *The Ivory Tower* promises to cut all too close to the bone.

In contrast, *The Sense of the Past* at first looks like 'mere fiddlesticks' (Lubbock ii. 462). Lubbock's explanation of the appeal of its 'unreality' and James's comment that it offers an 'antidote' to present worries (*Letters* iv. 716) make the novel appear a piece of irresponsible escapism, a retreat from the difficulty of attempting to express either the experience of wartime life, or James's new interpretation of pre-war experience. However, in a letter to Edith Wharton James suggests that the novel may be a way of confronting, rather than evading, the problems of the present. He sees it 'as perhaps offering a certain defiance of subject to the law by which most things now perish in the public blight. This does seem to kind of intrinsically resist—and I have hopes' (Lubbock ii. 442). In what way may *The Sense of the Past* be seen as offering resistance to the reality of the war, or to the processes which have brought it about? At first the novel seems to be guided by a purely nostalgic impulse, as the hero, Ralph Pendrel, embarks on a piece of time-travel which allows him to fulfil a lifelong ambition of recovering the experience of the past. His means of travelling through time is an old London house, left to him by a relative who wants to testify to his admiration for Ralph's book, 'An Essay in Aid of the Reading of History' (*SP* 41). Ralph's benefactor predicts that if he accepts the bequest, 'he would find himself master of a scene in which a chapter of history—obscure, though not so remote as might perhaps have been wished—would perhaps by his intervention step more into the light' (42). When, on entering the house, he thereby enters the year 1820, Ralph's experience literally enacts the belief expressed in his essay that we can be put into communication with the past through the spell of particular places. While the impulse which inspires Ralph to accept the opportunity for time-travel is a desire to retrieve historical experience, intact and authentic, the creation of a fiction in which it is possible for him to do this involves a willingness to take liberties with history, to leave it in a state other than that in which it was found. The idea of time-travel involves a declaration of imaginative immunity from the laws of time and history, and the fiction resists the idea of the irreversible and inexorable movement of time which underwrote James's distressed sense of the causes of the war. Ralph re-enters the stream of time much as James, in preparing the *New York Edition*, exercised his privilege to 'remount the stream of composition' (*LC* ii. 1059), and the novel makes history, like one of James's own fictions, imaginatively susceptible to revision.

The past is changed simply by Ralph's presence in it, but it is changed much more radically when he begins to depart from the script laid down for him by the historical figure he has replaced. The extant portion of the novel deals only with Ralph's early experience as he finds that he can successfully live into the past, taking whatever liberties he wants and finding that the documents fall into place afterwards—as when he refers to a portrait of his fiancée, and then finds in his pocket the object which confirms his words (132–3). The fragment ends with his meeting with his cousin Nan, his ignorance of whose existence represents his only lapse so far from an uncanny ability to know what the past requires of him. In his notes for the continuation of the novel, James planned to establish a growing atmosphere of 'malaise' (291) as the people of 1820 vaguely realize that Ralph is alien, not what he should be, and Ralph, the man of 1910, realizes that he cannot accept the implications of his decision to live in another time. His sense of 'horror' at being trapped in the past (288) is directed against the reasserted power of historical inevitability. He may have had the chance to break the laws of time once, but once placed in the past he is expected to abide by the rules of the game and repeat what the man of 1820 did. When he breaks these rules by ending his engagement to Molly, his *alter ego* comes back to accuse him of 'practical treachery' (316). The atmosphere of terror and malaise grows until a sacrifice on Nan's part wins back Ralph's freedom to return to 'his own original precious Present' (288).

The whole issue of the relation between time-travel and historical inevitability becomes a serious compositional and intellectual problem for James. His notes for the novel show him struggling with the question of whether he ought to make Ralph strictly repeat the actions of his predecessor or *alter ego* (questions of precedence, as of tense, become confused) 'without which where is definitely that Past, that made and achieved, that once living and enacted Past which is the field of his business?' (334). Against the inevitability of history is opposed 'the uncontrollability of his modernism' (334), 'Ralph's insuperable and ineffaceable margin of independence, clinging taint of modernity' (316). James's notes to the novel do not make clear quite how much authority he intended to give in the end to the untouchability of the events of history, and how much to the individual's power to revise them. What is clear from the notes is that the great effect of the novel would be to create a nightmarish sense of history as a trap; in this it promised to be a kind of companion piece to *The Turn of the Screw* (to which James often makes reference in the notes as he searches for the right tone (*SP* 288, 300–1, 304)), for whereas that novella had explored the horrors of being governed by fiction, this turn of the narrative screw (301) sets out the horrors of being trapped in history.

In its experiments with time, causation, and inevitability, *The Sense of the Past* is itself 'An Essay in Aid of the Reading of History' (41) which produces ambivalent effects. On the one hand it plays with the idea that the stream of time (which James, with horror, realized had been leading to the 'Niagara' of the war (*Letters* iv. 713)) could be re-entered and diverted as a result of human desire; on the other hand, it presents this as a hubristic act, a Faustian delving into unnatural knowledge, which is punishable by a reassertion of the very forces the imagination had tried to overcome. Ralph's escape from the inevitability of history is accompanied by an affirmation of the values of his present (1910), which is interesting in the light of the disgust with recent civilization expressed in James's early war letters. Nan is set apart from the other characters of the past because she possesses a finer, 'modern' sensibility, while from the perspective of 1820 Ralph sees the absolute superiority of his own age, 'of which he now sees only the ripeness, richness, attraction and civilisation, the virtual perfection without a flaw' (331). Informed anticipation therefore 'composes' the nineteenth century for Ralph in exactly the opposite way from that in which enlightened retrospection composed it for James in the first months of the war, and the novel re-establishes the meliorist myth that the war had smashed.

As well as using fictional narrative as a mode of resistance, James produced non-fictional accounts of his wartime experience which imaginatively oppose his greatest fears about the war. In August 1914 he wrote to Lucy Clifford of the dangers of dwelling too much on the present horrors: 'That way madness lies, and one must try to economise, and not disseminate, one's forces of resistance—to the prodigious public total of which I think we can each of us, in his or her own way, individually, and however obscurely, contribute' (Lubbock ii. 412). James's public statements about the war, collected in *Within the Rim* (1918), contrast with many of his private utterances expressed in letters, in that they seek imaginatively to restore to their places the values and beliefs which had been set adrift by the shock of war. The title essay of the collection describes the author's immediate reactions to the outbreak of war and uses devices derived from his novels to create a different narrative version of the relation between the war and the pre-war world from the hopelessly ironic one articulated in many of the letters.

In 'Within the Rim', the first thing James is anxious to establish is his 'immunity from illusion' about the 'immensities', 'monstrosities', and 'immeasurabilities' of suffering that the war will bring (*WR* 12). Unlike most English people, who had lived in an era of peace and would not know 'what a big war was going to mean', James's memories of the American Civil War put him in the position of 'literally knowing "by experience" ' (12) what to expect. However, the security derived from this is soon taken away by the realization that the attempt to use this 'vision of similitude' (15) to predict the horrors of the war will not work—'the moment anyhow came soon enough at which experience felt the ground give way and that one swung off into space, into history, into darkness, with every lamp extinguished and every abyss gaping' (13–14). The breadth of involvement in the conflict and the technological advances which have created 'unprecedented engines' of destruction (15) have conspired to create conditions which have never been known before. It is as if history is inventing new kinds of horror for which there is no touchstone in memory, and so the only means of coping with them is by recourse not to what one may derive from 'literally knowing "by experience" ' but to what one may create in imaginative response. 'It was the season of sensibility now' (27) and James had reason to be grateful for his resources of imagination:

> Never in all my life, probably, had I been so glad to have opened betimes an account with this faculty and to be able to feel for the most part something to my credit there; so vivid I mean had to be one's prevision of the rate at which drafts on that source would require cashing. (21)

The use to which he needs to put his imagination is the restoration of values thrown into disarray by the war (18); what he is doing, James implies, is not creating a counter-reality but re-establishing a prior reality disoriented and displaced by the false perspective of war. To do this he makes use of the familiar ironic trope of the discrepancy between the beauty of the English summer and the brutality of the events taking place in Europe. But James does not, as in his private letters, allow the irony to recoil on England itself, exposing the sinister undertone to its beautiful and placid surface. Rather, he keeps the two regions distinct, separated by the 'rim' of the essay's title, the English Channel. Geographical space becomes emotional and imaginative space, and the idea of the rim is all-important in dividing the region of peace and civilization from the region of war and barbarism:

> Just on the other side of that finest of horizon-lines history was raging at a pitch new under the sun; thinly masked by that shameless smile the Belgian horror grew; the curve of the globe toward these things was of the scantest, and yet the hither spaces of the purest, the interval representing only charm and calm and ease. (16–17)

The chance splendour of the season helps 'the reparatory, the re-identifying process' of restoring the value of English civilization:

> 'This, as you can see better than ever before,' the elements kept conspiring to say, 'is the rare, the sole, the exquisite England whose weight now hangs in the balance, and your appreciation of whose value, much as in the easy years you may have taken it for granted, seems exposed to some fresh and strange and strong determinant, something that breaks in like a character of high colour in a play.' (18)

The contrast with the horror of Europe 'composes' England by intensifying, rather than undermining, its formerly accepted value. The near-side of the rim thus becomes a saving space, a region of asylum for the civilized values threatened by the war. James uses architectural imagery, reminiscent of his 'house of fiction' metaphors, to show how, under the stress of events, he sets about transforming his old 'house of the spirit' (19) into 'a fortress of the faith, a palace of the soul, an extravagant, bristling, flag-flying structure which had quite as much to do with the air as with the earth' (20). The process recalls the way in which Nick Dormer, in *The Tragic Muse*, builds up an architectural sense of the value of England, as much fictional as representative, which reinforces his commitment to enter politics (*TM* ii. 27–8). Later in the essay 'one's individual inward state as determined by the menace' is described as a church filled with candles and choirs (30), an image which echoes the use of the cathedral as a precinct of imaginative immunity in *The Ambassadors*. In that novel, Notre Dame had been a privileged space where fictional values could be nourished without menace before being taken out to do battle with the realities of the world. A similar set of spatial relations operates here. Within the rim, 'England', increasingly synonymous with the author's personal inward state, is reserved for the establishment of fictions (dealing romantically with the air as well as realistically with the earth (20)) which reaffirm the old values of civilization, order, and peace. Across the rim in 'Europe' history is taking place in the form of 'unutterable things, massacre and ravage and anguish, all but irresistible assault and cruelty' (20). The saving fictions will make it possible to repel the devastating facts. For once in his life James had found a use for English insularity (23).

The spatial imagery of 'Within the Rim' externalizes the threat to culture posed by the war, something James was unable to do in the letters which described war as the 'treacherous' intention of his own society. The essay also reassigns the roles of truth and delusion. The enemy, externalized as Germany, is observed by James in 'the insolence of his dream and the depth of his delusion' (35). In making the agent of destruction the victim of his own delusions, James is able to cast his own 'side' in the role of the restorer, not only of value, but of realism. In rewriting the narrative relations produced by the war, James's point of view shifts from the retrospective, which dominates his letters, to the prospective, as he anticipates the victory that will recapture the ground of historical truth—although not of historical horrors—for his own culture.

'Within the Rim' is a response to James's 'dismay at the awful proposition of a world squeezed together in the huge Prussian fist and with the variety and spontaneity of its parts oozing in a steady trickle, like the sacred blood of sacrifice, between those hideous knuckly fingers' (29–30). This image suggests some of the most lurid 'anti-Hun' posters of the war, for the device of an absolute opposition between the civilization of 'us' and the barbarism of 'them' was a staple of Britain's propaganda campaign. 'Within the Rim' shows an attempt at imaginative resistance to history becoming part of the wartime culture of propaganda, and when James describes his 'fortress of the faith' as a 'flag-flying structure' (20), we realize that something is wrong with the house of fiction. Indeed, R. P. Blackmur sees James's response to the war as 'the violation of a great sensibility', and claims that James 'withstood nothing, but sucked up the horror like a vacuum' and 'in the end resorted to hatred and fury and utter surrender of his sensibility to every idea and device of the Allied cause'.[17] But this

---

[17] R. P. Blackmur, 'Henry Adams: Three Late Moments', in *A Primer of Ignorance*, ed. Joseph Frank (New York: Harcourt, Brace & World, 1967), 263.

judgement is too simple, too dismissive; above all, it assigns to James too passive a role and ignores the active and impassioned way in which he explored the possibilities for fiction to resist, as well as to acknowledge, the 'nightmare' (*Letters* iv. 715) of historical inevitability.

James's wartime writings show imaginative and narrative modes worked out in the context of nineteenth-century fiction attempting to come to terms with the particularly violent forces of twentieth-century history. However imperfect his success—and it seems impossible to deny that, in 'Within the Rim', the oppositional imagination is subsumed by a propagandist rhetoric —James strenuously defended the basis of the attempt. His quarrel with H. G. Wells in 1915, prompted by the attack on him in Wells's *Boon* (itself responding to the values expressed in James's 'The New Novel'), centred on the two novelists' opposed views of the relation between fiction and history. For Wells, who believed that artistic concerns displaced social involvement, the war exposed the futility and danger of the devotion to the art of fiction that James represented. In rejecting this view, James was rejecting the doubts about the value of his work as a novelist expressed in his private letters upon the outbreak of war.[18] In the bleak winter of early 1915 he offered his most eloquent defence of his fictional method and vocation: 'It is art that *makes* life, makes interest, makes importance, for our consideration and application of these things, and I know of no substitute whatever for the force and beauty of its process' (*Letters* iv. 770). The war had posed a massive challenge to James's novelistic enterprise, and to his late theory that fiction could operate most powerfully by defying the authority of history. Yet, at the same time, the situation in 1915 made it seem less than ever desirable that fiction should exist simply to repeat history. In defending the view that 'art . . . *makes* life', James was not advocating escapism or an aesthetic retreat from history, but the necessity of entering into imaginative negotiations with history. His theoretical challenge to the fixed binary opposition of history and fiction, and his attempts to apply this challenge to actual, urgent historical prob-

---

[18] The often neglected similarities between the views of art and civilization expressed in *Boon* and those expressed in James's early wartime letters are emphasized by Samuel Hynes in *A War Imagined: The First World War and English Culture* (New York: Athenaeum, 1991), 20–4.

lems, identify him with the concerns of twentieth-century novelists such as E. L. Doctorow, who writes:

I could claim that history is a kind of fiction in which we live and hope to
survive, and fiction is a kind of speculative history, perhaps a superhis-
tory, by which the available data for the composition is seen to be greater
and more various in its sources than the historian supposes.[19]

James's early use of a historiographical model for the novel grew
out of a culture which was deeply anxious about fiction; his late
rejection of that model anticipated the concerns of novelists in a
century which is even more worried about history.

[19] E. L. Doctorow, 'False Documents', *American Review*, 26 (1977), 229–30.

Bibliography

1. *Works by James*

The Ambassadors (London: Methuen, 1903).

The American, first pub. 1877 (London: Macmillan, 1879).

The American Scene (London: Chapman & Hall, 1907).

'The Art of Fiction', *Longman's Magazine*, 4 (1884), 502–21.

The Complete Tales of Henry James, ed. with introd. by Leon Edel, 12 vols. (London: Hart-Davis, 1962–4).

The Europeans: A Sketch, 2 vols. (London: Macmillan, 1878).

The Golden Bowl, first pub. 1904 (London: Methuen, 1905).

Henry James and Edith Wharton: Letters: 1900–1915, ed. Lyall H. Powers (New York: Scribner's, 1990).

Henry James: Letters, ed. Leon Edel, 4 vols. (i–iii: London: Macmillan, 1974–81; iv: Cambridge, Mass.: Belknap Press, 1984).

Henry James: Literary Criticism, ed. Leon Edel and Mark Wilson, 2 vols. (New York: Library of America, 1984); i: *Essays on Literature, American Writers, English Writers*; ii: *French Writers, Other European Writers, the Prefaces to the New York Edition*.

In the Cage (London: Duckworth, 1898).

'Is There a Life After Death?', in W. D. Howells *et al.*, *In After Days: Thoughts on the Future Life* (New York: Harper, 1910), 199–233.

The Ivory Tower (London: Collins, 1917).

The Letters of Henry James, ed. Percy Lubbock, 2 vols. (London: Macmillan, 1920).

The Novels and Tales of Henry James: New York Edition, first pub. 1907–9; 24 vols. (London: Macmillan, 1908–9).

Parisian Sketches: Letters to the New York Tribune *1875–1876*, ed. with introd. by Leon Edel and Ilse Dusoir Lind (London: Hart-Davis, 1958).

The Portrait of a Lady, 3 vols. (London: Macmillan, 1881).

The Princess Casamassima: A Novel, 3 vols. (London: Macmillan, 1886).

The Question of Our Speech, The Lesson of Balzac: Two Lectures (Boston: Houghton, Mifflin, 1905).

Roderick Hudson, first pub. 1876, rev. edn., 3 vols. (London: Macmillan, 1879).

The Sacred Fount (London: Methuen, 1901).

Selected Letters of Henry James, ed. with introd. by Leon Edel (London: Hart-Davis, 1956).

The Sense of the Past (London: Collins, 1917).

A Small Boy and Others (London: Macmillan, 1913).

The Tragic Muse, 3 vols. (London: Macmillan, 1890).

The Two Magics: The Turn of the Screw, Covering End (London: Heinemann, 1898).

Washington Square, The Pension Beaurepas, A Bundle of Letters, 2 vols. (London: Macmillan, 1881).

Within the Rim and Other Essays 1914–15 (London: Collins, 1918).

2. *Criticism and Biography of James*

ANDERSON, CHARLES R., *Person, Place, and Thing in Henry James's Novels* (Durham, NC: Duke University Press, 1977).

ARMSTRONG, PAUL B., *The Challenge of Bewilderment: Understanding and Representation in James, Conrad, and Ford* (Ithaca, NY: Cornell University Press, 1987).

BANTA, MARTHA (ed.), *New Essays on* The American (Cambridge: Cambridge University Press, 1987).

BEIDLER, PETER G., *Ghosts, Demons, and Henry James:* The Turn of the Screw *at the Turn of the Century* (Columbia: University of Missouri Press, 1989).

BERSANI, LEO, 'The Jamesian Lie', *Partisan Review*, 36 (1969), 53–79.

BEWLEY, MARIUS, *The Complex Fate: Hawthorne, Henry James and Some Other American Writers* (London: Chatto & Windus, 1952).

BLACKALL, JEAN FRANTZ, *Jamesian Ambiguity and* The Sacred Fount (Ithaca, NY: Cornell University Press, 1965).

——— 'James's *In the Cage*: An Approach through the Figurative Language', *University of Toronto Quarterly*, 31 (1962), 164–79.

BROOKE-ROSE, CHRISTINE, *A Rhetoric of the Unreal: Studies In Narrative and Structure, Especially of the Fantastic* (Cambridge: Cambridge University Press, 1981).

CAMERON, SHARON, *Thinking in Henry James* (Chicago: University of Chicago Press, 1989).

CHAPMAN, SARA S., *Henry James's Portrait of the Writer as Hero* (Basingstoke: Macmillan, 1990).

CHATMAN, SEYMOUR, *The Later Style of Henry James* (Oxford: Blackwell, 1972).

CLAIR, JOHN A., *The Ironic Dimension in the Fiction of Henry James* (Pittsburgh: Duquesne University Press, 1965).

CONRAD, JOSEPH, 'The Historian of Fine Consciences' (1905), in *The Question of Henry James: A Collection of Critical Essays*, ed. F. W. Dupee (London: Allan Wingate, 1947), 62–3.

EDEL, LEON, *The Life of Henry James*, 5 vols. (London: Hart-Davis, 1953–72).

FELMAN, SHOSHANA, 'Turning the Screw of Interpretation', *Yale French Studies*, 55–6 (1977), 94–207.

GARGANO, JAMES W., 'James's *The Sacred Fount*: The Phantasmagorical Made Evidential', *Henry James Review*, 2 (1980), 49–60.

GARIS, ROBERT E., 'The Two Lambert Strethers: A New Reading of *The Ambassadors*', *Modern Fiction Studies*, 7 (1961–2), 305–16.

GOODE, JOHN (ed.), *The Air of Reality: New Essays on Henry James* (London: Methuen, 1972).

HOCKS, RICHARD A., *Henry James and Pragmatistic Thought: A Study in the Relationship between the Philosophy of William James and the Literary Art of Henry James* (Chapel Hill: University of North Carolina Press, 1974).

HOLLAND, LAURENCE BEDWELL, *The Expense of Vision: Essays on the Craft of Henry James* (Princeton, NJ: Princeton University Press, 1964).

JONES, VIVIEN, 'James and Trollope', *Review of English Studies*, NS 33 (1982), 278–94.

—— *James the Critic* (London: Macmillan, 1985).

KASTON, CARREN, *Imagination and Desire in the Novels of Henry James* (New Brunswick, NJ: Rutgers University Press, 1984).

KIMBROUGH, ROBERT (ed.), The Turn of the Screw: *An Authoritative Text, Backgrounds and Sources, Essays in Criticism* (New York: Norton, 1966).

KROOK, DOROTHEA, *The Ordeal of Consciousness in Henry James* (Cambridge: Cambridge University Press, 1963).

LUCAS, JOHN, 'Conservatism and Revolution in the 1880s', in *Literature and Politics in the Nineteenth Century*, ed. Lucas (London: Methuen, 1971), 173–219.

MCMASTER, JULIET, 'The Portrait of Isabel Archer', *American Literature*, 45 (1973), 50–66.

MCWHIRTER, DAVID, *Desire and Love in Henry James: A Study of the Late Novels* (Cambridge: Cambridge University Press, 1989).

MARGOLIS, ANNE T., *Henry James and the Problem of Audience: An International Act* (Ann Arbor, Mich.: UMI Research Press, 1985).

MOON, HEATH, 'Saving James from Modernism: How to Read *The Sacred Fount*', *Modern Language Quarterly*, 49 (1988), 120–41.

NORRMAN, RALF, *The Insecure World of Henry James's Fiction: Intensity and Ambiguity* (London: Macmillan, 1982).

NUSSBAUM, MARTHA CRAVEN, 'Flawed Crystals: James's *The Golden Bowl* and Literature as Moral Philosophy', *New Literary History*, 15 (1983), 25–50.

PETRY, ALICE HALL, 'Jamesian Parody, *Jane Eyre*, and "The Turn of the Screw" ', *Modern Language Studies*, 13 (1983), 61–78.

POIRIER, RICHARD, *The Comic Sense of Henry James: A Study of the Early Novels* (London: Chatto & Windus, 1960).

RICHARDS, BERNARD, 'Henry James's "Fawns" ', *Modern Language Studies*, 13 (1983), 154–68.

RIMMON, SHLOMITH, *The Concept of Ambiguity—The Example of James* (Chicago: University of Chicago Press, 1977).

ROBBINS, BRUCE, 'Shooting Off James's Blanks: Theory, Politics, and *The Turn of the Screw*', *Henry James Review*, 5 (1984), 192–8.

ROWE, JOHN CARLOS, *Henry Adams and Henry James: The Emergence of a Modern Consciousness* (Ithaca, NY: Cornell University Press, 1976).

—— *The Theoretical Dimensions of Henry James* (London: Methuen, 1984).

RUBIN, LOUIS D., JR., 'One More Turn of the Screw', *Modern Fiction Studies*, 9 (1963–4), 314–28.

SABISTON, ELIZABETH, 'Isabel Archer: The Architecture of Consciousness and the International Theme', *Henry James Review*, 7 (1986), 29–47.

SAMUELS, CHARLES THOMAS, *The Ambiguity of Henry James* (Urbana: University of Illinois Press, 1971).

SCHRERO, ELLIOT M., 'Exposure in *The Turn of the Screw*', *Modern Philology*, 78 (1981), 261–74.

SEARS, SALLIE, *The Negative Imagination: Form and Perspective in the Novels of Henry James* (Ithaca, NY: Cornell University Press, 1968).

SELTZER, MARK, *Henry James and the Art of Power* (Ithaca, NY: Cornell University Press, 1984).

SINGH, AMRITJIT, and PANIKER, K. AYYAPPA (eds.), *The Magic Circle of Henry James: Essays in Honour of Darshan Singh Maini* (New Delhi: Sterling, 1989).

STOEHR, TAYLOR, 'Words and Deeds in *The Princess Casamassima*', *Journal of English Literary History*, 37 (1970), 95–135.

THOMAS, WILLIAM B., 'The Author's Voice in *The Ambassadors*', *Journal of Narrative Technique*, 1 (1971), 108–21.

TILFORD, JOHN E., JR., 'James the Old Intruder', *Modern Fiction Studies*, 4 (1958), 157–64.

TINTNER, ADELINE R., *The Book World of Henry James: Appropriating the Classics* (Ann Arbor, Mich.: UMI Research Press, 1987).

TRILLING, LIONEL, '*The Princess Casamassima*', *The Liberal Imagination: Essays on Literature and Society* (London: Secker & Warburg, 1951), 58–92.

WEINSTEIN, PHILIP M., *Henry James and the Requirements of the Imagination* (Cambridge, Mass.: Harvard University Press, 1971).

WILSON, EDMUND, 'The Ambiguity of Henry James', *Hound and Horn*, 7 (1934), 385–406.

YEAZELL, RUTH BERNARD, *Language and Knowledge in the Late Novels of Henry James* (Chicago: University of Chicago Press, 1976).

3. *Other Works*

'A.A.', 'On the Practice of Novel-Reading', (letter), *Christian Observer*, 14 (1815), 512–17.

ALTICK, RICHARD D., *The English Common Reader: A Social History of the Mass Reading Public 1800–1900* (Chicago: University of Chicago Press, 1957).

'Antiquus' [J. S. MILL], 'What is Poetry?', *Monthly Repository*, NS 7 (1833), 60–70.

BALDICK, CHRIS, *The Social Mission of English Criticism 1848–1932* (Oxford: Clarendon Press, 1983).

BANN, STEPHEN, *The Clothing of Clio: A Study of the Representation of History in Nineteenth-Century Britain and France* (Cambridge: Cambridge University Press, 1984).

BARTHES, ROLAND, 'The Reality Effect', in *French Literary Theory Today: A Reader*, ed. Tzvetan Todorov, trans. R. Carter (Cambridge: Cambridge University Press, 1982), 11–17.

—— *S/Z: An Essay*, trans. Richard Miller (New York: Hill & Wang, 1974).

BESANT, WALTER, *The Art of Fiction* (London: Chatto & Windus, 1884).

—— 'Candour in English Fiction', *New Review*, 2 (1890), 6–9.

BIRLEY, G., 'Thoughts on Reading Novels', *Methodist Magazine*, 42 (1819), 606–9.

BLACKMUR, R. P., 'Henry Adams: Three Late Moments', in *A Primer of Ignorance*, ed. Joseph Frank (New York: Harcourt, Brace & World, 1967), 251–73.

BOOTH, WAYNE C., *The Rhetoric of Fiction* (Chicago: University of Chicago Press, 1961).

BRAUDY, LEO, *Narrative Form in History and Fiction: Hume, Fielding and Gibbon* (Princeton, NJ: Princeton University Press, 1970).

BROOKS, PETER, *Reading for the Plot: Design and Intention in Narrative* (Oxford: Clarendon Press, 1984).

BROWNING, ROBERT, *The Ring and the Book*, first pub. 1868–9, ed. Richard D. Altick (Harmondsworth: Penguin, 1971).

BUCKLE, HENRY THOMAS, 'General Introduction', *History of Civilization in England*, 2nd edn., vol. i (London: Parker, 1858), 1–35 (2 vols. 1858–64).

CAINE, HALL, 'The New Watchwords of Fiction', *Contemporary Review*, 57 (1890), 479–88.

CERTEAU, MICHEL DE, 'History: Science and Fiction', *Heterologies: Discourse on the Other*, trans. Brian Massumi (Manchester: Manchester University Press, 1986), 199–221.

CHISHOLM, HUGH, 'How to Counteract the "Penny Dreadful" ', *Fortnightly Review*, NS 58 (1895), 765–75.

COLBY, ROBERT A., ' "Rational Amusement": Fiction vs. Useful Knowledge in the Nineteenth Century', in *Victorian Literature and Society: Essays Presented to Richard D. Altick*, ed. James R. Kincaid and Albert J. Kuhn (Columbus: Ohio State University Press, 1983), 46–73.

COLERIDGE, S. T., *Seven Lectures on Shakespeare and Milton*, ed. with introd. by J. Payne Collier (London: Chapman & Hall, 1856).

DALBERG-ACTON, JOHN EMERICH EDWARD, 'Inaugural Lecture on the Study of History', *Lectures on Modern History*, ed. with introd. by John Neville Figgis and Reginald Vere Laurence, first pub. 1906 (London: Macmillan; New York: St Martin's Press, 1960), 1–28.

DAVIS, LENNARD J., *Factual Fictions: The Origins of the English Novel* (New York: Columbia University Press, 1983).

DOCTOROW, E. L., 'False Documents', *American Review*, 26 (1977), 215–32.

EDGEWORTH, MARIA, and R. L., *Essays on Practical Education*, new edn., 2 vols. (London, 1815).

ELIOT, GEORGE, *Adam Bede*, 3 vols. (Edinburgh: Blackwood, 1859).

—— 'The Natural History of German Life', *Westminster Review* (July 1856); reprinted in *Essays of George Eliot*, ed. Thomas Pinney (London: Routledge & Kegan Paul, 1963), 266–99.

ELLMANN, RICHARD, *Oscar Wilde* (London: Hamish Hamilton, 1987).

'Excubitor', 'On the Expediency of Novel-Reading', (letter), *Christian Observer*, 16 (1817), 298–301.

FIELDING, HENRY, *The History of Tom Jones, a Foundling*, first pub. 1749, ed. Fredson Bowers with introd. by Martin Battestin, 2 vols. (Oxford: Clarendon Press, 1974).

FISHER, HERBERT A. L., 'Modern Historians and their Methods', *Fortnightly Review*, NS 56 (1894), 803–16.

FLINT, KATE, 'Reading the New Woman', *Browning Society Notes*, 17 (1987–8), 55–63.

FOUCAULT, MICHEL, 'What is an Author?', trans. Josué V. Harari, *The Foucault Reader*, ed. Paul Rabinow (Harmondsworth: Penguin, 1984), 101–20.

FRIERSON, WILLIAM C., 'The English Controversy over Realism in Fiction 1885–1895', *PMLA*, 43 (1928), 533–50.

FROUDE, JAMES ANTHONY, 'The Science of History', *Short Studies on Great Subjects*, vol. i (London: Longmans, Green, 1867), 1–36 (2 vols.).

FULLER, LON L., *Legal Fictions* (Stanford, Calif.: Stanford University Press, 1967).

FUSSELL, PAUL, *The Great War and Modern Memory* (London: Oxford University Press, 1975).

GALLAWAY, W. F., JR., 'The Conservative Attitude toward Fiction, 1770–1830', *PMLA*, 55 (1940), 1041–59.

GISSING, GEORGE, *New Grub Street: A Novel*, 3 vols. (London: Smith, Elder, 1891).

GOODE, JOHN, 'The Art of Fiction: Walter Besant and Henry James', in *Tradition and Tolerance in Nineteenth-Century Fiction: Critical Essays on Some English and American Novels*, ed. David Howard, John Lucas, and John Goode (London: Routledge & Kegan Paul, 1966), 243–81.

GOSSE, EDMUND, 'The Tyranny of the Novel', *National Review* (Apr. 1892); reprinted in *Questions at Issue* (London: Heinemann, 1893), 1–31.

GOSSON, STEPHEN, *The School of Abuse, Containing a Pleasant Invective against Poets, Pipers, Players, Jesters, &c.*, first pub. 1579 (London: Shakespeare Society, 1841).

GRAHAM, KENNETH, *English Criticism of the Novel 1865–1900* (Oxford: Clarendon Press, 1965).

[GREG, PERCY], 'Mr. Trollope's Novels', *National Review*, 7 (1858), 416–35.

[GREG, W. R.], 'False Morality of Lady Novelists', *National Review*, 8 (1859), 144–67.

GRIEST, GUINEVERE L., *Mudie's Circulating Library and the Victorian Novel* (Bloomington: Indiana University Press, 1970).

HARDY, THOMAS, 'Candour in English Fiction', *New Review*, 2 (1890), 15–21.

—— 'The Profitable Reading of Fiction', *Forum* (Mar. 1888); reprinted in *Life and Art: Essays, Notes and Letters*, ed. with introd. by Ernest Brennecke, Jr. (New York: Greenberg, 1925), 56–74.

HARRISON, FREDERIC, 'On the Choice of Books', *Fortnightly Review*, NS 25 (1879), 491–512.

[HARWOOD, PHILIP], 'The Modern Art and Science of History', *Westminster Review*, 38 (1842), 337–71.

[HITCHMAN, FRANCIS], 'Penny Fiction', *Quarterly Review*, 171 (1890), 150–71.

HOGARTH, JANET E., 'Literary Degenerates', *Fortnightly Review*, NS 57 (1895), 586–92.

HUGO, VICTOR, *Notre-Dame of Paris*, first pub. 1831, trans. John Sturrock (Harmondsworth: Penguin, 1978).

HUIZINGA, J., *Homo Ludens: A Study of the Play-Element in Culture*, trans. R. F. C. Hull (London: Routledge & Kegan Paul, 1949).

HYNES, SAMUEL, *A War Imagined: The First World War and English Culture* (New York: Athenaeum, 1991).

JAMES, WILLIAM, *Pragmatism: A New Name for Some Old Ways of Thinking. The Meaning of Truth: A Sequel to* Pragmatism, first pub. 1907, 1909 (Cambridge, Mass.: Harvard University Press, 1978).

—— 'The Teaching of Philosophy in Our Colleges', *Nation*, 23 (1876), 178–9.

JANN, ROSEMARY, *The Art and Science of Victorian History* (Columbus: Ohio State University Press, 1985).

KEATING, PETER, *The Haunted Study: A Social History of the English Novel 1875–1914* (London: Secker & Warburg, 1989).

KENDALL, JOHN, *Remarks on the Prevailing Custom of Attending Stage Entertainments; Also on the Present Taste for Reading Romances and Novels; and on Some Other Customs*, 3rd edn. (London, 1801).

LAUTERBACH, CHARLES E., and EDWARD S., 'The Nineteenth Century Three-Volume Novel', *PBSA*, 51 (1957), 263–302.

LEE, VERNON [VIOLET PAGET], 'A Dialogue on Novels', *Contemporary Review*, 48 (1885), 378–401.

—— *The Handling of Words and Other Studies in Literary Psychology* (London: John Lane, Bodley Head, 1923).

—— *Vital Lies: Studies of Some Varieties of Recent Obscurantism*, 2 vols. (London: John Lane, Bodley Head, 1912).

LEIGH, JOHN GARRETT, 'What Do the Masses Read?', *Economic Review*, 14 (1904), 166–77.

LILLY, W. S., 'The New Spirit in History', *Nineteenth Century*, 38 (1895), 619–33.

LINTON, E. LYNN, 'Candour in English Fiction', *New Review*, 2 (1890), 10–14.

LODGE, DAVID, *Working with Structuralism: Essays and Reviews on Nineteenth- and Twentieth-Century Literature* (London: Routledge & Kegan Paul, 1981).

LUBBOCK, PERCY, *The Craft of Fiction* (London: Jonathan Cape, 1921).

MAILLOUX, STEVEN, 'The Rhetorical Use and Abuse of Fiction: Eating Books in Late Nineteenth-Century America', *Boundary 2*, 17 (1990), 133–57.

MANGIN, EDWARD, *An Essay on Light Reading, as It May be Supposed to Influence Moral Conduct and Literary Taste* (London, 1808).

[MANSEL, H. L.], 'Sensation Novels', *Quarterly Review*, 113 (1863), 481–514.

MATTHIESSEN, F. O., *The James Family: Including Selections from the Writings of Henry James, Senior, William, Henry, and Alice James* (New York: Alfred A. Knopf, 1947).

MAXWELL, HERBERT, 'The Craving for Fiction', *Nineteenth Century*, 33 (1893), 1046–61.

[MILLAR, J. H.], 'Penny Fiction', *Blackwood's Magazine*, 164 (1898), 801–11.

MILLER, J. HILLIS, 'Narrative and History', *Journal of English Literary History*, 41 (1974), 455–73.

'Mr. Colburn's List', *Athenaeum*, 47 (1828), 735–6.

MOORE, GEORGE, *Literature at Nurse or Circulating Morals* (London: Vizetelly, 1885).

—— preface to *Piping Hot! (Pot-Bouille): A Realistic Novel*, by Émile Zola, trans. from the 63rd French edn. (London: Vizetelly, 1885), pp. v–xviii.

[MOZLEY, ANNE], 'On Fiction as an Educator', *Blackwood's Magazine*, 108 (1870), 449–59.

MURRAY, H., *Morality of Fiction; Or, an Inquiry into the Tendency of Fictitious Narratives, with Observations on Some of the Most Eminent* (Edinburgh, 1805).

NOBLE, JAMES ASHCROFT, 'The Fiction of Sexuality', *Contemporary Review*, 67 (1895), 490–8.

NORDAU, MAX, *Degeneration*, trans. from the 2nd German edn. (London: Heinemann, 1895).

'A Novel Education', *Punch*, 109 (1895), 255.

'Novels as Sedatives', *Spectator*, 73 (1894), 108–9.

OGDEN, C. K., *Bentham's Theory of Fictions* (London: Kegan Paul, Trench, Trubner, 1932).

ORIANS, G. HARRISON, 'Censure of Fiction in American Romances and Magazines, 1789–1810', *PMLA*, 52 (1937), 195–214.

'Our Female Sensation Novelists', *Christian Remembrancer*, NS 46 (1863), 209–36.

'Penny Novels', *Macmillan's Magazine*, 14 (1866), 96–105.

PETERSON, M. JEANNE, 'The Victorian Governess: Status Incongruence in Family and Society', in *Suffer and Be Still: Women in the Victorian Age*, ed. Martha Vicinus (Bloomington: Indiana University Press, 1972), 3–19.

PLATO, Book 2, *Republic*, *The Dialogues of Plato*, trans. B. Jowett, 4th edn., vol. ii (Oxford: Clarendon Press, 1953), 198–229 (4 vols.).

POOVEY, MARY, 'The Anathematized Race: The Governess and *Jane Eyre*', *Uneven Developments: The Ideological Work of Gender in Mid-Victorian England* (London: Virago, 1989), 126–63.

PRICE, MARTIN, *Forms of Life: Character and Moral Imagination in the Novel* (New Haven, Conn.: Yale University Press, 1983).

QUILTER, HARRY, 'The Gospel of Intensity', *Contemporary Review*, 67 (1895), 761–82.

[RAE, W. F.], 'Sensation Novelists: Miss Braddon', *North British Review*, 43 (1865), 180–204.

ROGERS, WINFIELD H., 'The Reaction against Melodramatic Sentimentality in the English Novel, 1796–1830', *PMLA*, 49 (1934), 98–122.

ROUND, J. H., 'Historical Research', *Nineteenth Century*, 44 (1898), 1004–14.

SAID, EDWARD W., *Beginnings: Intention and Method*, first pub. 1975 (New York: Columbia University Press, 1985).

SAINTSBURY, GEORGE, *Essays on French Novelists* (London: Percival, 1891).

SALMON, EDWARD G., 'What Girls Read', *Nineteenth Century*, 20 (1886), 515–29.

—— 'What the Working Classes Read', *Nineteenth Century*, 20 (1886), 108–17.

SIDNEY, PHILIP, Sir, *A Defence of Poetry* (1595), reprinted in *Miscellaneous Prose of Sir Philip Sidney*, ed. Katherine Duncan-Jones and Jan Van Dorsten (Oxford: Clarendon Press, 1973), 59–121.

SPILKA, MARK, 'Henry James and Walter Besant: "The Art of Fiction" Controversy', in *Towards a Poetics of Fiction*, ed. Spilka (Bloomington: Indiana University Press, 1977), 190–208.

—— 'Ian Watt on Intrusive Authors, or the Future of an Illusion', *Hebrew University Studies in Literature*, 1 (1973), 1–24.

STANG, RICHARD, *The Theory of the Novel in England 1850–1870* (London: Routledge & Kegan Paul, 1959).

STEVENSON, ROBERT LOUIS, *Essays in the Art of Writing* (London: Chatto & Windus, 1905).

—— 'A Humble Remonstrance', *Longman's Magazine* (Dec. 1884); reprinted in *Memories and Portraits* (London: Chatto & Windus, 1887), 275–99.

STIERLE, KARLHEINZ, 'The Reading of Fictional Texts', trans. Inge Crosman and Thekla Zachrau, in *The Reader in the Text: Essays on Audience and Interpretation*, ed. Susan R. Suleiman and Inge Crosman (Princeton, NJ: Princeton University Press, 1980), 83–105.

STRAHAN, A., 'Bad Literature for the Young', *Contemporary Review*, 26 (1875), 981–91.

STUTFIELD, HUGH E. M., 'Tommyrotics', *Blackwood's Magazine*, 157 (1895), 833–45.

TAYLOR, JOHN TINNON, *Early Opposition to the English Novel: The Popular Reaction from 1760 to 1830* (New York: King's Crown Press, 1943).

THACKERAY, WILLIAM MAKEPEACE, *Vanity Fair: A Novel without a Hero* (London: Bradbury & Evans, 1848).

THORNTON, WILLIAM T., 'History, and its Scientific Pretensions', *Macmillan's Magazine*, 8 (1863), 25–35.

TODOROV, TZVETAN, *The Fantastic: A Structural Approach to a Literary Genre*, trans. Richard Howard (Ithaca, NY: Cornell University Press, 1975).

—— *The Poetics of Prose*, trans. Richard Howard (Oxford: Blackwell, 1977).

TROLLOPE, ANTHONY, *An Autobiography*, 2 vols. (Edinburgh: Blackwood, 1883).

—— *Barchester Towers*, 3 vols. (London: Longman, 1857).

—— 'Novel-Reading', *Nineteenth Century*, 5 (1879), 24–43.

—— 'On English Prose Fiction as a Rational Amusement' (1870), in *Four Lectures*, ed. Morris L. Parrish (London: Constable, 1938), 91–139.

—— *Thackeray* (London: Macmillan, 1879).

WELSH, ALEXANDER, *Strong Representations: Narrative and Circumstantial Evidence in England* (Baltimore: Johns Hopkins University Press, 1992).

WHITE, ALLON, *The Uses of Obscurity: The Fiction of Early Modernism* (London: Routledge & Kegan Paul, 1981).

WHITE, HAYDEN, *Metahistory: The Historical Imagination in Nineteenth-Century Europe* (Baltimore: Johns Hopkins University Press, 1973).

Index